Letters to
Paul's
Delegates

THE NEW TESTAMENT IN CONTEXT

Friendship and Finances in Philippi
THE LETTER OF PAUL TO THE PHILIPPIANS
Ben Witherington III

Walking in the Truth: Perseverers and Deserters
THE FIRST, SECOND, AND THIRD LETTERS OF JOHN
Gerard S. Sloyan

Church and Community in Crisis
THE GOSPEL ACCORDING TO MATTHEW
J. Andrew Overman

Letters to Paul's Delegates
1 TIMOTHY, 2 TIMOTHY, TITUS
Luke Timothy Johnson

Letters to Paul's Delegates

1 TIMOTHY, 2 TIMOTHY, TITUS

Luke Timothy Johnson

THE NEW TESTAMENT IN CONTEXT

Howard Clark Kee and J. Andrew Overman, editors

TRINITY PRESS INTERNATIONAL

Valley Forge, Pennsylvania

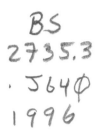

BS
2735.3
. J64Ø
1996

Trinity Press International, P.O. Box 851, Valley Forge, PA 19482-0851
Trinity Press International is part of the Morehouse Publishing Group

Library of Congress Cataloging-in-Publication Data
Johnson, Luke Timothy.
    Letters to Paul's delegates : 1 Timothy, 2 Timothy, Titus / Luke Timothy Johnson.
        p. cm. – (The New Testament in context)
    Includes bibliographical references and index.
    ISBN 1-56338-144-3 (alk. paper)
    1. Bible. N.T. Pastoral Epistles – Commentaries. I. Title.
II. Series.
BS2735.3.J64 1996
227'.83077–dc20   96-42303
                                                                CIP

Printed in the United States of America

96 97 98 99 00 01   10 9 8 7 6 5 4 3 2 1

Contents

Preface

The three letters of Paul to his delegates Timothy and Titus do not make easy reading for the obvious reason that they are written from a context completely different than our own; getting at their meaning involves the willingness to struggle with foreign words and even more foreign symbols and concepts. They are also not easy for contemporary readers in particular because the symbols and concepts of these letters offend many sensibilities of the present age. Ours is an age that likes to think of itself as egalitarian and inclusive and nonsexist. Whatever else they are, these compositions are hierarchical, exclusive, and androcentric, if not actually sexist. Reading them, therefore, also involves a struggle of another sort, namely, the effort to read them fairly and without prejudice. Here is a good reason to make that effort: we grow more from what is unlike us than we do from what is like us. The biggest gift these ancient writings make to present-day readers is their otherness, their refusal to say what we might like them to say.

This commentary appears in a series dedicated to providing an intelligent reading of the New Testament "in context." As I point out in the introduction, that task is especially complicated in the case of these compositions because so much of the scholarly attention they have received has been a debate of what that context might be. I have taken it as my task to do two things: first, to offer a consistent reading of the texts from the perspective of a single context and, second, to provide the reader with the information and references needed to make an informed judgment concerning other theories.

Although the style of the commentary is, I hope, reasonably

accessible to all readers, two aspects of it may seem forbidding. In order to offer some sense of where to go for information and views other than my own, I strew a fair amount of bibliographical data through the text. I hope the reader's ability to pick through the prose is not thereby terminally hampered. Then there is the matter of Greek words — many Greek words, often in long lists. Why? Because for some readers, this is the raw data that needs to go into the study of these letters. For readers who do not know Greek, my advice is to read just the summary statements concerning style and diction and then move on.

The commentary provides a new translation, which is divided into units for discussion. The first part of the analysis of each unit (Notes on Translation) consists of technical matters: the state of the Greek text, diction, and style. Readers tempted to leap over this part may find, however, that it contains valuable pieces of information, for example, the reasons for specific translation decisions. The second part of the analysis (Literary Observations) deals with a variety of issues pertinent to the literary context of the writing: allusions to Scripture, for example, or similarities to other bodies of literature. The last part of the analysis (Comment) provides broader discussions concerning the historical realities and religious ideas revealed by the passage.

Those willing to struggle with these writings of Paul will find themselves richly rewarded, for beneath what is repelling in them is also something deeply appealing, and profoundly pertinent to our own age.

Introduction

Meaning is contextual. Words have meaning within sentences, sentences within arguments or narratives, arguments and narratives within literary compositions, literary compositions within language, language within the complex world of social structures, dynamics, and symbols that we call *culture*. The more we understand these multiple and overlapping contexts, the more we can discover and determine meaning. The interpretation of any writing, therefore, demands engaging the contexts — historical, social, literary — within which its meaning is to be found. Engaging the contexts of ancient compositions requires the reconstruction of at least partially lost or forgotten historical and literary worlds. The work is frustrating because the surviving evidence is fragmentary and often free-floating. In the case of New Testament (NT) writings, the process also involves an inevitable circularity, for the information concerning the context is often derived from the very documents that the context is then asked to interpret.

It should be no surprise, then, that even after the passage of many centuries and the efforts of many interpreters, the precise context, and therefore the precise meaning of NT writings, so often remains disputed. Some debates are virtually intractable. Take the Synoptic Problem for example. No matter how many scholars affirm the two-source solution (that Matthew and Luke used Mark plus another written source), there will always be voices to challenge that position for the simple reason that even theories enjoying wide acceptance do not cover all the data and alternative explanations can always be defended. The consequences for interpretation are real. A different account of how

1

the synoptic Gospels are related to each other yields distinct or even contradictory understandings of the compositions and the process by which they were produced, that is, of their historical and literary contexts.

The letters to Paul's delegates Timothy and Titus (usually referred to as the Pastoral Letters) offer one of the most dramatic examples of how different understandings of the context of composition lead to widely divergent interpretations of the writings. There are two basic ways to place these writings within early Christianity. The more traditional view is that they are authentic letters written by Paul himself during his lifetime. They should, therefore, be read in the context of Paul's ministry between the years 49–68 C.E. and interpreted in light of the other Pauline letters. The situations suggested by the compositions, the circumstances of author and addressees, the range of nuance for the various subjects discussed, are all to be discerned within a *Pauline context.*

A second view is much more prominent today, indeed is almost universal among contemporary scholars. It holds that these three letters are not authentic, but are pseudonymous compositions produced by an admirer of Paul several generations after his death. The shift in perspective affects one's understanding of the compositions' literary form, the situations they address, and the reasons why they were written. Thus the letters are "Pauline" in a very different sense, for the context is one of *pseudonymity.* Moreover, Paul's other letters (the "authentic," or, more neutrally, "undisputed" letters) are less the frame of reference and more the point of contrast for the interpretation of these three writings.

For a commentary on the letters to Paul's delegates to have integrity, its author must make a clear choice between these options and provide reasons why the choice has been made. In this introduction, I sketch the arguments that lead me to interpret these letters as authentically Pauline and to read them within the context of the first generation of the Christian movement. By no means do I hold this position without reservation. For many years, in fact, I shared the majority position that I had learned from earlier scholars. Only when I tried to communicate to students the logic underlying the majority position, and found that I could not make it convincing, did I adopt — with considerable hesitation — the traditional position as the more elegant and reasonable hypothesis. I have subsequently argued this position even more vigorously than I hold it (as in Johnson, *Writings of the New Testament*, 381–405), simply because I am convinced that the position now in favor is deeply flawed and in need of reexamination. At the very least, the majority view needs to become something more than what it too often is today, an assumed and unexamined verity. For a position on these compositions to be responsible, all the data must be taken into account, and arguments as well as assertions must be made.

The Background

Paul's letters to Timothy and Titus were first termed "the Pastorals" in the eighteenth century, but as early as the Muratorian Canon (ca. 170 C.E.) their special character was noted. They were singled out as having to do with "ecclesiastical discipline." Their absence from an early manuscript (MS) of the Pauline Epistles ($\mathfrak{P}^{46}$), in fact, may have something to do with the distinction between the letters Paul wrote to churches and those he wrote to individuals. Early Christian writers read and interpreted the Pastorals as genuinely Pauline. The major exception was Marcion (ca. 150), who, according to Tertullian, "rejected (*recusavit*) the two epistles to Timothy and the one to Titus" (*Adversus Marcionem* 5.21). Marcion undoubtedly objected to a number of themes in the letters, including their clear teaching on God's will to save all, the goodness of the created order, and the positive nature of marriage.

The Pauline character and authenticity of these letters were otherwise not challenged seriously until the German theologian F. Schleiermacher in *Über den sogennanten Ersten Brief des Paulus an den Timotheus* (1807) challenged the authenticity of 1 Timothy on the basis of its vocabulary (see especially 1:3 and 6:3), which Schleiermacher took as proof of composition after Paul's time. A more sustained attack on the authenticity of all three letters was launched by F. C. Baur in *Die sogennanten Pastoralbriefe des Apostels Paulus* (1835), who argued that both the vocabulary and the historical setting were non-Pauline. Baur took the reference to "falsely called knowledge (*gnōsis*)" in 1 Timothy 6:20 to be a clear reference to Marcion. The opponents of all three letters, therefore, were not those of Paul's time but were second-century Gnostics. If the Pastorals were written in response to the Gnostic challenge, they would naturally also be pseudonymous.

Despite the impressive rebuttal of Baur by scholars such as T. Zahn (*Introduction to the New Testament*, 3:1–133), the enormous prestige of Baur and the Tübingen School among historical critics helped the more radical position to become the dominant one (see Schweitzer, *Paul and His Interpreters*). The theory that the Pastorals are pseudonymous productions of the second century currently holds sway in NT scholarship except among some conservative scholars (see Ellis, "The Authorship of the Pastorals"). The resulting disappearance of the Pastorals from serious scholarly consideration is indicated by a 1989 survey of NT scholarship, sponsored by the Society of Biblical Literature, *The New Testament and its Modern Interpreters*. In V. P. Furnish's article "Pauline Studies" (pp. 321–50), the Pastorals appear in one line with reference to their inauthenticity (p. 326). More remarkably, they are treated nowhere else, even though the volume contains extensive essays on the NT Apocrypha (pp. 429–56) and the apostolic fathers (pp. 457–500).

Tendencies in the Debate

Such an overwhelming consensus regarding the Pastorals suggests that the term "debate" is too strong a word for the present situation. But the reader should be aware that until very recently there was a vigorous discussion and that fashions in scholarship by no means guarantee the truth. Before we consider in some detail the data that must be examined in reaching a responsible decision on the appropriate context for these letters, it may be helpful to sketch some of the tendencies that have shaped the discussion.

Seeking a Congenial Apostle

For many scholars, Paul is the first and best witness to the Christian religion to which they themselves are also committed. He is simply "the apostle" (see, e.g., the essays in Meeks, *The Writings of St. Paul*). There has been a natural tendency to seek for a Paul that corresponds with the scholar's own sense of what is essential to Christianity and to reject as inauthentic what does not meet that measure. On the one hand, those who think that the principle of righteousness by faith is not only at the heart of Paul but also of Christianity find the Pastorals to be disappointingly moralizing. Those who can deal with Paul's occasional suppression of women in other letters because of his fundamental commitment to equality find nothing in the Pastorals to redeem a sexist attitude. On the other hand, those who treasure conformity to doctrine, and a strong sense of tradition, and church structure, and the inspiration of Scripture tend to find these values in the undisputed as well as in the Pastoral Letters. Scholars who are believers would like to find a Paul who is the mirror of themselves. Their scholarship is not necessarily determined by such bias, but neither is it unaffected by it (see, e.g., Beker, *Heirs of Paul*, 36–47, 83–86, 105–8).

Authenticity and Acceptance

For those whose theological evaluation of writings is attached not to their canonical status but to their connection with the apostolic age, the determination of authenticity or inauthenticity also affected the appreciation or depreciation of the Pastorals as Christian witnesses. This tendency can be found on both sides of the debate. One cannot help but think that some scholars fight the authenticity of the Pastorals because they think that such a recognition would demand an acceptance of their message as well and that others defend their authenticity as a way of championing their teaching. The two issues ought to be held separate, but too seldom are.

Tests of Authenticity

The discussion of the authenticity of Paul's letters generally has operated with premises that increasingly appear, in the light of better scholarship, as simplistic and perhaps even misguided. The various criteria that are used to test for authenticity — placement in Paul's career, style, development of ecclesiastical order, consistency in thought — are based on an anachronistic model of authorship. Moreover, the image of Paul as a solitary correspondent is probably mistaken. The composition of all of Paul's letters is far more complex than has sometimes been appreciated. His letters were frequently cosponsored or dictated, and they use community traditions. Passages within them reveal traces of the hellenistic teaching style called the *diatribe* and the Jewish mode of scriptural interpretation called *midrash*, suggesting a social setting of a teacher working out materials with his disciples. It is reasonable to suppose that, in the production of all his letters, more hands and minds were at work than Paul's alone. The "Pauline School," in other words, did not need to arise after Paul's death, for it was already at work in the composition of his letters during his lifetime.

Specific criteria, such as *style* for example — diction, sentence structure, the use of particles, the citation of Scripture — make sense if Paul's undisputed letters either uniformly demonstrate a unique mode of expression or were the spontaneous outpouring of an individual consciousness. But in fact, even the undisputed letters are widely diverse in their style. More significantly, the romantic ideal of "the style is the person" was unknown in antiquity. In Paul's world, the rhetorical ideal was *prosōpopoiia*, which meant, whether in drama, narrative, or speeches, to "write in character," an ideal that applied to the writing of letters as well (see Stowers, "Romans 7:7–25 as a Speech in Character"). Rhetorical handbooks like those of Pseudo-Demetrius and Pseudo-Libanius provide samples of diverse letter-forms appropriate to different situations and social relations (see Malherbe, "Ancient Epistolary Theory"). Style, in Paul's time, was less an expression of the inner self than of a social presence. In writers of such differing gifts as Luke the evangelist and Lucian the satirist, we can observe the easy manipulation of multiple "styles."

Consequences of Grouping

The Pastorals are always treated as a group, rather than as separate and distinct letters. This tendency has several consequences. The first is that characterizations are drawn from the evidence of all the letters together and then (inappropriately) applied to each of them equally, even though a particular letter may have little evidence of that trait. For example, the Pastorals are often said to bear witness to a more elaborate church order than do the undisputed letters. But 2 Timothy has nothing at all about church order, and Titus only a bit more. As another example, one finds discussion of the "opponents in the Pastorals," even though the profile of the opposition in each letter is distinctive (e.g., Spicq, *Les Epîtres Pastorales*, 85–119; Brox, *Die Pastoralbriefe*, 31–42; Lock, *Commentary on the Pastoral Epistles*, xvi–xviii).

Such generalizations blur the distinctions between the letters and strengthen the perception of them as a single literary production. This, in turn, has two further consequences. One is that the sense of distance from the undisputed Pauline corpus is heightened. A similar effect could be achieved by treating the Thessalonian letters as a separate group without ever relating them to their points of contact with other Pauline letters. If Titus is read next to Galatians, or if 2 Timothy is read next to Philippians, or 1 Timothy next to 1 Corinthians, the strangeness of each is greatly diminished.

Finally, once the letters have been isolated and read as a single entity, then the decision for authenticity or inauthenticity would seem to include all of them or none of them. In fact, however, it is possible to consider the letters separately and as distinct literary productions. It is possible as well, therefore, to decide for the authenticity or inauthenticity of the letters individually. As I will point out later, however, such a separate treatment is resisted by the majority opinion, which absolutely requires the simultaneous production of the letters for its theory to work (see, e.g., Trummer, "Corpus Paulinum — Corpus Pastorale"). If, for example, 2 Timothy were authentic, while

1 Timothy and Titus were written pseudonymously in imitation of it, the conventional wisdom on the correspondence would collapse.

Even when such prejudicial tendencies are acknowledged and taken into account, the very real problems presented by these letters are by no means eliminated. Everyone recognizes that the Pastorals are in some sense Pauline. They are, after all, written in his name, seek to advance his cause, and contain elements which are distinctive to Paul in earliest Christianity. Everyone also recognizes that each of these letters contains just enough divergence, or difference, from what the reader instinctively takes to be "authentically Paul" to demand some accounting. It is the way this combination of similarity and difference, of the familiar and the strange, is diversely reckoned that leads to the wide difference of opinion among scholars.

Factors to Be Considered

The distinguishing features of each of these letters will be considered in the commentary itself. In order to understand the current state of scholarship on "the Pastorals" as such, however, it is necessary to continue the practice of considering them as a group, if only to show, by taking each point in turn, how such a grouping may not be appropriate and how the data can support more than one position.

The Letters and Paul's Ministry

We can begin with the question of placement within Paul's ministry. Can the Pastorals be fitted within that framework such as it is known to us from the Acts of the Apostles and Paul's undisputed letters? Of all the criteria for authenticity, this is the only one that is truly "hard." If these letters contained a gross anachronism, or if they flatly contradicted the evidence of our other sources, then this criterion would disqualify them. If, for example, we had a complete account of Paul's imprisonment in Rome, day by day, and we knew that no one named Onesiphorus had ever visited him, then we would know, when 2 Timothy

1:16 mentions such a person visiting Paul, that the document was fictionalizing or that Paul himself was forgetful or mistaken or lying. The problem with this hard criterion is that it is hard in theory only. In the case of Paul, neither Acts nor his extant letters provide us with anything close to a comprehensive account of his ministry or movements.

Nevertheless, we can say some things. First Timothy and Titus presuppose Paul's active ministry. In 1 Timothy, we are given very little information: Paul has left his delegate in Ephesus while he travels to Macedonia (1 Tim. 1:3); Timothy is to deal with affairs there until Paul returns within a short time (3:14). In principle, such a letter could have been written anytime during Paul's fairly extensive Aegean ministry. Our other sources indicate that Paul spent some two years in Ephesus (Acts 19:10) and made at least two trips from there to Macedonia (see Acts 20:1–3; 2 Cor. 1:16; 2:12–13; 7:5–6). Titus is more problematic. It is written to Paul's delegate whom Paul had "left" in Crete (Titus 1:5). Paul's whereabouts are not revealed, although he plans to winter in Nicopolis (3:12), which could be one of several cities of that name. That there should be a church in Crete is in itself not surprising, but we have no other evidence of Titus's working there. More significantly, Paul's only personal contact with Crete, according to Acts 27:7–15, was a brief stopover as a prisoner on his way to Rome.

In 2 Timothy, Paul writes from captivity, most probably in Rome (2 Tim. 1:16–17). This can be fitted into the account of Acts 28:30–31. But does his reference to a "first defense" (2 Tim. 4:16) indicate that he is now in a second imprisonment, after he had been released from a first (4:17)? In contrast to 1 Timothy and Titus, 2 Timothy contains information about some fifteen of Paul's helpers (4:9–21). Their movements, as recorded here, do not seem to contradict what we know of them from other sources, although some scholars cavil over the apparent discrepancy in the matter of Trophimus: Acts 21:29 places Trophimus with Paul in Jerusalem before his arrest in the temple; 2 Timothy 4:20 says that Paul left Trophimus ill in Miletus (see Acts 20:17–37). On the face of it, this would *seem* to be one of those impossible-to-resolve contradictions, until we examine the several possibilities more closely. Other information in 2 Timothy startlingly confirms data found in other letters, such as the short remark, "Erastus remained in Corinth" (4:20), which fits with Romans 16:23.

The autobiographical data provided by these compositions can be evaluated in several ways. The options are more difficult if, as is usually done, a hypothesis must include all three letters. Those who consider the letters to be pseudonymous have two basic ways of viewing this personal information. Some consider it entirely fictional, a dimension of pseudepigraphic literature. The presence of such autobiographical information as we find in 2 Timothy and Titus has even been proposed as a sign of pseudepigraphy (Donelson, *Pseudepigraphy and Ethical Argument*, 23–66), despite the presence of intensely autobiographical passages in some of Paul's undisputed letters, above all Galatians, 2 Corinthians, and Philippians. Others think the information to be at least broadly historical, whether preserved in the form of fragments from genuine Pauline letters (see Harrison, *The Problem of the Pastoral Epistles*) or as developed folklorically in oral tradition, like that found also in the second-century apocryphal writing the *Acts of Paul and Thecla*, whose dramatis personae resemble those in 2 Timothy (see D. R. MacDonald, *The Legend and the Apostle*).

Those who consider the letters genuine have three options available. First, they can try to squeeze the documents into the framework provided by Paul's other letters and Acts, although this requires considerable ingenuity (see J. A. T. Robinson, *Redating the New Testament*, 67–85). Second, they can try to expand the time of Paul's active ministry by invoking the ancient tradition (see *1 Clem.* 5:7) that Paul was released from a first Roman imprisonment and preached in Spain before being taken captive again and put to death. This helps especially in accounting for Titus and the movements in 2 Timothy (see, e.g., Knight, *Commentary on the Pastoral Epistles*, 15–20). Unfortunately, however, those letters refer to movements of Paul and his associates in the East, whereas the tradition speaks of a ministry in the West.

A final option appears to be the most reasonable. It recognizes that neither Acts nor Paul's letters give us a full account of Paul's ministry and also acknowledges that these letters do not fit easily within that framework. But it leaves open the possibility that these compositions may provide us with important additional information about Paul's career and captivity not found in the other sources. Just as 2 Corinthians tells us that Paul experienced other imprisonments that we would not otherwise have suspected, so these letters tell us about Pauline missionary endeavors — such as in Crete — we would not otherwise know. I mentioned above how the casual connection of Erastus with Corinth is confirmed by Romans 16:23; so also is the fact that Paul's associates worked in the territory of Dalmatia, otherwise known as Illyricum (see 2 Tim. 4:10), corroborated by Romans 15:19. In short, if the Pastorals are difficult to fit within Paul's lifetime because of the biographical information they contain, they are no more problematic in this respect than such undoubted letters as Galatians, Philemon, and Philippians.

Style

Even if we grant its validity, the criterion of style is particularly difficult to apply in the case of the Pastorals. Statistical studies of vocabulary (see, e.g., Graystone and Herdan, "The Authorship of the Pastorals") are not helpful, even when carried out with some degree of rigor (see, e.g., Cook, "The Pastoral Fragments Reconsidered"), for they fail to account for the smallness of the sample and wide variability in the undisputed Pauline corpus (see T. A. Robinson, "Graystone and Herdan's 'C' Quantity Formula"). Most of all, vocabulary studies do not recognize the influence of such factors as distinctive subject matter and the stylistic ideal of *prosōpopoiia*. That the Pastorals as a group contain a large number of words not found in other Pauline letters, and share a certain number of terms not otherwise attested in the NT, is indisputable. But here is a case where the grouping of the letters leads to misperception. The vocabulary of 2 Timothy is close to that of the other Pauline letters, whereas the diction in Titus and 1 Timothy diverges more markedly. Since the distinctive vocabulary of the Pastorals as a group resembles that in Luke-Acts, some scholars have drawn the conclusion that Luke was the author of the Pastorals (see Wilson, *Luke and the Pastoral Epistles*), perhaps even as the third volume of Luke-Acts (see Quinn, "The Last Volume of Luke"). It would be more accurate to say that the Pastorals and Luke-Acts share a broader sample of koine Greek than is attested in the undisputed letters.

Stylistic analysis involves more than counting words. It entails the analysis of clauses, connectives, and sentences. The syntax of the Pastorals, taken as a group, is generally flatter and smoother than in letters such as Galatians, 1 Corinthians, and Romans. Sentences in the Pastorals tend to be longer and more regular, and the use of particles is less varied and rich. Yet the question immediately presents itself: how much of the style of Galatians, Romans, and 1 Corinthians is due to Paul's use of the diatribal mode in those letters? If the Pastorals are compared rather to 1 Thessalonians or to Philippians, the contrast is not so extreme.

The issue of style is further complicated by the fact that the Pastorals do not manifest a single "hand" that is consistent throughout, in the manner of Colossians and Ephesians. Instead, they present a mixture of "Pauline" and "non-Pauline" elements (that is, elements that we *recognize* as Pauline and non-Pauline), sometimes in alternating sentences. It is this phenomenon which led to the theory that authentic Pauline fragments were taken up into later pseudonymous compositions (see Harrison, *The Problem of the Pastoral Epistles*). Far too little attention has been paid to the way in which elements that are considered non-Pauline tend to cluster precisely in those places where the Pastorals deal with subjects that are not considered in the undisputed letters. It may be worth noting that no one in the ancient church challenged the authenticity of the Pastorals on the basis of style, a point more worth noting because criticism on this issue was not lacking when it came to the attribution of Hebrews, and because we might suppose the sense of Greek style to be better among those who continued to be schooled in the same system of *paideia* than among those who learned their Greek in a German gymnasium or American prep school or seminary.

Identification of Opponents

One of the early reasons for questioning the genuineness of the Pastorals was the identity of the opponents they dispute or the nature of the "heresy" espoused by the opponents. Those who understood the *gnōsis* of 1 Timothy 6:20 as referring to the second-century movement called Gnosticism, and who took the "antitheses" in the same verse as a reference to the work by Marcion, had good reason to date the Pastorals in the middle of the second century and see it as a response to these movements (see, e.g., Bauer, *Orthodoxy and Heresy*, 222–28). Unfortunately, the matter is not that simple. It is by no means obvious that the terms in 1 Timothy 6:20 have such a specific referent. The question of whether all the letters oppose the same teachers or teaching, furthermore, should be an open one, for the combination of elements (the resurrection already past [2 Tim. 2:17–18], forbidding marriage and certain foods [1 Tim. 4:3], advocating physical asceticism [1 Tim. 4:8], being concerned for the law [1 Tim. 1:7; Titus 3:9], practicing circumcision and purity regulations [Titus 1:10, 15]) does not match precisely the profile of known heresies. Taken separately, each of these elements can be traced back to Paul's own ministry (see, e.g., 1 Cor. 7:1; 8:1–3; 15:17–19; Gal. 4:8–10; Col. 2:20–22). The composite sketch, moreover, ignores the fact that each of the letters deals with a different set of "opponents," whether they are real or simply literary foils.

The manner in which the Pastorals respond to opponents has also been considered uncharacteristic of the genuine Paul. They rely on polemic, it is said, rather than logical refutation. This is not entirely the case since 1 Timothy does engage in substantive theological refutation at least four times (1:8; 4:3–5, 7–8; 6:5–10), and the genuine Paul is certainly capable of using invective against rival teachers (see, e.g., 2 Cor. 11:13–15; Gal. 5:12; 6:13; Rom. 16:17–18; Phil. 3:2, 18–19). What is distinctive to the Pastorals is the amount of polemical material they employ, its stereotypical character, and, above all, its literary function in 1 and 2 Timothy.

Church Structure

A major reason for doubting the authenticity of the Pastorals is the elements of church order they are thought to contain (see, e.g., von Campenhausen, *Ecclesiastical Authority and Spiritual Power*). Here, it is argued, we find more than a shift in emphasis, such as taking the image of the body of Christ from 1 Corinthians and altering it in Colossians by making Christ the head of the body (cf. 1 Cor. 12:12–27 to Col. 1:18–19). Here, the Pauline *ekklēsia* as God's convocation filled with the gifts of the Holy Spirit is replaced by an organizational chart for "the household of God" (1 Tim. 3:15), which has a hierarchical ministry of bishops, elders, and deacons, as well as orders of women deacons and widows. For some scholars, such attention to structure virtually defines the Pastorals and locates them in the development of early Christianity from a sect to a church (see, e.g., M. Y. MacDonald, *The Pauline Churches*). No clearer evidence could be found, it is asserted, that these letters address and help to create a context in which, to use Max Weber's terms, "charism has been routinized" and Christianity has come to grips with the delay of the parousia, diminished eschatological expectation, and the necessity of continued life in the world.

Attention to church order can also be read as a defensive reaction to powerful egalitarian forces within Christianity, especially among women (see D. R. MacDonald, "Virgins, Widows, and Paul," and Davies, *The Revolt of the Widows*), which accounts for the markedly sexist attitudes found particularly in 1 Timothy (see Bassler, "The Widow's Tale"). According to this understanding, the church order in the Pastorals should be compared to that found in the letters of Ignatius of Antioch (ca. 115), in which a monarchical episcopate and hierarchical order are essential instruments in the unification of the church against what is perceived as deviance (see Ign. *Eph.* 2.2; Ign. *Magn.* 3.1; Ign. *Trall.* 2.2; 3.1). No matter how widely held, this perception is fundamentally flawed and goes considerably beyond the evidence offered by the writings themselves. The commentary will consider the evidence in detail. At this point only a series of summary points should be made.

1. It is inaccurate to speak of the church order of the Pastorals as such. There is none in 2 Timothy, and the little there is in Titus does not exactly match what we find in 1 Timothy.

2. The organizational elements touched on (*not* defined or described) by 1 Timothy can scarcely be called elaborate. They do not approach the hierarchical structure found in

Ignatius. Rather, the simple structure that we can reconstruct on the basis of hints in 1 Timothy resembles the
synagogal structure of diaspora Judaism, an organizational
arrangement which in turn closely resembled that found in
Greco-Roman *collegia*. Such a structure was obviously available to Christians in Paul's ministry and did not require a
long period of internal development to emerge.

3. The organizational structure in 1 Timothy and Titus is
   given no legitimation. It is neither theologically defended
   nor interpreted; there is nothing "sacral" about it. Indeed, the various positions and functions appear entirely
   practical and quotidian.

4. The letters, in fact, do not prescribe but rather presume
   a certain organization or order. No job descriptions are
   given. Instead, there is a concern for the mental and moral
   capacities of those who are to fill certain already established positions. This point is important because it cuts to
   the heart of the position that the Pastorals assert organization as a response to crisis. Nothing in these letters suggests
   the *creation* of an organizational structure. In fact, we cannot even construct a complete community structure from
   the hints given by 1 Timothy. The casual references suggest
   that the readers were already aware of the realities about
   which the author speaks.

5. Common sense and sociology alike confirm the validity
   of the observation that intentional groups move progressively from simpler to more elaborate, and eventually more
   legitimated, structures. But it by no means follows that
   such development requires decades. Analyses of communes
   have shown that they cannot survive much beyond a few
   years without strong boundaries, mechanisms for decision
   making, and social control (see Kantor, *Community and
   Commitment,* and Kephart, *Extraordinary Groups*). The assumption of a great time-lapse between the founding of a
   Pauline church and the development of a stable structure
   is counterintuitive. We find just as often that charismatic
   communities are highly structured. When the produc-

tion of the Pastorals up to a century after Paul's death is attributed to a new need for structure, some form of sociological fantasy is at work.

6. Closer attention to the undisputed letters of Paul reveals not only that he refers by name to the same offices that appear in 1 Timothy and Titus (bishops and deacons in Phil. 1:1; a woman deacon in Rom. 16:1), but that he is far more concerned with the presence and the recognition of authority figures in local churches than is sometimes imagined (see Rom. 12:8; 1 Cor. 6:2–6; 12:28; 16:15–17; Gal. 6:6; Col. 4:17; 1 Thess. 5:12; Phil. 4:3). The idea that Pauline communities existed, even during his lifetime, as free-floating bodies of charismatic activity, is unsupported by the evidence.

7. The elements of church order found in 1 Timothy and Titus are far closer to that in the undisputed letters of Paul than to the ecclesiastical structure found in the letters of Ignatius of Antioch. For that matter, the data resembles that in Paul more than that found in the writings from the Qumran community, which was contemporary with Paul and had a rigid hierarchical structure that was also highly legitimated theologically (see Reicke, "The Constitution of the Early Church").

8. The elements of organization and order that we find in 1 Timothy and Titus can be accounted for, not by the passage of time and new circumstances, but by the nature of the compositions and the identity of the addressees, who were Paul's delegates to local churches.

When all of these points are taken into account, the issue of church order turns out to be nondeterminative. If it does not prove that 1 Timothy and Titus were written by Paul, neither does it by any means exclude that possibility. In my judgment, the elements of community structure we find in 1 Timothy and Titus most resemble what we know about the first-century diaspora synagogue and Pauline churches.

Consistency in Teaching

The most telling objection to the authenticity of the Pastorals is the criterion of consistency in theology and moral teaching (see, e.g., Kümmel, *Introduction to the New Testament*, and Lohfink, "Paulinische Theologie"). Even when full credit is given to Paul's great range on these points, fair-minded readers must grant that in the Pastorals there are elements that seem to push the margins of what would be possible for Paul and do so in sufficient combination to present a genuine issue. Certainly, these letters contain a number of themes that are genuinely and distinctively Pauline, such as the mission to the Gentiles, the apostolic example, the necessity of suffering in order to share in God's glory. There are also Pauline expressions that are used in ways that seem slightly different from their usage in the undisputed letters. First Timothy speaks of "law" as something that can be used "lawfully" (1 Tim. 1:8), "faith" seems less an obediential response to God and more a common conviction and commitment (Titus 1:1; 1 Tim. 5:8) or a virtue (2 Tim. 2:22). "Righteousness" (*dikaiosynē*) appears, not as a characteristic of God's activity or as a state of right relations between God and humans, but as a virtue in the Greek sense of "justice" (1 Tim. 6:11; 2 Tim. 2:22). "Tradition" seems to connote a deposit of truth that is to be protected (1 Tim. 6:20; 2 Tim. 1:12–14) rather than a process of transmission within the community (1 Cor. 11:2, 23; 15:3). The Christology of the Pastorals seems to emphasize Jesus' role as "savior" (2 Tim. 1:10; Titus 1:4; 3:6) and his "appearance" (1 Tim. 6:14; 2 Tim. 1:10). Now, it must be emphasized that virtually every one of these aspects can be found in the undisputed letters as well, but not in the same combination or concentration, and therein lies the difference that must be adjudicated.

A similar point can be made about the moral teaching of these letters. The single most important gain in our understanding of Paul over the past twenty years has been in the recognition of the ways in which he *is* a moralist, using many of the techniques and some of the perspectives of Greco-Roman moral teachers (see esp. Malherbe, *Paul and the Popular Philosophers*). But here again, there are points of emphasis in the Pastorals that seem, in the eyes of some readers, to represent something new and different. We don't meet, for example, anything like Paul's admonition to the Corinthians to live in the world "as though not." In the Pastorals, the attitudes and aptitudes of those living in households are appropriate to the life of the community as well. The distinctive Pauline theme of "conscience" (*syneidēsis*) is here, but not in terms of "weak" and "strong" so much as in terms of "good" (1 Tim. 1:5, 19) in contrast to "soiled" (Titus 1:15) and "cauterized" (1 Tim. 4:2). Especially characteristic of the Pastorals is the contrast between "healthy teaching" (1 Tim. 1:10; 6:3; 2 Tim. 1:13; 4:3; Titus 1:9; 2:1) and "sick" (2 Tim. 2:17; 1 Tim. 4:2), expressed respectively by a life filled with virtue (1 Tim. 1:10; 3:2–4, 11; 4:12; 2 Tim. 2:22, 24; 3:10; Titus 1:7–9; 2:7) or vice (1 Tim. 1:8–10; 2 Tim. 3:2–5; Titus 3:3). Once more, it is possible to find each of these elements in the undisputed letters, if not in the same degree and distribution.

Evaluating these thematic points is not easy. Neither an appeal to the outlook of an aging apostle (for this, see Malherbe, "Paulus Senex") nor an appeal to the adjustments of a later generation seems adequately to account for them. What is indisputable is that these three letters have a more distinctly "Greek" feel to them than the "biblical" feel of many of Paul's other letters. Before drawing precipitous conclusions from this, remember that the biblical style is not to be equated with Paul's "natural" style and outlook. Indeed, the distinctively biblical idiom is concentrated in some of his letters (especially Galatians and Romans) while being virtually absent from others (such as 1 Thessalonians, Philippians, and Philemon).

Paul's "voice" in each of his letters is very much affected by his subject matter, his audience, the traditions he employs, and the literary conventions demanded by the circumstances. Can the same factors help to account for the distinctive combination of theological and moral emphases in these three letters to Paul's delegates? Does the fact that both Titus and Timothy have at least partly hellenistic backgrounds, and both play the role of teachers in Pauline churches, help locate the kind of language and the choice of themes found in the letters purporting to be written to them? How would Paul speak and write when among his more hellenistically educated associates? Before pursuing this line of inquiry, we should consider more fully the conventional solution to the problem presented by the Pastorals.

The Conventional Solution

How do the majority of scholars account for the combination of Pauline similarity and difference in the Pastorals? They attribute the similarity to the influence of a Pauline School, which is deeply attached to the figure and teaching of Paul. They ascribe the difference to the fact that this school produced the three letters pseudonymously several decades, perhaps even a century, after Paul's death, when the situation faced by his communities was greatly altered from the days of their first founding and nurturing by the apostle.

It is essential for this theory that all three letters be viewed as *a single literary production* (see Dibelius and Conzelmann, *The Pastoral Epistles,* 5) in which each letter plays a different role. The "letters," then, are not real correspondence, but the fictional re-creation of correspondence. They are not to be read with reference to other Pauline letters from several generations earlier, but only with reference to each other, and possibly to other literature that is regarded as contemporaneous with their production.

In this scenario, 2 Timothy is the key, since it provides the portrait of an aged apostle who wants to hand over the tradition to his delegates, and through them to others (2 Tim. 2:2). We thus have the cipher for the situation proposed: the "faithful teachers" to whom the delegate Timothy handed on the tradition are the sponsors of this correspondence. The personal information in the three letters is entirely fictional, based on the imitation of Paul's genuine letters for the purpose of persuading readers of Pauline authorship. The real point of the literary production is found in the instructions, which represent the beginning of church orders, that is, manuals of discipline that regulate the behavior of communities. First Timothy and Titus find their closest parallels, then, in such works as Polycarp of Smyrna's *Letter to the Philippians,* which in turn is related to the *Didache,* the *Didascalia Apostolorum,* and the *Apostolic Constitutions.*

Why were the Pastorals written? There are a number of possible explanations provided by the scholars who hold that they are pseudonymous. One is that the literary production is a natural response to what might be called a generational crisis within Pauline Christianity. Communities bereft of their founder need to adjust to new circumstances, so disciples of the founder produce a literature in his name to assist the community in its adjustment (see, e.g., M. Y. MacDonald, *The Pauline Churches;* Wolter, *Die Pastoralbriefe als Paulustradition;* Brown, *Churches the Apostles Left Behind,* 31–46). An alternative position emphasizes the development of a conservative reaction within Paulinism. In this view, Paul is being claimed as a hero by groups that the author regards as dangerous. Perhaps Paul is the champion of ascetic Christians who celebrate the active and itinerant mission of women, the way Thecla is associated with Paul in the *Acts of Paul and Thecla* (see D. R. MacDonald, *Paul,* and Davies, *The Revolt of the Widows*). The author of the Pastorals claims Paul as the source for a patriarchal, household-based Christianity in which women's roles are suppressed. Another variation: Paul is being co-opted by heretical movements such as that of Marcion, whose extreme asceticism and world renunciation appeals to many. The author seeks to claim Paul for the more conservative, world-affirming view we see in these letters (see de Boer, "Images of Paul," and Barrett, "Pauline Controversies"). It has even been proposed that Polycarp of Smyrna, an opponent of Marcion, was the author of the Pastorals (von Campenhausen, "Polykarp von Smyrna")!

The author of the Pastorals, therefore, sought to adapt the Pauline message for a new generation, emphasizing structure and order, while resisting ascetical and egalitarian tendencies. In the process, he showed how Christianity was coming to grips with a diminished eschatological expectation, a growth in organization, and an increased accommodation to the world. The "Paulinism" of the Pastorals is one refracted through the prism of second- and third-generation concerns (see Redalié, *Paul après Paul*). Paul has receded to the status of a legendary hero, whose authentic genius is diminished to an echo, whose startling insights have become part of the "deposit" of faith for future generations, whose eschatological rigor has been transformed into "good citizenship" (Dibelius and Conzelmann, *The Pastoral Epistles*, 8).

The obvious appeal of this reconstruction is attested to by its many adherents. It provides a sense of development and conflict within the Pauline tradition. It also helps account for the emergence of the "catholic church" of the mid-second century. The Pastorals, together with Acts and Ephesians, are taken as part of the movement of "early catholicism" that resisted Gnosticism while domesticating the radical Paul, enabling his more challenging letters to remain the heart of the NT canon (see Käsemann, "Paul and Early Catholicism").

Problems with the Conventional Wisdom

The majority opinion is appealing but is not without serious difficulties. In fact, these difficulties are so real that it makes one wonder whether so many hold the position because they are convinced by its arguments, or because it is simply more convenient.

Selective Data

The use of data is selective and slanted. Elements supporting non-Pauline views are emphasized, but elements suggesting continuity with the undisputed letters are slighted. Examples of continuity include Paul's consistent desire for good order, his use of himself as an example for imitation, the way Paul employed his delegates as representatives to local churches, his mixed views on the role of women in the assembly, his affirmation of marriage and the created order, his insistence on strong boundaries, his concern for the reputation of the community, his hostility toward opponents and rivals, his emphasis on the transformative power of grace, his expectation that leaders in local communities would exercise real functions and receive real respect. The list could be extended. My point is simply that these elements also need to be taken into account, and not merely ignored, when making a decision for or against authenticity.

Composite Constructs

The contrast between the Pastorals and the "authentic Paul" is based on artificial and simplified constructs on both ends. Comparison is not made between each of these letters and the whole range of Paul's other letters, but between a composite portrait (drawn unevenly from the three letters) and a composite also of the "authentic Paul." The very real differences between the three letters are simply ignored. In his recent monograph, for example, Y. Redalié refers to the delineation of differences by J. Murphy-O'Connor ("2 Timothy Contrasted") but never discusses what implications these differences might have for his theory of unitary literary construction (*Paul après Paul*, 18). The majority opinion must insist on an all-or-nothing decision regarding authenticity, for the theory relies precisely on such packaging. If, for example, 2 Timothy could be shown with some probability to be authentic, the current explanation for the appearance and function of the Pastorals would fall apart.

Naive Literary Assumptions

The production of pseudonymous literature is regarded as non-problematic for the Christian movement. Nobody who knows the literature of antiquity will deny that large numbers of pseud-epigraphal writings were produced, both within Judaism and within Greco-Roman culture. Virtually without exception, however, such productions amounted to transparent fictions, since authorship was attributed, not to a near contemporary, but to a figure of the distant past. Such is the case with Jewish apocalyptic and wisdom traditions that ascribe authorship to Enoch and Ezra and the Sybil; such is the case also with the letters from the hellenistic period that are attributed to Socrates and Plato. But the assumption that pseudonymity was regarded as benign among the first Christians remains only an assumption (see Aland, "The Problem of Anonymity and Pseudonymity"), which needs seriously to be questioned (see Metzger, "Literary Forgeries and Canonical Pseudepigrapha"). Specifically in the case of Paul, whose letters were so specific and circumstantial, it appears that efforts to advance compositions as his would not be met entirely uncritically (see 2 Thess. 2:2).

Particularly if the Pastorals are dated between 100 and 150, as is currently common, the ready reception of such writings as Pauline by the larger community seems to contradict what evidence we have from that period. We note that the Pastorals appear in *all* the canonical lists of antiquity, whereas other productions attributed to Paul (*Third Corinthians, Letter to Laodiceans, Letters of Paul and Seneca*) or dealing with him (*Acts of Paul and Thecla*) were just as universally rejected. No one knows exactly how to date the NT writing known as 2 Peter, but everyone agrees that it has to have been one of the latest NT compositions, possibly written in the second century. Second Peter 3:16 clearly suggests, not only that Paul wrote from an earlier generation, but that his letters exist in some form of collection ("all his letters") and had already been subject to a history of interpretation (and "misinterpretation").

The *Letter of Clement,* usually dated around 95, is equally conscious of the distance between the apostolic age and Clement's own, and consciously quotes from 1 Corinthians (47:1-7). Ignatius of Antioch (writing around 115) also echoes at least one of Paul's letters in his own (see the allusions to 1 Cor. in Ign. *Eph.* 18.1; Ign. *Magn.* 10.2; Ign. *Trall.* 5.1; 9.2; Ign. *Rom.* 9.2; Ign. *Phld.* 3.3) and makes a sharp distinction between the kind of authority that Paul had as an apostle and his own authority as a bishop, between the apostolic age and his own (Ign. *Eph.* 12.2; Ign. *Rom.* 4.3). Most impressively, Polycarp of Smyrna's *Letter to the Philippians* (Pol. *Phil.,* written shortly after Ignatius's death to accompany the sending of his letters to the Philippians) cites 1 Timothy 6:7 and 6:10 in a passage which, as he clearly indicates, is a florilegium drawn from Paul's letters (Pol. *Phil.* 4.1). The position that Polycarp and the Pastorals are merely drawing from the same wisdom tradition (Dibelius and Conzelmann, *The Pastoral Epistles,* 2, 84–86) fails to account for Polycarp's literary framing and for the specific wording, which is closer in Polycarp and the Pastorals than in any of the other parallels. Finally, a late dating must deal with Tertullian's explicit statement that Marcion "rejected" (*recusavit*) the Pastorals, signifying at the very least that they were already in existence and available to be rejected on account of the teaching that displeased Marcion (*Adversus Marcionem* 5.21). In the light of this sort of hard data, we must ask how likely it would be for these letters to have been produced as late as 100–150 and to have been widely distributed and accepted as genuinely Pauline. In my view, the burden of proof lies on the shoulders of those who hold the majority opinion. This data does *not*, of course, demonstrate that the Pastorals are authentic, but it does suggest that they at least come from a period considerably earlier than is now commonly asserted.

Social Context of Composition

A satisfactory social setting for the composition of three such similar and yet quite different letters has not been provided. Even if the motivations suggested for the writings — the rehabilitation of Paul or the domestication of his tradition or the mastering of a generational crisis — make sense, the process of composition eventually has to touch ground. Someone had to have written the documents and disseminated them to readers as Pauline. Under what circumstances could this take place? Unless we think that literary compositions of this complexity simply appear, we must think in terms of specific human authors and readers. Indeed, the appeal of the Polycarp hypothesis is that it provides a specific situation and person. If he were the author, of course, then we would truly be dealing with a deliberate forgery. Does this fit what we know otherwise of Polycarp's character? And would such a ploy have worked at a time when Paul was a figure of controversy and when Polycarp's opponent Marcion was challenging the authenticity of parts of Paul's letters? And if Polycarp was able to invoke Paul anyway as support for his instructions (which so resemble those in the Pastorals) and, in fact, was able to quote from authentic letters as authority, why should he have needed also to forge these letters?

It has also been suggested that the Pastorals were produced in a school setting, where the imitation of literary models was a common feature of rhetorical education and where a corpus of pseudonymous letters (such as those attributed to Socrates) could be produced for a specific pedagogical purpose (see Fiore, *The Function of Personal Example*, 107–126, 229). This is an attractive alternative to the options of charismatic mist and deliberate forgery. But a closer look reveals its limitations. What evidence do we have for the existence of such a Pauline School after the apostle's death *apart from the very documents that are in question?* We have far more evidence that Paul's disciples were at work in his correspondence during his lifetime, than that they produced letters in his name after his death. The imitation of literary models, furthermore, took place at a fairly elementary level of rhetorical training. It is a long leap from school exercises to compositions meant to serve the functions assigned to these documents. Furthermore, if authentic letters of Paul were being imitated, why were not letters to churches produced (as is hypothesized in the case of Colossians and Ephesians), rather than letters to Paul's delegates, for which there are no prototypes in the undisputed letters? For that matter, why, if imitation was at work, were the language and thought of the undisputed letters not followed more closely? The fragment hypothesis (see p. 12) is of little help. It is difficult to understand why tiny fragments of authentic Pauline notes should be lifted into new compositions so clumsily. We are to suppose an author with a literary sensitivity so acute as to recognize Paul's style in a tiny fragment, yet so clumsy as to be incapable of reproducing it.

Variety in Composition

The irreducible variety in the Pastorals is not taken into account. If these letters are *both* pseudonymous *and* a single literary composition, then we are dealing with an artist of considerable imagination, indeed one not unworthy to be considered Kierkegaard's predecessor. Each letter is directed to a situation that close analysis shows to be at once internally consistent, yet completely inconsistent with the situation addressed by the other two letters. Our pseudonymous author would need to have the ability to capture precisely the psychology of a prisoner who feels abandoned and alone (with slight shades of difference in mood from the self-presentation of the apostle in Philippians) and to create the verisimilitude of an established church (in

Ephesus) and a new foundation (in Crete), with a portrait of opposition appropriate to each circumstance and positive directions fitted to precisely those diverse situations, yet not have the ability to imitate more convincingly the Pauline samples being used for imitation.

I am not suggesting that these problems cannot be answered. It is the failure even to recognize that they are problems, or to engage them with a serious examination of the evidence, that makes the present state of scholarship on the Pastorals so discouraging.

An Alternative Approach

I don't think it is possible to *demonstrate* that the Pastoral letters are authentic, but I do think a legitimate case can be made to read them within the context of Paul's own lifetime and ministry. In the following paragraphs, I sketch four important considerations for establishing that context. Only the careful analysis of specific passages in the letters themselves will reveal which context makes better sense. Is 1 Timothy 2:11-15 intelligible within the context of Paul's experiences with the Corinthian church, or *must* it be read as the work of a later and more sexist author? Is 1 Timothy 5:3-16 better understood as a response to a classic problem in a community's organized charity efforts — and therefore intelligible in the context of the diaspora synagogue — or *must* it be understood as the repression of a protofeminist movement among women in the second century? The real demonstration is in the details. These four framing comments, however, set the stage for such arguments in the commentary proper, by stating some of the fundamentals that the majority position too regularly overlooks.

Character of Paul's Ministry

Paul's mission was both more extensive and more complex than we might suppose from a casual reading of Acts, which focuses on Paul as a prophetic figure (see Johnson, *The Acts of the Apostles,* 11-14). It is more extensive: we learn from Romans 5:19 that

Paul's mission extended to Illyricum (the coast of erstwhile Yugoslavia), information that is absent from Acts. We also know that Paul founded churches in Galatia, although Acts barely provides him the opportunity to do so. Not all of these foundations were carried out by Paul personally. He writes to the Colossians as one of his churches, although it was founded by Epaphras. Paul had a network of associates in the field that numbered at least forty persons (see Johnson, *Writings of the New Testament*, 248–49).

Paul's ministry, furthermore, was not primarily that of the theologian but of the pastor. He founded churches, stayed with them for a time, then put them in the hands of others, as he sought to preach Christ where no one else had gone (Rom. 15:20). His "daily care for all the churches" (2 Cor. 11:28) is legitimately listed among his sufferings, for oversight of communities across such an expanse of territory must have been extraordinarily stressful. Paul's letters to these communities indicate how central the goal of edification was for him. For Paul, the essential thing was the "building of a house," that is, the creation and maintenance of a community of character that manifested the holiness of the God who called it into being (1 Thess. 4:3). To shape the character of his communities, Paul played the role of the *moral teacher* of antiquity. Recent scholarship has shown just how pervasively Paul used the techniques and topoi of Greco-Roman philosophers (see Malherbe, "Hellenistic Moralists and the New Testament"). The point I am making is simply this: when the pastorals portray Paul as "teacher of the Gentiles" and emphasize life in the community as life in a household and contain the style and substance of moral instruction that looks remarkably Greco-Roman, they are entirely consistent with the ministry of Paul as found in the undisputed letters.

Character of Paul's Correspondence

Paul's letters are one of the instruments he employed to shape these communities of character. But they were neither his first nor his preferred mode of pastoral presence. Paul's preferred way of dealing with difficulties in local communities was by a personal visit (see Funk, "The Apostolic *Parousia* "). When such a visit was not possible, his next step was the sending of a trusted delegate — among whom Timothy and Titus stand out — to represent him personally to that community. Only as a third step did Paul write a letter.

That Paul's letter writing was not always successful is shown by the fact that his letters sometimes needed to be followed by others because of misunderstandings generated by the first (see 2 Thessalonians and 2 Corinthians). The letters that Paul wrote to communities, therefore, were *occasional,* not simply because they were written to diverse locations and populations, but because they were written in response to specific kinds of difficulties which, by the time of the writing, were sometimes at a critical stage. The impossibility of systematizing Paul's "thought" — even if there were anything systematic about it — is directly connected to this contingent character of his correspondence (see Beker, *Paul the Apostle*).

His letters were also *official* in character, that is, they were written not simply from Paul to personal friends but from the apostle to "the church of God" in one location or another. They are, from beginning to end, religious literature produced with the aim of securing a people with a certain identity in the world. Finally, his letters were also *complex* in composition. Some aspects of this I have touched on already: that Paul's letters use the forms found in rhetorical handbooks, that the principle of *prosōpopoiia* affects his style, that the use of traditional materials affects wording and content, that cosponsorship and dictation mean at the very least that more minds than his own were involved in such composition (note that Timothy, for example, is cosender of 2 Corinthians, Philippians, Colossians, 1 Thessalonians, 2 Thessalonians, and Philemon). Such complexity makes each of Paul's letters distinctive.

There is no such thing as a generic Pauline letter, but only this collection of unique missives. Equally, there is no such thing as a Pauline theology standing outside these discrete compositions, but only the specific rhetoric of a pastor responding in writing to situations presented by his churches. It may be appropriate to speak of "the theological perspective of Romans," for it can be located within the rhetoric of that composition. To attempt larger statements about Paul's theology is to risk a form of abstraction that distorts the lively and flexible thought found in ✓ his letters. The point of these remarks for the Pastorals should be clear. No more than we can collapse Romans and Galatians and declare them to be saying the "same thing" — despite all their thematic similarities — should we be allowed to collapse the Pastorals and declare them to be saying the "same thing."

Identity and Role of Paul's Delegates

For the majority view on the Pastorals, the identity of Paul's addressees is incidental; Timothy and Titus serve as literary types for second-generation disciples who are to hand on the tradition to a third generation (2 Tim. 2:2). Yet a closer look at the role played by delegates in Paul's ministry should give us pause (see, in particular, Mitchell, "New Testament Envoys").

Timothy played a central role in the Pauline mission. I have already indicated that he was cosponsor of five undisputed letters. Timothy also served at various times as Paul's representative to the Macedonian churches (see Acts 18:5; 19:22) of Thessalonica (1 Thess. 3:2) and Philippi (Phil. 2:19), as well as to the Corinthians (see 1 Cor. 4:17; 16:10–11; Rom. 16:21). According to 1 Timothy 1:3, he played the same role in the Ephesian church. Acts 16:1 says that Timothy had a Greek father, which would make it likely that he had a Greek style of education as well. From Paul's references to him in the undoubted letters, his special role and his place in Paul's affection are obvious. When Paul tells the Corinthians to "imitate me" (1 Cor. 4:16), he adds, "Therefore I sent to you Timothy, my beloved and faithful child in the Lord, to remind you of my ways in Christ, as I teach them everywhere in the church." We take note in this passage of the role of memory and imitation, the portrayal of Paul as teacher, and Timothy's role as the "reminder" of Paul's teaching and example to a local community. Timothy may not have possessed much personal presence and confidence, for Paul also tells the Corinthians (1 Cor. 16:10–11), "When Timothy comes, see that you put him at ease among you, for he is doing the work of the Lord as I am. Let no one despise him." When writing to the Philippians in 2:19–23, Paul says of Timothy,

I hope in the Lord Jesus to send Timothy to you soon, so that I may be cheered by news of you. I have no one like him, who will be genuinely anxious for your welfare. They all look after their own interests, not those of Jesus Christ. But Timothy's worth you know, how as a son with a father, he has served with me in the Gospel. I hope therefore to send him just as soon as I see how it will go with me.

Finally, in 1 Thessalonians 3:2, Paul writes of Timothy, "And we have sent Timothy, our brother and God's servant in the gospel of Christ, to establish you in your faith and to exhort you, that no one be moved by these afflictions."

There is the most remarkable correlation between these random notes concerning Timothy in the authentic letters of Paul and the portrayal of Timothy in the two letters addressed to him. In them, he appears as young, timid, and easily despised (1 Tim. 4:12; 2 Tim. 1:7). He is a "beloved" (2 Tim. 1:2) or "genuine" son (1 Tim. 1:2) of Paul's. He is a "servant of God" (*diakonos* in 1 Thess. 3:2, *doulos* in 2 Tim. 2:24 and Phil. 1:1). He is to "exhort" others (1 Tim. 6:2; 2 Tim. 4:2) and to "remind" churches of Paul's teaching (2 Tim. 2:14), as well as to provide them an example they can imitate (1 Tim. 4:12), just as he has an example to follow in Paul (2 Tim. 1:13).

Two reasonable explanations can be offered for this coincidence of details. The first is that the letters to Timothy contain Paul's characteristic and habitual perceptions of his delegate and faithfully report them. The second is that a pseudepigrapher had available to him the full range of such epithets and functions, and captured them with unerring accuracy. The more important point — too often overlooked in discussions of the Pastorals — is that the character and function of the delegate Timothy as presented in these letters corresponds perfectly to the context of Paul's ministry.

The undisputed letters tell us much less about Titus. He also was of Greek background (Gal. 2:3), and Paul makes much of Titus's not having to be circumcised when he accompanied Paul to Jerusalem (Gal. 2:1). Although the connection cannot be certain, he may be the Titus (or Titius) Justus, whom Acts 18:7 calls a God-fearer and whose house Paul uses after leaving the synagogue in Corinth. Titus is, in any case, notably associated with Paul's Corinthian ministry (2 Cor. 2:13; 7:6, 13-14), and seems to have been especially heavily involved in Paul's collection efforts (2 Cor. 8:6, 16, 23; 12:18). He is not the representative of a local church, but is Paul's "associate/partner" (*koinōnos*). Paul never speaks of him in the same terms of affection he uses for Timothy.

These few details match well what little we learn of Titus in the letter addressed to him. He is not a "beloved" but a "genuine son" who shares a "common faith" (*koinēn pistin*) with Paul (Titus 1:4). Titus has been sent to Crete to carry out administrative oversight (Titus 1:5) until he is replaced in that position by Artemas or Tychichos (3:12). His duty in Crete may also have included some fund-raising (see Titus 3:14). According to 2 Timothy 4:10, Titus also worked in Dalmatia, which would fit within the broad range of the Pauline mission (see Rom. 15:19).

We have no other letters of Paul written to delegates. Only Philemon is addressed to an individual, and like 1 Timothy and Titus, it seems to have intended a public audience as well as the individual addressed. Therefore, we can only speculate about what sort of letters Paul would write to delegates with such back grounds and such responsibilities. We would, I suggest, expect personal encouragement for the hard task of dealing with lively and often refractory Pauline churches, reminders of the ideal they should follow, hostile dismissals of rival teachers, *ad hoc* directions concerning leadership positions. For fellow workers of Greek education, we might well expect a shaping of the gospel that emphasized its godliness/piety (*eusebeia*) and a Christology in which the appearance of a savior figured prominently, as well as ethical teaching that stressed the pursuit of virtue and the avoidance of vice. Such a shaping would in part be an adaptation to Paul's readers, but we should not assume that the private Paul did not have views similar to these. We would expect letters to such delegates to combine attention to their personal disposition and character, as well as specific direction regarding particular issues. As so often in the hellenistic world, there were precedents for letters such as these.

Literary Character of the Respective Letters

This consideration is particularly important, for the categorization of the compositions can profoundly affect the degree to which it is plausible that they could have been written by Paul in his lifetime. As we shall see, it is commonly asserted that 2 Timothy has the literary form of a *testament* or *farewell discourse.* There are real arguments that can be made in favor of such a designation, which we shall consider in the appropriate place. The point to be noted here is that this literary genre tends to demand the presumption of pseudonymity, since virtually without exception such farewell discourses were put into the mouths of heroes of the past. If, however, 2 Timothy appears to fit even more closely the form of the personal *paraenetic letter,* as I will argue, then this is a form that was available to Paul in his lifetime and, if anything, tilts the balance in favor of authenticity. Likewise, if 1 Timothy and Titus are categorized as *church orders,* then it makes sense to see them as a development from a later period than Paul's own ministry. If, however, they are seen to fit even better the form of a *mandate letter,* that genre was also certainly available to Paul during his lifetime.

The Approach of This Commentary

In the pages that follow, I will read the Pastorals as much as possible in terms of their literary self-presentation. First, I will treat them as real rather than fictional letters. This means, second, that the literary form of each letter, the circumstances of composition that it suggests, and the responses it gives to those circumstances will be considered individually and in particular, rather than in general and as a group. Third, I will use the rest of the Pauline corpus as the appropriate comparative context for the analysis of these letters. Fourth, when this approach finds itself in difficulties — as it does in some passages — I will discuss the relative strengths and weaknesses of the alternative approach. Fifth, I will consider the theology, ethics, and church order of these letters only as each emerges from the specific argument of the respective compositions, since the premise that these are real letters places them in the same category of the occasional and contingent as the rest of the Pauline Epistles. Sixth, in order to sharpen the perception of the letters as separate and distinct compositions, I will deal with 2 Timothy first, and then 1 Timothy and Titus.

Works Cited in Introduction

Aland, K. "The Problem of Anonymity and Pseudonymity in Christian Literature of the First Two Centuries." *JTS*, n.s., 12 (1961): 39–49.

Barrett, C. K., "Pauline Controversies in the Post-Pauline Period." *NTS* 20 (1973–74): 229–45.

Bassler, J. "The Widow's Tale: A Fresh Look at 1 Tim 5:3–16." *JBL* 103 (1982): 23–41.

Bauer, W. *Orthodoxy and Heresy in Earliest Christianity.* Edited by R. A. Kraft and G. Krodel. Philadelphia: Fortress Press, 1971.

Beker, J. C. *Heirs of Paul: Paul's Legacy in the New Testament and in the Church Today.* Minneapolis: Fortress Press, 1991.

———. *Paul the Apostle: The Triumph of God in Life and Thought.* Philadelphia: Fortress Press, 1980.

Brown, R. E. *The Churches the Apostles Left Behind.* New York: Paulist Press, 1984.

Brox, N. *Die Pastoralbriefe.* Regensburger Neues Testament. Regensburg: F. Pustet, 1969.

von Campenhausen, H. *Ecclesiastical Authority and Spiritual Power in the Church of the First Three Centuries.* Translated by J. Baker. Stanford: Stanford University Press, 1969.

———. "Polykarp von Smyrna und die Pastoralbriefe." In *Aus der Früzeit des Christentums,* 197–252. Tübingen: J. C. B. Mohr (Paul Siebeck, 1993).

Cook, D. "The Pastoral Fragments Reconsidered." *JTS* 35 (1984): 120–31.

Davies, S. L. *The Revolt of the Widows: The Social World of the Apocryphral Acts.* Carbondale, Ill.: Southern Illinois University Press, 1980.

de Boer, M. C. "Images of Paul in the Post-Apostolic Period." *CBQ* 42 (1980): 359–80.

Dibelius, M., and H. Conzelman. *The Pastoral Epistles.* Edited by H. Koester. Translated by P. Buttolph and A. Yarbro. Hermeneia. Philadelphia: Fortress Press, 1972.

Donelson, L. R. *Pseudepigraphy and Ethical Argument in the Pastoral Epistles.* Hermeneutische Untersuchungen zur Theologie 22. Tübingen: J. C. B. Mohr (Paul Siebeck, 1986).

Ellis, E. E. "The Authorship of the Pastorals: A Resume and Assessment of Recent Trends." In *Paul and His Recent Interpreters,* 49–57. Grand Rapids: Eerdmans, 1961.

Epp, E. J., and G. W. MacRae, eds. *The New Testament and Its Modern Interpreters.* Atlanta: Scholars Press, 1989.

Fiore, B. *The Function of Personal Example in the Socratic and Pastoral Epistles.* Analecta Biblica 105. Rome: Biblical Institute Press, 1986.

Funk, R. W. "The Apostolic *Parousia:* Form and Significance." In *Christian History and Interpretation: Essays Presented to John Knox,* edited by W. B. Farmer, et al., 249–69. Cambridge: Cambridge University Press, 1967.

Furnish, V. P. "Pauline Studies." In *The New Testament and Its Modern Interpreters,* edited by E. J. Epp and G. W. MacRae, 321–50. Atlanta: Scholars Press, 1989.

Graystone, K., and G. Herdan. "The Authorship of the Pastorals in the Light of Statistical Linguistics." *NTS* 6 (1959–60): 1–15.

Harrison, P. *The Problem of the Pastoral Epistles.* London: Oxford University Press, 1921.

Johnson, L. T. *The Acts of the Apostles.* Sacra Pagina 5. Collegeville, Minn.: Liturgical Press, 1992.

———. *The Writings of the New Testament: An Interpretation.* Philadelphia: Fortress Press, 1986.

Käsemann, E. "Paul and Early Catholicism." In *New Testament Questions of Today,* 236–51. Philadelphia: Fortress Press, 1969.

Kantor, R. *Community and Commitment.* Cambridge: Harvard University Press, 1973.

Kephart, W. *Extraordinary Groups: The Sociology of Unconventional Life-Styles.* New York: St. Martin's Press, 1976.

Knight, G. W. *Commentary on the Pastoral Epistles.* New International Greek Testament Commentary. Grand Rapids: Eerdmans, 1992.

Kümmel, W. G. *Introduction to the New Testament.* Rev. ed. Translated by H. C. Kee. Nashville: Abingdon Press, 1975. 366–87.

Lock, W. *A Critical and Exegetical Commentary on the Pastoral Epistles.* International Critical Commentary. New York: T. & T. Clark, 1924.

Lohfink, G. "Paulinische Theologie in der Rezeption der Pastoralbriefe." In *Paulus in den neutestamentlichen Spatschriften,* edited K. Kertelge, 70–121. Quaestiones disputatae 89. Freiburg: Herder, 1981.

MacDonald, D. R. *The Legend and the Apostle: The Battle for Paul in Story and Canon.* Philadelphia: Westminster Press, 1983.

———. "Virgins, Widows, and Paul in Second-Century Asia Minor." In *1979 SBL Seminar Papers,* edited by P. Achtemeier, 1:165–84. Missoula, Mont.: Scholars Press, 1979.

MacDonald, M. Y., *The Pauline Churches: A Socio-Historical Study of Institutionalization in the Pauline and Deutero-Pauline Writings*. Society for New Testament Studies Monograph Series. Cambridge: Cambridge University Press, 1988.

Malherbe, A. J. "Ancient Epistolary Theory." *Ohio Journal of Religious Studies* 5 (1977): 3–77.

———. "Hellenistic Moralists and the New Testament." *ANRW* II, 26, 1 (1992): 267–333.

———. *Paul and the Popular Philosophers*. Minneapolis: Fortress Press, 1989.

———. "Paulus Senex." *Restoration Quarterly* 36 (1994): 197–207.

Meeks, W. A. *The Writings of St. Paul*. New York: W. W. Norton, 1972.

Metzger, B. M. "Literary Forgeries and Canonical Pseudepigrapha." *JBL* 91 (1972): 3–24.

Mitchell, M. M. "New Testament Envoys in the Context of Greco-Roman Diplomatic and Epistolary Conventions: The Example of Timothy and Titus." *JBL* 111 (1992): 641–62.

Murphy-O'Connor, J. "2 Timothy Contrasted with 1 Timothy and Titus." *RB* 98 (1991): 403–10.

Quinn, J. D. "The Last Volume of Luke: The Relation of Luke-Acts to the Pastoral Epistles." In *Perspectives on Luke-Acts,* edited C. H. Talbert, 62–75. Danville, Va.: Association of Baptist Professors of Religion, 1978.

Redalié, Y. *Paul après Paul: le temps, le salut, le morale selon les epîtres à Timothée et à Tite*. Geneva: Labor et Fides, 1994.

Reicke, B. "The Constitution of the Early Church in the Light of Jewish Documents." In *The Scrolls and the New Testament,* edited by K. Stendahl, 143–56. New York: Harper and Row, 1957.

Robinson, J. A. T. *Redating the New Testament*. Philadelphia: Westminster Press, 1970.

Robinson, T. A. "Graystone and Herdan's 'C' Quantity Formula and the Authorship of the Pastorals." *NTS* 30 (1984): 282–88.

Schweitzer, A. *Paul and His Interpreters*. Translated by W. Montgomery. New York: Macmillan Co., 1912.

Spicq, C. *Les Epîtres Pastorales*. Paris: J. Gabalda, 1969.

Stowers, S. K. "Romans 7:7–25 as a Speech in Character (*prosopōpoiia*)." In *Paul in His Hellenistic Setting,* edited by T. Engberg-Peterson, 180–202. Minneapolis: Fortress Press, 1995.

Trummer, P. "Corpus Paulinum — Corpus Pastorale: zur Ortung der Paulustradition in den Pastoralbriefen." In *Paulus in den neutestamentlichen Spätschriften,* edited by K. Kertelge, 122–45. Quaestiones disputatae, no. 89. Freiburg: Herder, 1981.

Wilson, S. G. *Luke and the Pastoral Epistles*. London: SPCK, 1979.

Wolter, M. *Die Pastoralbriefe als Paulustradition.* Forschungen zur Religion und Literatur des Alten und Neuen Testaments, 146. Göttingen: Vandenhoeck & Ruprecht, 1988.

Zahn, T. *Introduction to the New Testament.* 3 vols. Translated by M. W. Jacobs et al. New York: Charles Scribner's Sons, 1909.

Chapter One _____

2 Timothy

_____

Paul is writing to his delegate Timothy from prison (2 Tim. 1:16; 2:9; 4:16). The most likely supposition is that this is a Roman imprisonment (1:17), possibly the one reported by Acts 28:30. We are not told where Timothy is at the time of writing, although Paul hopes that he will come before winter (4:21), which may be close at hand in view of Paul's concern to have Timothy bring the cloak that Paul had left with Carpus (4:13). Although Paul's conditions are such that he can receive visitors (1:16; 4:21) and carry out some business, namely, the sending out of associates (4:12) as well as study and correspondence (4:13), he does not view his situation optimistically. The apostle has already had one hearing (a "first defense," 4:16), but thinks that his life is very nearly spent (4:6). His only realistic hope is for the "crown of righteousness" (4:8) and the "heavenly kingdom" (4:18). Nevertheless, he struggles to continue proclaiming the gospel (4:17).

The situation sketched by this letter in many respects resembles that found in Philippians, which is also written (in all likelihood) from a Roman imprisonment (see Phil. 1:12–14; 4:22) and is cosponsored by Timothy (Phil. 1:1). As I will show later (see p. 60), the mode of argument in 2 Timothy 1:8–2:13 particularly resembles that in Philippians 2:1–3:17. The difference between the two letters is mainly one of tone. In Philippians, Paul has some optimism about the mission, despite rivalry among his coworkers (Phil. 1:12–18; 4:2–3). His dismissal of rival teachers is preemptory (Phil. 1:28; 3:2–3, 18–19). Although Paul is willing to die, he is certain that he will survive to continue working for his readers' welfare (Phil. 1:19–

26). He sends Timothy as a delegate to them, hoping to receive
him back with news (Phil. 2:19–24). In 2 Timothy, the mood
is much grimmer. It is not simply that Paul expresses no hope
of this-life deliverance. His mission, which faced opposition in
the past from Alexander the coppersmith (2 Tim. 4:14), continues to be under assault from rival teachers, who now confront
and challenge Timothy. They include men named Hymenaios
and Philetos (2 Tim. 2:17), who teach that the resurrection is
already past (v. 18). The worst news is that they are enjoying
considerable success (2 Tim. 2:18; 3:1–5, 13; 4:3–4).

At this critical juncture, Paul considers himself abandoned by
some of his allies. He names Phygelus and Hermogenes from
Asia (2 Tim. 1:15), and Demas, who is "in love with this present
world" (4:10). Paul complains that at his first defense, "No one
took my part; all deserted me" (4:16). It is clear from the fact
that Onesiphorus has come to visit him (1:16), and that he is
still supported by Luke (4:11) and Eubulus and Pudens and Linus
and Claudia and "all the brethren" (4:21), that Paul's abandonment is as much emotional as it is physical. It is impossible to
avoid the impression as well that he fears for the stability of
his beloved son Timothy, perhaps concerned about his timidity/
cowardice (1:6) in the face of opposition.

Paul writes, then, to encourage his favorite delegate in his
struggles. By so doing, the apostle also fights for the success of
his own ministry and demonstrates that "the word of God is not
chained" (2 Tim. 2:9). The letter is noteworthy for its unswerv-
ing attention to Timothy, his character and his role as a teacher.
Only one verse suggests that Timothy should hand on what he
has learned to allies who are equally faithful and able to teach
others (2:2). Otherwise, everything in the letter, including the
attacks on opponents, bears on Timothy himself. The letter is
personal not only in tone but in focus.

The image of an aging, perhaps dying, religious leader who
before his death instructs his follower on the struggles still to
come and on the need for perseverance in the face of opposition reminds most scholars of the literary genre known as the
farewell discourse, or testament (see Wolter, *Die Pastoralbriefe als
Paulustradition,* 222–41; Redalié, *Paul après Paul,* 101–7). Building on the farewell of Jacob to his twelve sons in Genesis 49,

the form became elaborated into such full-fledged literary productions as the *Testaments of the Twelve Patriarchs, Testament of Abraham,* and *Testament of Job* (see Kurz, *Farewell Addresses*). The NT contains a clear example of the form in Paul's farewell address to the elders at Ephesus in Acts 20:17–35. A constant feature of the genre is that the eponymous ancestor is a figure of the past, whose dying words thus take on the character of prophecy. The presence of such a discourse in Acts 20:17–35 is taken to be one of the surest signs that Acts was composed after the death of Paul. Understandably, then, those who are convinced that 2 Timothy is a testament are also confident that it was written after Paul's death and is, therefore, necessarily a pseudonymous composition.

The decision to regard 2 Timothy as a farewell discourse may, however, be precipitous on two counts. The first is that some elements in the composition do not fit the genre terribly well. Paul's death, for example, is only intimated, and the letter does not portray him as ceasing from his efforts for the mission. He is not really "handing over" anything to Timothy in an explicit generational transition. The attention given to the opponents, furthermore, is far more detailed than is usual in such compositions, which usually cast their "predictions" in terms suitably vague and portentous. The degree of specific detail in 2 Timothy is impressive. The second reason for doubting that 2 Timothy is a testament is the existence of another literary form, one not requiring pseudonymity, that fits the evidence in 2 Timothy even better, namely, the personal paraenetic letter.

In the rhetorical handbooks composed by Pseudo-Demetrius and Pseudo-Libanius, there is listed a type of letter called *epistolē parainetikē* (paraenetic letter). Pseudo-Libanius says such a letter is written "to exhort someone, advising him to pursue something and to abstain from something." In the model letter he provides, Pseudo-Libanius makes clear that such paraenesis involves above all moral behavior:

> Always be an emulator, dear friend, of virtuous men. For it is better to be well spoken of when imitating good men, than to be reproached by all for following evil men. (in Malherbe, "Ancient Epistolary Theory," 71)

The short sample contains many of the elements of the moral exhortation that is broadly referred to as paraenetic (see Malherbe, *Moral Exhortation*, 122–24). We notice that the form involves the imitation of a model, contains an antithesis between pursuing good and avoiding evil, and makes explicit a concern for good reputation in the eyes of others.

We are fortunate also to have the treatise *To Demonicus* by Pseudo-Isocrates, in which an uncle of a young man whose father had died writes to him what he explicitly calls a paraenetic treatise, which actually takes a form very similar to a letter. The uncle proposes the young man's father as the perfect model for him to imitate and calls that paradigm to Demonicus's memory (*To Demonicus* 3–11). Notice again—memory, model, and imitation. The author then fleshes out this model by means of a long series of maxims, which, as so frequently in paraenesis, tend to fall naturally into a positive and negative alternation: "Do this, avoid that." Throughout these maxims, there is a constant stress on the need for a young man to maintain a good reputation in the eyes of others (*To Demonicus* 12–49). At the conclusion of the treatise, the author again proposes a series of models that young Demonicus can imitate (50–51).

In 2 Timothy, likewise, we find Paul presenting himself as father to his beloved son Timothy. The apostle evokes Timothy's memory of the models that he can imitate, among whom Paul includes himself. Then, Paul explicates the model with a series of maxims. At the end, he once more presents himself as a model. Second Timothy fits as closely as anything in the ancient world the form of the personal paraenetic letter, such as we find it described in the rhetorical handbooks and exemplified by *To Demonicus*.

One dimension of 2 Timothy that does not seem to fit within the framework of the paraenetic letter is the polemic against false teachers. It has been recognized for some time that a great deal of this polemic is stereotypical and should be understood, not as specific descriptions of the opponents, but as the kind of vituperation that commonly took place in hellenistic schools between rival teachers of every sort (see Karris, "Background and Significance") and can be found in the NT also in the form of slander against fellow Jews (see Johnson, "The New Testament's Anti-Jewish Slander"). The first social function of such polemic was the disparagement of opposing teachers in order to recommend one's own teaching. In 2 Timothy, however, Paul does not attack these opponents directly. Instead, he contrasts their character and methods to those of his delegate, Timothy, constantly returning to his personal instruction ("but you...."). The false teachers become the negative model that Timothy is to avoid.

The identical use of polemic as a negative foil can be found in hellenistic protreptic discourses encouraging young men to pursue the life of philosophy. In works such as Lucian of Samosata's *Demonax* and *Nigrinus,* in Dio Chryostom's *Oration 77/78,* and in Epictetus's discourse on the ideal Cynic (*Discourse* III, 22), we find the same combination of elements as in 2 Timothy: the memory of the respected teacher, who is a model for the aspirant to imitate, and then the presentation of maxims ("do this, avoid that") employing the stereotyped polemic against false teachers in order to portray in vivid colors that which should be avoided.

Second Timothy, then, has the overall form of the paraenetic letter. But since Paul is concerned, not simply with Timothy's personal virtue, but above all with his character as a delegate, that is, as a teacher of churches, he uses polemic in the way it is used in protreptic discourses, as a negative foil to the ideal image represented by Paul himself. The structure of 2 Timothy, therefore, is (a) the presentation of Paul as a model together with other exemplars (1:3–2:13); (b) maxims for Timothy as a teacher, presented in contrast to the false teachers (2:14–4:5); and (c) the re-presentation of Paul as a model (4:6–18).

The Greeting — 1:1–2

1:1 From Paul, an apostle of Christ Jesus, because God wills it and based on the promise of life found in Christ Jesus, **2**to Timothy my beloved child. May you have grace, mercy, and peace, from God who is Father and from Christ Jesus, our Lord.

Notes on Translation

There are no significant textual variants in these two verses. The reading in verse 1 of some MSS, "Jesus Christ" rather than "Christ Jesus," is understandable, since Paul's usage elsewhere varies. Each of the Pastorals has "Christ Jesus" in the greeting, as do 2 Corinthians, Philippians, Philemon, Colossians, and Ephesians. In Galatians, 1 Thessalonians, and 2 Thessalonians, in contrast, Paul uses "Jesus Christ." In Romans and 1 Corinthians, we find the same textual variation as here. The diction of the greeting is entirely Pauline, with none of the terms unattested in the universally recognized letters. The term *eleos* (mercy) in v. 2 is used by Paul elsewhere (Rom. 9:23; 11:31; Gal. 6:16), but not as part of his usual formula, "grace and peace." Likewise, Paul normally makes *"our* God who is father" explicit by the use of the possessive pronoun *hēmōn,* but the pronoun is absent in v. 2 and is (probably) lacking in 2 Thessalonians 1:2 as well as in 1 Timothy 1:2 and Titus 1:2. Precisely these small touches are what analysts of style in the Pastorals must consider, and, as here, the evidence is almost always mixed: the Pastorals appear as a "little different," but not so far off the range of Pauline possibility as to make the criterion of style definitive. The translation "because God wills it" in v. 1 is a free rendition of *dia thelēmatos theou* (literally, "through God's will"). The hardest phrase to render is *kat' epangelian zōēs* (v. 1), which could be taken as "according to [or, with a view to] the promise of life." I have chosen to read it as equivalent to "in virtue of" (cf. Heb. 7:16): the promise of life in Christ Jesus is the basis of Paul's apostleship together with the choice of God.

Literary Observations

Within the wide range of compositions that were counted as letters in antiquity, ranging from short business notes to philosophical treatises (see Seneca's *Moral Epistles* or *Letter of Aristeas*), the greeting was the most important signal of an author's intention that a writing be regarded as correspondence, a personal written exchange between a (real or fictive) author and a (real or fictive) reader. The greeting also signalled the social relationships that obtained between the parties and even some of the social functions of the correspondence (see Stowers, "Social Typification"). In the present case, the social relationship is that of a (fictive) father and his (fictive) son.

The greeting of hellenistic letters had a definite form: from author to addressee, greetings (*chairein;* see, e.g., 1 Macc. 10:18; 11:30; 12:6; 2 Macc. 9:19; 11:16). Paul's greetings follow this basic form. Rather than use the secular "greetings" (*chairein*), however, he uses the more religiously colored "grace" (*charis*) and combines this with the "peace" (*eirēnē*) characteristic of Jewish letter greetings. It is also common for Paul to elaborate one or the other elements of the greeting. These variations can provide clues as to his circumstances, to those of the readers, or to Paul's intentions for writing. In Corinth, for example, where the problems presented by the church were so central, we find the part of the greeting concerning the church elaborated. In Romans and Galatians, where Paul's apostolic standing is important, the first element of the greeting is given fuller treatment. Among the Pastorals, 2 Timothy's greeting holds a middle position. It is more complex than that in 1 Timothy, but simpler than the one in Titus.

Comment

Although the greeting is relatively short and straightforward, it announces a set of complex relationships that pervade the letter. What is most striking is the thoroughly religious character of these relationships. Paul does not identify himself in personal terms but rather in terms of his religious calling and office. The designation "apostle" (*apostolos*) is used absolutely in Romans 1:1, but is specified as "of Christ Jesus" or "of Jesus Christ" in the greetings of 1 and 2 Corinthians, Galatians, and Ephesians, as well as 1 Timothy and Titus. The title is absent from the greeting in Philippians, Philemon, and 1 and 2 Thessalonians. As the etymology of *apostolos* and its usage in the NT suggest, being an apostle meant being a representative of the one who sends out with a commission. In this case, Paul designates himself as the official representative of "Messiah Jesus." Since Paul's apostolic credentials were frequently in question, the fact that he was personally sent out by Christ Jesus is important to him (see Gal. 1:1–4, 11–12). Paul specifies his apostolic authority further by the phrase *dia thelēmatos theou* ("because God wills it"). This is the only time the phrase occurs in the Pastorals, but it appears in the greeting of 1 and 2 Corinthians, Galatians, Colossians, and Ephesians; the theological warrant for Paul's authority could hardly be made more explicit.

Paul's apostleship is grounded further in "the promise of life found in Christ Jesus." The language of promise is prevalent in the NT (see, e.g., Luke 24:49; Acts 2:33; 7:17; 13:23; 23:21; 26:6; Rom. 4:13–21; 9:4; 15:8; 2 Cor. 1:20; Gal. 3:14–29; 4:28; Eph. 1:13; Heb. 4:1; 6:13; James 1:12), but is remarkably absent from the Old Testament (see only LXX Ps. 55:9; 2 Macc. 2:18). The phrase "promise of life" is found otherwise only in 1 Timothy 4:8 ("a promise of life both now and in the future"), although the same combination of ideas is found also in Titus 1:2 ("eternal life, which was promised by the truthful God") and James 1:12. That this "life" is more than biological, and is to be understood precisely in terms of a gift from the "living God," is clear from Paul's usage elsewhere (see Rom. 5:21; 6:23; Gal. 6:8). That this life comes through the gift of Jesus as Messiah and risen Lord is also emphasized by Paul (Rom. 5:17–18, 21; 8:2; 1 Cor. 15:19; 2 Cor. 4:11; Col. 3:3).

Apart from 1 Peter 3:16, 5:10, and 5:14, the phrase "in Christ Jesus" (*en christō Iēsou*) is found only in the Pauline literature. The phrase does not occur in Titus, but it appears in 2 Timothy 1:1, 9, 13; 2:1; 3:12, 15 and in 1 Timothy 1:14 and 3:13. Typically, then, 2 Timothy's usage is closer to Paul's own (see esp. Rom. 3:24; 15:17; 1 Cor. 1:4; 4:17; Gal. 2:4; Phil. 2:1; 3:14; Col. 1:4; 1 Thess. 5:18; Philem. 8), although the two occurrences in 1 Timothy also fall within the range of Pauline diction. The precise way in which the phrase is used in the Pastorals, however, has been contrasted to that found in the undisputed letters (see Allen, "The 'In Christ' Formula"). The distinction, in my opinion, is overdrawn.

The greeting defines Paul's relationship with Timothy as one of father to child. The phrase "beloved child" (*agapētō teknō*) strikingly echoes Paul's characterization of this delegate to the Corinthians, "For this reason I am sending to you Timothy, who is my beloved child and faithful in the Lord" (1 Cor. 4:17). The use of fictive kinship language is common in Paul's letters (see Meeks, *The First Urban Christians*, 87, 225) and seems to be based on the sense that Paul "gave birth" to his communities by means of the gospel (see 1 Cor. 4:15; Gal. 4:19; and esp. Philem. 10). Paul does refer to others among his associates and readers as "beloved" (see Rom. 16:5, 8–9, 12; 1 Cor. 4:14; 15:58; Phil. 2:12; Col. 1:7; Philem. 16). The filial relationship with Timothy involves more than a shared commitment to Christ. It involves as well the fact that Timothy is Paul's representative and, as such, must teach communities in his place. There is, then, a teacher/disciple relationship between them that is critical to the understanding of this letter. Note that in 1:11 Paul designates himself, not only as "preacher and apostle," but also as "teacher" (*didaskalos*), and it is Timothy's character and behavior in the same role that Paul seeks to encourage here.

The specifically religious character of the correspondence is signalled, finally, by the fact that the greeting concludes in a prayer. Even though "grace and peace" are formulaic, it is worth noting that they are specified as qualities that Timothy should claim or pursue (*charis*, 1:9; 2:1; 4:22; *eirēnē*, 2:22). As for "mercy" (*eleos*), as we shall see, Paul suggests that it will be given to those who are not ashamed to share in suffering...the very point he wishes to impress on Timothy (see 1:16, 18).

The Thanksgiving — 1:3–5

1:3I thank the God whom I serve, as did my fathers, with a pure conscience. I hold you constantly in my memory as I pray night and day. **4**I long to see you, so that I might be filled with joy, as I remember your tears, **5**holding in memory your sincere faith, the same kind that dwelt in your grandmother Lois and in your mother Eunice before you. I trust it is in you as well.

Notes on Translation

The Greek text of this passage is stable. A few MSS read the present participle *lambanōn* in v.5, rather than the aorist *labōn*, but the difference in meaning is negligible. The personal names Lois and Eunice are not found elsewhere. Acts 16:1 tells us that Timothy's mother was a "faithful Jewish woman."

The passage provides a fine example of how statistical analyses of vocabulary — so often applied to the Pastorals — can be misleading. In these three verses, there are three *hapax legomena,* that is, words otherwise not attested in the NT. But two of them are proper names (Lois and Eunice), and the third, "grandmother," is not one that naturally occurs with any frequency — notice its absence from the LXX, except in 4 Maccabees 16:9. Another term, *progonos* (ancestor, v. 3) is found only in 1 Timothy 5:4, so it is part of the special Pastorals vocabulary. And the noun *hypomnēsis* (remembrance) in v. 5 appears only here in the Pauline corpus.

Of the sixty-one words in these three verses, therefore, there are five that do not appear elsewhere in Paul. All the other words are attested in the undisputed letters. The variation in vocabulary in this small sample seems insignificant. But here is where factors other than vocabulary come into play. Three of the phrases that contain all Pauline words do so in phrases that do not occur as such in letters other than the Pastorals. Thus, Paul can say "thanks be to God" (*charis tǭ theǭ,* see Rom. 6:17; 7:25; 1 Cor. 15:57), but never elsewhere says "I thank God" with this same combination of words (*charin echō tǭ theǭ*). Likewise, Paul does not use the exact phrase "holding you in memory" elsewhere, although he uses each of the words in that phrase, and Romans 1:9 comes fairly close: *hōs adialeiptōs mneian hymōn poioumai.* Finally, the term "conscience" (*syneidēsis*) is used some eleven times by Paul, but he never refers to a "pure" conscience, a phrase that reappears only in 1 Timothy 3:9. The variations, then, are more significant than shown by a mere word count.

On the other hand, much of the phrasing in the passage is completely consistent with Paul's usage elsewhere. For "praying night and day," see 1 Thessalonians 3:10; for "longing to see you," see Romans 1:11, Philippians 2:26, and 1 Thessalonians 3:6; for "filled with joy," see Philippians 2:2; for "sincere faith," compare "sincere love" in Romans 12:9; for a quality "dwelling in" someone, see Romans 7:17, 8:11, 2 Corinthians 6:16, and Colossians 3:16; for *prōton* as "earlier," see Romans

1:16 and 1 Corinthians 12:28; for "I trust," see Romans 8:38, 14:14, and 15:14.

The main difficulty in translating vv. 3–5 is turning one long sentence into several intelligible sentences of normal length for English usage, while retaining the proper relationship between modifiers and their referents.

Literary Observations

An analysis of the Pauline thanksgiving prayers (see Schubert, *Form and Function,* and O'Brien, *Introductory Thanksgivings*) shows that while they are certainly real prayer, and a further sign of the specifically religious character of Paul's correspondence, they are also rhetorically purposeful. They enable Paul to begin the process of persuasion by touching on concerns that he will later develop thematically. Not surprisingly, such analysis has not been applied systematically to the thanksgivings in the Pastorals. Nevertheless, we can see how this short prayer in 2 Timothy establishes the three major themes of Paul's letter. The first is that Paul can serve as Timothy's model. Thus, we see here Paul's prayer and worship, his loyalty to the tradition and his colleagues, his sincerity, and his affection. The second is that Timothy should imitate these qualities. Thus, we find stressed here his sincere faith and his own tradition of piety. Third, there is Paul's concern that Timothy may be deficient in some of these qualities. Thus, the cautionary tone of "I trust it is in you as well."

Comment

The thanksgiving is intensely personal, yet it begins the process of exhortation. The two are intimately connected, for moral instruction in the hellenistic world was very much a matter of imitating the personal qualities of others. Thus, it is precisely to the point that Paul twice notes how he remembers Timothy, for he also wants Timothy to remember and, by remembering, to renew his sense of commitment to his call (1:6). It is likewise not incidental that Paul expresses his longing to see Timothy, for he wants Timothy to come visit him as soon as possible (4:21) as Onesiphorus had already done (1:16–17). The same is true for Paul's mention of his worship in the tradition of his ancestors. The picture of Paul as faithful to his Jewish identity, not only corresponds to his presentation in Acts 26:4–21 and his self-presentation in Romans 9:1-5, 11:1, 2 Corinthians 3:4–5, and 11:22, but also serves a hortatory purpose. The thanksgiving itself suggests that Timothy also has a tradition of piety that comes to him from his grandmother and mother (1:5), and Paul will later remind Timothy to stick with the things he had learned from childhood since he knew from whom he learned them (3:14–15). Paul's "pure conscience," similarly, is to be matched by Timothy's "sincere [literally, unhypocritical] faith," for Paul will encourage Timothy to be among those "purified vessels" of the household (2:21) and to "pursue faith" (2:22), unlike those who are "unsound in faith" (3:8) and are "upsetting the faith of some" (2:18).

As so often happens in Paul's letters, the thanksgiving also suggests something of the reason why the apostle feels it necessary to write. His memory of Timothy is not casual, but is carried out in "prayers night and day." It is the expectation that Timothy will overcome his reluctance and visit him that will fill Paul with joy. To what can we attribute such intensity? I think the clue is found in the last line of the thanksgiving, which is then picked up in the very next sentence, namely, "I trust it is in you as well." The perfect of the verb *peithein* has the sense of "I am confident, I am persuaded." But it is difficult to avoid the impression that, in this place, such an affirmation, coming as it does at the very end, also expresses some doubt and concern. Paul will immediately declare that "for this very reason" (1:6) he is reminding Timothy, but if everything were fine, why would the reminder be necessary? No, Paul's language suggests that although these qualities of faith dwell in Timothy as in his maternal forebears, there is reason for concern and the need to exhort him to bring those qualities to life. There is the sense, then, that the network of personal loyalty that Paul here invokes is critical to his moral exhortation: Paul appeals to that loyalty dormant within Timothy, to his grandmother and mother and to Paul himself, as motivation for the delegate's further faithful effort for the good news.

Paul as Model of Suffering — 1:6–14

1:6 For this reason, I am reminding you to revivify that special gift for service God gave you. It came to you through the imposition of my hands. **7**God did not give us a spirit that leads to cowardice. He gave us a spirit which leads to power, to love, and to self-control. **8**Do not be ashamed, therefore, of bearing witness to our Lord or to me, a prisoner for him. But as God gives you power, take your share of suffering for the good news. **9**God saved us and called us by a holy calling. He did this, not on the basis of our accomplishments, but on the basis of his own stated purpose and gift. The gift was given us before the ages in Christ Jesus. **10**But it has been revealed now through the appearance of our savior, Christ Jesus. He has abolished death. He has manifested life and immortality, and this through the good news **11**whose herald, apostle, and teacher, I have been appointed. **12**For this reason I suffer even these things. But I am not ashamed. For I know the one I have trusted. I am positive he is able to preserve that which has been entrusted to me until that day. **13**Keep holding fast to the example of healthy teaching which you heard from me. In the faith and love that are in Christ Jesus, **14**protect the precious deposit through the Holy Spirit that dwells in us.

Notes on Translation

There are more textual variants here than in the earlier verses, but they present no significant interpretive difficulties. A number of MSS read *hypomimnēskō* in 1:6, rather than *anamimnēskō,* which occurs elsewhere in Paul (1 Cor. 4:17; 2 Cor. 7:15; see 1 Cor. 11:24–25); scribes reading *hypomimnēskō* could easily have been influenced by the presence of *hypomnēsis* in the preceding verse. A considerable number of witnesses have "Jesus Christ" in v. 10 instead of "Christ Jesus"; since the order of these words is so irregular both in the Pastorals and in the undisputed letters, textual confusion is understandable. A great many MSS have "teacher of the Gentiles" in v. 11, rather than the simple "teacher" adopted here. The shorter text is to be preferred even though it has scanter external attestation because the longer text undoubtedly is influenced by 1 Timothy 2:7. Finally, some MSS and versions lack the emphatic *kai* in v. 12, which is translated either as "even these things" or "these things also." In this case, the longer text is to be preferred because it is also the harder (i.e., more awkward) reading.

We find here a few more terms that are unattested elsewhere in Paul's letters. The verb "to revivify" (*anazōpyrein*) in v. 6 actually means to "rekindle/set aflame again." This is its only use in the NT. The same is true for the word *deilia* (v. 7), which I have translated as "cowardice" (see LXX Lev. 26:36; Ps. 54:4; and esp. Sir. 4:17).

A third term presents distinctive problems. In opposition to cowardice in v. 7, Paul puts power, love, and *sōphronismos,* another NT hapax legomenon. The precise meaning of the term is debatable. I have chosen the path of caution by translating it as "self-control," placing it in the semantic field of the *sōphron*-words occurring so frequently in the Pastorals: *sōphronein* in Titus 2:6; *sōphronizein* in Titus 2:4; *sōphronōs* in Titus 2:12; *sōphrosynē* in 1 Timothy 2:9, 15; and *sōphrōn* in 1 Timothy 3:2 and Titus 1:8, 2:2, 5. Of these terms, only *sōphronein* is used by Paul in the undisputed letters (see Rom.12:3; 2 Cor. 5:13). The entire range of words is, however, widely attested in Greek moral philosophy. It refers to what might be called in the broadest sense "moral right thinking," including among its nuances prudence, temperance, self-control, sobriety, and moderation. The translation here, therefore, makes it equivalent to the noun *sōphrosynē;* note that the Vulgate translates it as *sobrietas.* It is tempting, however, to follow the lead of the Syriac Version, which translates *sōphronismos* as "moral teaching," which is the more consistent meaning of the term in ordinary hellenistic discourse (see Plutarch *Table Talk* III, 6 [*Mor.* 653C]; Strabo *Geography* 1.2.3; Philo *Allegorical Laws* 3.193). The translation "moral teaching" would also fit perfectly the program of this letter.

The term *synkakopathein* (to take a share in suffering) in v. 8 is also a NT hapax legomenon. The closest parallel is the use of *kakopathein* (to suffer hardship) in 2 Timothy 2:9, 4:5, and James 5:13. The noun *keryx* (herald) in v. 11 is likewise not found in Paul's undisputed letters. The noun *hypotypōsis* (example/model) is found only here in v. 13 and in 1 Timothy 1:16, although Paul expresses the same idea in Philippians 3:17: "you have an example (*typos*) in us." The noun *parathēkē* is found only in the Pastorals (v. 14; see also 1 Tim. 6:20). As the form of the word suggests, it refers to anything put in trust, such as a deposit (see, e.g., Herodotus *Persian War* 6.86; LXX Lev. 5:21; *The Sentences of Pseudo-Phocylides* 135).

Apart from the noted exceptions, the diction of the passage falls comfortably within the Pauline range, with the unusual terms accountable largely on the basis of the subject matter. The noun *epiphaneia* (appearance) in 1:10 is found frequently in the Pastorals with reference either to the past or the future presence of Jesus (see 1 Tim. 6:14; 2 Tim. 4:1, 8; Titus 2:13), but is also used by Paul in 2 Thessalonians 2:8 with reference to the *parousia tou kyriou* (coming of the Lord). The use of *sōtēr* (savior, v. 10) is likewise characteristic of the Pastorals (1 Tim. 1:1; 2:3; 4:10; Titus 1:3, 4; 2:10, 13; 3:4, 6), as applied both to Jesus and to God. It can be found also in other letters of Paul with reference to Jesus (Phil. 3:20; Eph. 5:23).

Some specific translation decisions: The term *charisma* in v. 6 I have rendered with the pleonastic "special gift for service" because it better captures the virtually technical sense of the term as it is used by Paul in Romans 1:11, 12:6, 1 Corinthians 1:7, 7:7, 12:4, 9, 28, 30–31. Apart from the single instance of 1 Peter 4:10, the term *charisma* is exclusively Pauline in the NT, appearing also in 1 Timothy 4:14. I have taken the phrase *martyrion tou kyriou* in v. 8 as objective, that is, as a witness borne *to* the Lord, since that is what Paul fears Timothy might be ashamed of in his own ministry. In the contrast between *charis* and *erga* in 1:9, I have translated the first as "gift," and the second as "accomplishments," trying to avoid the more technical sense of "works" that Paul sometimes employs (see Gal. 2:16) in favor of the broader sense of "human deeds" that Paul also employs (see Rom. 2:6–7). Otherwise, I have again tried to render long Greek sentences into idiomatically more appropriate English ones, resisting the invitation of the Nestle-Aland critical text (27th ed.) to treat vv. 9–10 as (possibly cited) hymnic material.

Literary Observations

Although by implication the thanksgiving already presented
Paul as a model for Timothy's imitation, this section, which
begins the body of the letter, makes the theme explicit. The
paraenetic function of the exemplar is also clear. It is "for this
reason" that Paul writes, namely, to stir up Timothy's memory
of his own calling and commitment by contemplating his mentor and model Paul. Precisely the same purpose was served in *To
Demonicus* by the presentation to the young man of his father
as an example of the virtues he was to pursue. Paul is actually
the first in a series of models for Timothy's imitation. We will
see the others in 1:15–2:13 and find the climax in the example
of Jesus himself.

The passage is carefully crafted, weaving together three
things: the good news which Paul and Timothy were called
to proclaim, Paul's willingness to bear the suffering his role as
teacher requires, and his exhortation to Timothy to claim his
own "special gift for service." The extended kerygmatic statement in 1:9–10 is bracketed on one side by the double command
"do not be ashamed" and "take your share in the suffering" for
the good news (1:8) and on the other by the assertion that although Paul "suffers even these things" for the good news, he
is "not ashamed" (1:12). In similar fashion, Paul's confidence
concerning what was entrusted to him in v. 12 is matched by his
concern that Timothy guard what was entrusted to him in v. 14.

The kerygmatic statement itself has carefully balanced
clauses, with a major contrast between that which God determined "before the ages" (v. 9) and the revelation of salvation
"now" through Christ (v. 10). The same contrast is found in
Romans 16:25–27 and seems standard for revelational discourse
(see Dahl, "Form-Critical Observations").

Comment

The context in which this passage is placed profoundly affects its
interpretation. If 2 Timothy is pseudonymous, then this entire
section is fictional, an act of imagination by an author writing
some 80–90 years after Paul's death. There is no "real Timothy,"

about whose courage and fidelity Paul is concerned, but only a "fictive Timothy" (the general believer of a later generation?) whom the author seeks to...what? Here we come to the real problem of the majority position on the Pastorals: it works much better at the level of generalities than at the level of specifics. If the purpose of this "correspondence" is simply to rehabilitate Paul, or to mediate his teaching to a new generation, then it is difficult to understand the subtle appropriateness of the specific language to another context, namely, that of an imprisoned and abandoned apostle who is fearful that his most trusted delegate lacks the courage to continue his ministry. If the passage is read in *this* context, then every single detail works. We may still wonder about the diction or the sentence structure, but the function of the writing makes perfectly good sense.

From the perspective of pseudonymity, Paul's reference to Timothy's "special gift for service" (*charisma*) given him by the laying on of Paul's hands (1:6) is highlighted in two ways. First, the majority position takes v. 6 as a sign of the routinization of charism in the post-Pauline period, since Paul never mentions such laying on of hands in his undisputed letters and since the ritual is mentioned repeatedly by Acts (6:6; 8:18; 13:3; 19:6). Second, the majority views the verse as part of a fictional apparatus because it appears to conflict with 1 Timothy 4:14, which says Timothy had hands placed on him by the whole board of elders. To the second point, we can say that the conflict is more apparent than real: there is no reason why Timothy could not have received authority as a delegate from Paul personally and also have been confirmed in his position by a local assembly. To the first point, we can say that the ritual of the laying on of hands for bestowing authority is ancient within Judaism (see, e.g., Num. 8:10); thus, early Christianity did not have to invent a routine already in place.

As so often happens, the attention to the detail that is supposed to indicate inauthenticity misses the real point of the passage. In 2 Timothy, at least, there is no "routinization" of charism. The charging of Timothy by Paul is direct and personal. The emphasis, furthermore, is not on office but on spiritual power. Notice the repetition: the spirit God gave "to us" is not one of cowardice, but of *dynamis* (1:7); Timothy is able to take his share of suffering for the good news "according to the *dynamis* of God" (1:8); God is *dynatos* to enable Paul to preserve what was entrusted to him; the Holy Spirit (which as we learn from 1:7 is the source of this *dynamis*) "indwells" Timothy so that he can likewise remain faithful. The emphasis here is on *power,* not on ritual or office.

Identifying *dynamis* as the proper emphasis also helps us make better sense of the rest of the passage. It enables us to understand, first, why Paul expands the note of suffering for the good news "as God gives you power" (1:8) into a full-blown kerygmatic statement. The apostle does it for the same reason he included such statements in passages like Romans 1:2–5, 2 Corinthians 5:11–21, and Colossians 1:9–23, namely, to show that the *power* at work in the ministry is not merely that of humans, but of God. Just as Paul was "not ashamed of the good news" in Romans 1:16 because it was "the power of God for salvation," so here the lack of shame that is his and to which he calls Timothy is linked to this good news that is from the power of God who saves (2 Tim. 1:8–9). Paul and Timothy are not the elected leaders of a Roman collegium, but have been "called by a holy call" from the one whose gifting them in Christ precedes their own age (cf. Gal. 1:15–16), not on the basis of their accomplishments, but on the basis of his own will (*prothesis;* cf. Rom. 8:28) and gift (*charis;* cf. Rom. 4:4, 16).

This power of God has been manifested "now" (cf. Rom. 3:26; 5:9; 8:1; 16:26; 2 Cor. 6:2) in the "appearance of the savior Christ Jesus" (1:10). Once more, scholars tend to focus on the combination of *epiphaneia* and *sōtēr,* and conclude that in the Pastorals we find a new development within Christianity, namely, the infiltration of Greco-Roman savior cults (see the discussion in Redalié, *Paul après Paul,* 157–74). I am not unwilling to recognize that the language here may well have been influenced by the Mediterranean religious milieu, and by the (probable) hellenistic education of Paul's addressee. But I am not willing to grant that such influence was not possible during Paul's own lifetime, as his use of both terms with reference to Jesus clearly indicates (see p. 51). More to the point, again, is that this passage specifies the way Jesus is savior through his death and resurrection: "He destroyed death [cf. 1 Cor. 15:26] and [literally] exposed to light life [see Rom. 5:10; 6:23; 2 Cor. 4:11] and immortality [*aphthar-sia;* see Rom. 2:7; 1 Cor. 15:42-54]." By bringing this statement back to "the gospel" in v. 11, Paul not only nicely frames the kerygma (see v. 8) but also repeats the point I have been trying to make: the call of Paul and Timothy to proclaim the good news is enabled by the power of God that was at work in the death and resurrection of Jesus.

The focus on personal agency and power also clarifies the meaning of the term *parathēkē* in 1:12 and 1:14, which I translated in the first instance as "that which has been entrusted to me," and in the second, "the precious deposit." As noted above, the noun is a Pauline hapax legomenon, appearing only here and in 1 Timothy 6:20. Scholars intent on reading 2 Timothy pseudonymously do two things with the term. First, they stress what they see as the "static" character of it, in contrast to the "dynamic" sense of tradition that is found in the genuine Paul (see, e.g., 1 Cor. 11:2, 23; 15:3). Second, they identify the deposit with a given body of teaching that is to be kept rather than developed in the Pauline churches, thus showing that the letters are addressed to a later stage in Pauline Christianity (see, e.g., Wolter, *Pastoralbriefe als Paulustradition,* 114-30). The problem with the first point is that it focuses on words rather than realities. In fact, Paul is capable of demanding conformity to a set body of teaching (in Rom. 6:17; 16:17; and indeed 1 Cor. 15:3-8) and is willing to expel those who teach another one (Gal. 1:8-9). The problem with the second point is that it interprets 2 Timothy 1:12-14 through the lens of 1 Timothy 6:20. In that place, I would agree that "the deposit" means true teaching as opposed to false teaching. But the assumption that it must mean the same thing here is based primarily on the premise that the Pastorals are a single composition, rather than separate letters whose meaning is determined by their historical and literary contexts.

It would patently be foolish to deny that "sound teaching" is somehow involved here as well, for Paul says that Timothy has a model of "healthy words" (1:13) in the ones he heard from Paul. We will see later how pervasive such medical imagery is in the Pastorals for distinguishing between "good" and "bad" teaching (see Malherbe, "Medical Imagery in the Pastorals"). But is the emphasis simply on Paul's words? I think not. First, we note that in v. 13 Paul adds "in the faith and love that are in Christ Jesus." Whether modifying Paul as example, or the mode of Timothy's hearing (it could be either), these terms point not to doctrinal content but to characterological traits. Paul presents, and Timothy imitates, a way of living, and not merely a package of teaching. Second, the use of *paratheke* in v. 12 cannot be separated from Paul's personal loyalty to the one who called him. The apostle's confidence that what has been entrusted to him will be preserved is rooted in the fact that *God* is strong enough to enable this "until that day," namely, the eschatological judgment. The language here simply recasts the same sentiments expressed in 4:8, where Paul expresses confidence that "in that day the righteous judge" will give to him and to all who love his coming the crown of righteousness (cf. 1 Cor. 1:8–9). It follows, then, that Paul's exhortation to Timothy to "protect the precious deposit" through the power of the Holy Spirit means more than handing on Paul's words. It includes loyalty to his way of life, which means suffering faithfully in behalf of the Gospel as Paul does.

More Examples to Consider — 1:15–2:7

1:15 You know that all those in Asia, among them Phygelos and Hermogenes, have abandoned me. **16**May the Lord grant mercy to Onesiphorus's household! Many times he refreshed me. He was not ashamed of my chains! **17**Rather, once in Rome, he sought me eagerly and he found me. **18**May the Lord grant him to find mercy in that day — and you know well how many services he rendered in Ephesus. **2:1**Be strengthened, therefore, my child, by the gift that is in Christ Jesus. **2**The things which you heard me say in the presence of many witnesses, these you must entrust to men who are faithful, and who are competent enough also to teach others. **3**Take your share of suffering as a good soldier of Christ Jesus. **4**No one gets entangled with the affairs of everyday life while he is serving in the army — so that he might please his recruiter. **5**And also, if anyone competes in an athletic contest, he won't be crowned unless he competes by the rules. ⁶The hardworking farmer ought to share first in the fruits of the harvest. ⁷Grasp what I am telling you. The Lord will give you quickness of understanding in all these matters.

Notes on Translation

The textual variants in this section present some possibilities for different nuances in meaning. The most interesting are those that affect Paul's portrayal of Onesiphorus. Some witnesses have the comparative adverb "more eagerly" to describe his search for Paul in 1:17, rather than "eagerly," a reading that would tend to cast Timothy's own reluctance in even greater shadow. Likewise, some MSS of v. 18 add the words "to me" after "how many services he rendered," making Onesiphorus's devotion to Paul even more dramatic (cf. Paul's comment on Onesimus in Philem. 13).

Some textual witnesses add the words "to/for God" (*tō theō*) in 2:4, clearly missing the character of the intended analogy, but carrying forward the "good soldier for Christ" in v. 3. Finally, in v. 7 some MSS have "May the Lord give you" rather than "the Lord will give you," making Paul's statement a prayer rather than an assurance. The future is the preferred reading, not only because of stronger external attestation, but also because the subjunctive can be explained by attraction from the double use of *dōe* in 1:16 and 1:18.

The number of distinctive words increases in this passage. Three of them are names otherwise unattested in the NT. Phygelos appears nowhere else in our literature. Onesiphorus reappears (with his household!) in 2 Timothy 4:19, as well as in the *Acts of Paul and Thecla*, once more in the role of householder and helper of Paul. Hermogenes also appears in the *Acts of Paul and Thecla*, but as "Hermogenes the copper-smith" who opposes Paul (see "Alexander the coppersmith" in 2 Tim. 4:14). The significance of these names will be discussed below.

Other new words are either ones that can be found in Paul but in different uses (cf. *paratithēmi* in 2:2 as meaning "hand on/entrust" to *paratithēmi* in 1 Cor. 10:27 as meaning "what is set at table") or ones that are largely determined by the subject matter (especially those dealing with soldiering, competing, farming). The only distinctively Pastoral term in the section is *nomimōs* (lawfully/according to rules) in 2:5, which is used also in 1 Timothy 1:8.

The passage calls for a number of translation decisions. The neuter comparative adjective *beltion* is used adverbially in 1:18 and can mean either "you know better [than I?]" or, as I have rendered it, "you know well." Much more difficult — and requiring some discussion below — is the way to translate *dia pollōn martyrōn* in 2:2. Literally, it means "through many witnesses," but it can also mean "in the presence of many witnesses" (see Moule, *Idiom Book,* 57). In 2:2 also, my translation "and who are competent enough" is an effort to catch the adjectival quality of *hoitines hikanoi esontai.* In 2:7, I have added "you" to Paul's more cryptic "know what I am saying" and have translated *synesis* as "quickness of understanding" (see Plato *Cratylus* 412A; *Philebus* 19D); even the etymology suggests "putting it together."

The reader will undoubtedly have noticed by this point (where it first becomes really obvious) that I am not attempting a gender-inclusive translation. Thus, although *pistois anthrōpois* in 2:2 certainly *can* be translated as "faithful people," I have rendered it "faithful men." The reason is simply that the androcentrism of the Pastorals is so profound and pervasive that a gender-inclusive translation is almost impossible. To the degree it succeeds, furthermore, it actually camouflages the true voice of the writing, which is unmistakably that of a male writing to another male within the Mediterranean culture of antiquity. For better or worse, the assumptions of that culture should accurately be conveyed by translation, leaving it to hermeneutics to decide what present-day readers should think or do about what it says.

Literary Observations

The appearance of the personal names Phygelos, Hermogenes, and Onesiphorus in 1:15-18 sets the stage for two kinds of literary observations. The first concerns the historical context suggested by the names themselves, especially since, as noted above, Hermogenes and Onesiphorus appear again in the apocryphal writing the *Acts of Paul and Thecla*. For that matter, so do Demas and Titus, who are named also in 2 Timothy 4:10. In 2 Timothy, all these except Onesiphorus are associates of Paul who have, in one way or another, left him. Phygelos and Hermogenes have abandoned him; Demas went to Thessalonika because he was "in love with this world"; Titus, on the other hand, simply went to Dalmatia (we presume on a mission). In the *Acts of Paul and Thecla*, Titus and Onesiphorus are loyal to Paul, and Onesiphorus provides hospitality to Paul in Iconium. Demas and Hermogenes, on the other hand, are jealous of Paul's success and seek to destroy him; they are, in fact, identified as those who say that "the resurrection has already taken place" (cf. 2 Tim. 2:17, where that statement is attributed to Hymenaios and Philetos). Each writing also has other characters that do not appear in the other.

What are we to make of this overlapping of dramatis personae? There is no question of real "literary dependence," in which one composition uses the other in a sustained fashion. It could be that the author of the *Acts of Paul and Thecla* knew 2 Timothy, simply drew the names from the Pauline letter, and elaborated them for his own purposes, which involved both the glorification of Thecla and the advancement of an ascetic form of Christianity. Conversely, the *Acts of Paul and Thecla* could have been the first written, and the author of the Pastorals used the same names in order to present, not a Paul who advanced asceticism, but a Paul who opposed it; not a Paul who cooperated (even if reluctantly) with free-spirited women evangelists, but a Paul who worried about women who "always studied and never learned." Finally, as advanced already by the historian A. von Harnack and recently argued by D. R. MacDonald, both 2 Timothy and the *Acts of Paul and Thecla* could have drawn independently from local or regional folk traditions concerning Paul and Thecla, with the two writings not responding to each other but rather advancing two competitive versions of Pauline Christianity in the mid-second century (see McDonald, *The Legend and the Apostle*). Lacking firm external controls, scholars judge such matters depending almost entirely on what seems reasonable, and readers can legitimately differ in such judgments. The position I have taken on the authenticity of 2 Timothy on other grounds clearly affects my judgment on this matter as well. But in my view, the way in which the names are elaborated in the *Acts of Paul and Thecla* makes it seem more likely that they represent the further elaboration of secondary and tertiary characters, some of whom were derived from 2 Timothy.

Also involving Onesiphorus, the second literary question considers the literary coherence of 2 Timothy. Put simply: is the mention of names in 1:15–18 a sign of the haphazard construction of the Pastorals, at best a bit of fictional adornment to persuade the reader that this came from Paul—even if the names don't appear anywhere else in his letters? Or does it serve another purpose? The literary shaping of 1:15–18 makes it clear that the mention of these names is purposeful. Paul asks Timothy not to be ashamed of his chains in 1:8 and, in effect, not to abandon him. Phygelos and Hermogenes stand for those who have abandoned Paul in Asia. Onesiphorus, in contrast, came to visit Paul (as the apostle wants Timothy to do; see 4:9, 21), and, to make the point obvious, "he was not ashamed of my [Paul's] chains" (v. 16). The mention of Onesiphorus, therefore, has the rhetorical function of presenting Timothy with another example for imitation. We notice also that Paul follows this in rapid succession with the examples of the soldier (2:3–4), the athlete (v. 5,) and the farmer (v. 6), concluding with the example of Jesus Christ (vv. 8–13). It is striking that the same three miniature analogies of soldier, athlete, and farmer are also used by Paul in 1 Corinthians 9:7 and 9:24–25. Even more impressive is 2 Timothy's presentation of the same sort of exemplary sequence that Paul forged in Philippians to convince those readers to look to others' interests rather than simply their own. In that case, the apostle began with the example of Jesus (Phil. 2:5–11), then himself (vv. 14–18), then Timothy (vv. 19–24), and then Epaphroditus (vv. 25–30), followed by a developed example of Paul himself once more (3:1–16) and concluding with the demand to imitate such models as these (v. 17). Given that the style and setting of 2 Timothy so much resemble those of Philippians, this similarity in rhetorical strategy is the more impressive.

Comment

This section of text provides another good sample for the testing of diverse approaches to the Pastorals. In the conventional view, 1:15–2:13 is an ill-coordinated series of statements, mixing together biographical and instructional materials without any logical organization: the mention of Onesiphorus (1:15–18) is intrusive as well as fictional, the analogies of 2:3–7 are botched adaptations of Pauline material. The real key to the passage — and indeed to the Pastorals as a whole — is provided by 2:1–2. Everything else is simply a fictional setting for this instruction, which is understood as setting the fundamental agenda of the Pastorals: Timothy is to "entrust" (*paratithēmi* is cognate with the *parathēkē* [deposit] that we saw in 1:12, 14) the things he heard from Paul to other faithful men, who in turn can teach others. What is going on here, in other words, is the passing of the Pauline tradition from one generation to another. The phrase *dia pollōn martyrōn* can be taken as strong evidence for this position, for if it means "through many witnesses," it suggests that the author himself stands at some distance from Paul. The author of 2 Timothy, in other words, is among those "faithful men" recruited by Paul's successors, and the readers of 2 Timothy are "the others" that are now being taught the things that Paul said, if in a more domesticated fashion.

What happens to 2:1–2, however, if we contextualize it within the setting suggested by the letter (that is, Paul the captive suffering abandonment) and the rhetorical strategy of personal paraenesis (teaching character through exemplars)? Now we read all of the personal elements, not as incidental ornamentation, but as the central point. What is the point that has already been established by 1:6–14? It is that Timothy should not give in to cowardice, but should take hold of the *power* that is his by gift; that he should not be ashamed of witnessing to Jesus or to Paul because of his chains; that he should preserve the teaching and character of Paul as he saw them displayed by Paul's own behavior; that he should take his share of suffering for the sake of the gospel, for such suffering is an intrinsic element of the good news. These four elements are all found in 1:15–2:7.

The references to Phygelos, Hermogenes, and Onesiphorus are

not, in this reading, incidental, but an intrinsic part of the argument. They represent antithetical ways of responding to Paul's
desperate situation. The first two abandoned him, as did the rest
of his followers in Asia. But Onesiphorus stands as an example
of fidelity to Paul. The subtle remark in 1:16 that "he was not
ashamed of my chains" is the critical clue to Paul's point. Onesiphorus was willing to seek Paul out eagerly and find him (v. 17)
and, thereby, took upon himself the danger of suffering with the
apostle. Clearly Paul expects Timothy to take the same chance
(4:9, 21). We see as well that Onesiphorus exemplifies the pattern of "suffering now, reward later": Paul prays that his loyalty
and that of his household will be rewarded by mercy "in that
day" (1:18).

This example of strength in loyalty immediately precedes
Paul's direct turn to Timothy: "Be strengthened, therefore, my
child" (2:1). The "therefore" is not incidental; it shows that the
point now being made builds on what preceded it. Timothy is to
"be empowered" by the gift/grace (*charis*) that is in Christ Jesus.
The note of empowerment must be seen in light of 1:6–14, where
the *power* of the gift given Timothy through the Holy Spirit was
iterated (1:7–8, 12). Paul wants Timothy to claim and use that
gift of courage and loyalty. As an expression of this, he is to further Paul's cause by the recruitment of other loyal people who
can in turn teach others. In this reading, Timothy's chore is the
most logical imaginable in a situation in which Paul's followers
are abandoning him and many people are following after false
teachers. Not only is Timothy expected to remain loyal himself,
but he is to build up the circle of those loyal to Paul. Read this
way, the phrase *dia pollōn martyrōn* can be taken as "in the presence of many witnesses" and can serve as a reminder to Timothy
of the living network of which he is a part and of which the
names of Onesiphorus and the others mentioned in chapter 4
stand as a reminder.

The soldier, athlete, and farmer in 2:4–6 are stock examples
in hellenistic moral discourse (see, e.g., Epictetus *Discourse* III,
15, 2–7; III, 24, 34–35; IV, 8, 35–40). The precise lesson to be
derived from these examples depends in great part on what aspect of their vocation is emphasized. When Paul used these same
three examples in 1 Corinthians 9, his point was that those who

worked deserved the reward for their labors. In the present case, the lesson is slightly different. Paul now wants to emphasize the necessity of doing one's job and of putting up with what it requires as the basis for the expectation of a reward. Thus, the example of the soldier is turned in the direction of discipline: if the soldier hopes to please his recruiting officer, he has to devote himself to the hardships of soldiering and not let the affairs of everyday life distract him. Likewise, the athlete needs to play by the rules if he hopes to be crowned, and these rules inevitably involve discipline and hardship. Finally, and most cryptically, Paul says it is the hardworking farmer who can expect to first have a share in the crop. The examples are tossed off in rapid-fire fashion. Timothy is himself a teacher; Paul expects he can get the point: you need to be willing to suffer if you want to win a reward.

Which context or perspective makes better sense of the passage? The conventional wisdom makes some sense of 2:1–2 but does not know what to do with the rest. The position I have argued here makes sense of everything

Jesus as Exemplar — 2:8–13

2:8Keep on remembering Jesus Christ. According to the good news I preach, he is raised from the dead, he is from the seed of David. 9For this good news, I am suffering even to the point of imprisonment, and this as a criminal. But the word of God is not enchained. 10This is why I endure all things for the sake of the chosen ones, that they also might attain salvation with eternal glory that is found in Christ Jesus. 11The word is faithful! For if we have died together, then we shall also live together. 12If we endure, we shall reign together. If we deny him, he will deny us. 13If we are unfaithful, he still remains faithful, for he is not able to deny himself.

Notes on Translation

A textual variant in 2:12 has little impact on meaning but is of interest. The MS evidence is almost evenly divided between

the present tense *arnoumetha* and the future tense *arnēsometha*.
The future, which is found in Nestle-Aland (27th ed.), is the
harder reading because it interrupts the sequence: the protasis
of the other three conditional sentences is either in the aorist or
present tense. Scribes would, therefore, be tempted to "correct"
the future, changing it back to the present, for the sake of consistency. In 2:13, the evidence is likewise divided on the question
of including *gar* (for), but since it is to be inferred in any case,
its inclusion makes little difference.

The diction throughout this passage is thoroughly Pauline,
with only three terms not appearing in the undisputed letters: *kakopathein* (to suffer hardship, v. 9; see 1:8), *kakourgos*
(a malefactor or an evildoer, v. 9; see Luke 23:32–33, 39), and
arnēsesthai (to deny, see Luke 12:9). In contrast, much of the
language is distinctively Pauline, for example, "according to my
gospel" (*kata to euangelion mou*, v. 8; see Rom. 2:16), "endur-
ing all things" (v. 10; see 1 Cor. 13:7), "dying with and living
with" (v. 11; see 2 Cor. 7:3; Rom. 6:8), "ruling together with"
(v. 12; see 1 Cor. 4:8), and the phrase "if we are unfaithful" in
v. 13, which resembles Romans 3:3, "What if some should prove
faithless?"

Although the phrase *pistos ho logos* in v. 11 is distinctive to the
Pastorals (see 1 Tim. 1:15; 3:1; 4:9; Titus 3:8), the use of *pistos* to
characterize God is typical of Paul (see 1 Cor. 1:9; 2 Cor. 2:18;
1 Thess. 5:24; 2 Thess. 3:3), and is applied in v. 13 to Jesus as
well. Similarly, the statement in v. 9 that "the word of God is
not enchained" expresses a confidence not unlike that in Romans
9:6: *ouch hoion de hoti ekpeptōken ho logos tou theou* ("but it is not
as though the word of God has fallen").

Only here in 2 Timothy 2:8 — if the textual determinations
have been correct — does the sequence "Jesus Christ," with the
personal name preceding the title, appear in the Pastorals (see
by contrast 2 Tim. 1:1–2, 9–10, 13; 2:1, 3, 10; 3:12, 15; 4:1). It is
striking because in this place Paul focuses attention on the person of Jesus rather than on the messianic reality. A similar sort
of alteration is also observable in Paul's undisputed letters (see,
e.g., Rom. 3:22, 26; 4:24; 5:1, in contrast to Rom. 6:3, 11, 23;
8:1–2). Finally, as in Romans (but in reverse order), the capsule
summary of the gospel touches on two things: Jesus' resurrec-

tion and his earthly descent from "the seed of David" (2:8; see Rom. 1:3–4).

Translation decisions: Although distinctions between tenses for the imperative mood were not strictly observed in hellenistic Greek, the translation of *mnēmoneue* as "keep on remembering" in 2:8 is appropriate in context, for Paul wants Timothy to keep this example before him. In v. 9, the phrase "for this good news" helps clarify the referent of the relative pronoun *en hō* and compensate for the awkward English word order. In v. 10, the phrase "with eternal glory" is placed last in the sentence with its referent unclear; I have attached it to "salvation." In v. 11, the hardest decision is whether to make explicit "with him," which is implied by the *syn*-constructions. I have chosen not to, but agree that such association with Christ seems logically to be intended.

Literary Observations

The use of "remembering" in particular (2:8), as well as the content of the passage in general, supports the contention that Jesus is being presented to Timothy as the last in a series of models for imitation, all of which have made (with slight variations) the same point: one must share in Jesus' death to share in his life; one must endure in order to enter the kingdom. The overall connection to the imitation of Paul, Timothy's mentor, is made by 2:9–10, which echoes 1:8 and 1:12.

More difficult problems are presented by 2:11–13. Is the phrase *pistos ho logos* in v. 11 simply the introduction of an implied citation (as it seems to be in its uses both in 1 Timothy and Titus), or should it be read primarily with reference to *ho logos tou theou* in v. 9? Methodologically, the issue is whether those other instances in the Pastorals should be determinative for the meaning of the phrase here. But if it is at least theoretically possible, as I am arguing, that 2 Timothy is authentic, then the use of *pistos ho logos* in v. 11 might be read intelligibly within its present context and also might have become the source for the "tradition introduction" function to which the phrase is put in the other two letters (see Duncan, *"Pistos ho Logos"*).

Also problematic is the determination of the literary form and function of 2:11–13. Taken individually, the statements resemble those that have been identified form critically as *sentences of holy law*, which propose that a human action is answered in response by the identical divine action (see Käsemann, "Säetze heiligen Rechts"). Examples include 1 Corinthians 3:17 and 14:38. The statement concerning denial in 2:12 has its closest counterpart in the synoptic saying, "If anyone is ashamed of me...of him will the Son of man be ashamed" (Mark 8:38).

By indenting 2:11b–13, the Nestle-Aland text (27th ed.) implies that the material is both traditional and at least quasi-poetic. It is a short step to calling it *hymnic* and considering it a crystallization of some Pauline themes that the author has put in his composition for additional Pauline coloration. Such editing implicitly supports the conventional view of the Pastorals. There is no question that the four balanced conditional sentences in sequence, with the last providing an extended reversal of the third, have a certain rhetorical power. But by no means are such sequences of balanced clauses unfamiliar in the undisputed letters. Sometimes, these too are considered as hymnic, as in the case of Philippians 2:5–11 or Colossians 1:15–20. It is not certain, however, what is gained by such designations. Other passages in Paul have at least equivalent poetic form and force, but are not termed traditional or poetic. I have in mind such passages as 1 Corinthians 13:1–3, Romans 8:31–39, 2 Corinthians 4:8–10, 6:3–10, and perhaps most impressive (because of the similar use of conditional sentences) 1 Corinthians 15:12--19 (RSV):

> [I]f Christ is preached as raised from the dead,
>   how can some of you say there is no
>   resurrection of the dead?
> ... [I]f there is no resurrection of the dead,
>   then Christ has not been raised;
> [I]f Christ has not been raised,
>   then our preaching is in vain and your
>   faith is in vain.
> . . . .
> [I]f the dead are not raised,
>   then Christ has not been raised.

If Christ has not been raised,
   your faith is futile and you are
   still in your sins.

. . . .

If for this life only we have hoped in Christ,
   we are of all men most to be pitied.

Everyone, I think, agrees that this passage from 1 Corinthians is Paul's own composition. Yet, such is its tone of affirmation that he could well have prefaced it also with the words *pistos ho logos*.

Comment

No one will deny that 2 Timothy has a different "feel" than some of Paul's other letters, yet it is also impossible to resist the sense that there is something particularly Pauline about this Pastoral letter. The present passage exemplifies that combination of similarity and difference. What is different here is the almost telegraphic mode of communication between author and addressee. The points are extraordinarily compressed, indeed re quiring a "putting it together" by someone presumably familiar with the author's thinking.

Paul presents Jesus as the final example that Timothy is to "keep on remembering," and by remembering, to keep imitating. Nothing could be more typical of Paul than presenting Jesus as the supreme model for Christian behavior, while also proffering himself as an example as well. For instance, after his long discussion of moral discernment in the matter of foods offered to idols in 1 Corinthians 8:1–10:31, Paul says: "Give no offense to Jews or to Greeks or to the church of God, just as I try to please all men in everything I do, not seeking my own advantage, but that of many, that they may be saved. Be imitators of me, as I am of Christ" (1 Cor. 10:32–11:1 RSV). In that discussion, Jesus is the model because he "died for the brother," that is — as the narrative fragment suggests — he gave his life in service to others rather than himself (1 Cor. 8:11). Paul imitated that model by "making myself a slave to all, that I might win the more" (1 Cor. 9:19). The Corinthians are instructed to imitate Jesus and Paul by seeking to build each other up in love: "Let each one seek not his own good, but the good of his neighbor" (1 Cor. 10:24). We find a very similar appropriation of the Jesus story (in particular its basic pattern of service unto death for others) as exemplary in Romans 15:1–13 and in Philippians 2:1–11.

What is different in 2 Timothy 2:8–13 is the cryptic quality of the presentation. When Paul summarizes the good news as "risen from the dead, out of the seed of David," the point is not immediately clear. First, the sequence reverses that in Romans 1:3–4, where the same two elements occur. Second, Paul immediately shifts to his own suffering of imprisonment "as a criminal." And perhaps that is the clue: Paul begins with the resurrection of Jesus, for that is the power of life he and Timothy share and can claim (see 1:10). But he then turns Timothy to Jesus' earthly existence and connects that to Paul's own suffering — in the pattern of rejection as a criminal experienced by Jesus. In contrast to those who claim the resurrection is already (2:18), Paul typically insists that the present time is one in which the transformative power of the Spirit manifests itself in enabling humans to follow the messianic pattern of suffering in behalf of others. Thus, Paul undergoes this suffering for the sake of the elect, that they might be saved (v. 10). The pattern of the messianic life is "life for others," which means, inevitably, a present life of faithful endurance rather than glory.

Paul calls Timothy to grasp two things at once: Paul himself is a prisoner, but the word of God is not imprisoned! The power of God at work in the world through the resurrection of Jesus is paradoxical and works through circumstances that by appearance seem to contradict the reality of that power (cf. 2 Cor. 4:7–12). When Paul turns to the cadenced rhythms of reminder, then, the phrase *pistos ho logos* does not seem, in this context, merely formal. He means the *logos tou theou* is faithful! Paul and his delegate can trust the pattern of suffering now, glory later, because it is confirmed in the story of Jesus, the power of whose Holy Spirit now indwells and strengthens them as they undergo suffering for the sake of that same good news.

Paul next goes through the steps of that pattern. First, "if we have died with him, we shall also live with him" (2 Tim. 2:11b). The line is remarkably close to Romans 6:8, "If we have died with

Christ, we believe that we shall also live with him." In Romans, the context of Paul's statement is the experience of baptism. The identification with the death and resurrection of Jesus in that ritual points to a new form of moral existence in obedience to God (6:13–14).

The new resurrection existence of v. 11b, however, is not one in which believers reign in power (1 Cor. 4:8), but it is one marked by service and suffering. Thus, "if we endure, we shall also rule with him" (v. 12a). The form of this statement resembles Matthew 10:22. For the theme of "endurance" in Paul, see Romans 2:7, 5:3, 8:24, 12:12, 15:4, 1 Corinthians 13:7, 2 Corinthians 1:6, 6:4, 12:12, 1 Thessalonians 1:3; 2 Thessalonians 1:4, 3:5, and Colossians 1:11. In the Pastorals, see 1 Timothy 6:11; 2 Timothy 3:10; Titus 2:2. Most pertinently for the present passage, we see that this "endurance" is one that Paul himself exemplifies: "This is why I endure all things for the sake of the chosen ones" (2:10).

As noted above in the Literary Observations, the next statement takes the form of a sentence of holy law, which posits a direct relationship between human action and divine response: "If we deny him, he will deny us" (v. 12b). The rigor of that conviction is especially pertinent in the context of this letter. Paul faces the abandonment of some of his disciples, and perhaps fears Timothy's lack of courage as well. Timothy in turn must face the popular success of charlatans who "have the form of piety but who deny its power" (3:5). Remarkably, however, this tight equation is broken by the greater fidelity of Jesus to those who have committed themselves to him. Even if they are unfaithful, Jesus remains faithful; to do otherwise would be to deny his very identity (2:13). This triumphant note of fidelity and mercy, one that dominates 2 Timothy, extends even to those who are opposing Paul and his delegate (see 2:24–25).

This passage concludes the first major section of 2 Timothy. Paul has presented himself as a model not only of healthy teaching but, above all, of a willingness to suffer for the sake of the good news to which he was appointed as a preacher and teacher. In order to persuade his delegate to be strengthened in his own gift of service, Paul has brought forth many witnesses who also serve as examples of suffering for the sake of a goal, and whom Timothy can imitate: Onesiphorus, the soldier, the athlete, the farmer, and Jesus Christ himself. In the next part of this personal paraenetic letter, Paul turns to the positive qualities that Timothy should exhibit as he carries out this vocation, in contrast to the negative qualities manifested by the opponents.

The Delegate as Proven Workman — 2:14-21

2:14Remind them of these things when you admonish them before God not to engage in polemics that are of no profit but lead to the destruction of those hearing them. 15Be eager to present yourself as a proven workman to God, one with no reason for shame, as you accurately delineate the word of truth. 16But keep avoiding profane chatter. Those people are going to make ever greater progress in impiety. 17And their teaching will spread like gangrene. Hymenaios and Philetos are among the ones 18who have missed the mark concerning the truth by saying that the resurrection has already happened. They are upsetting some peoples' faith. 19Nevertheless, God's firm foundation still stands, bearing this seal: "The Lord has known his own," and, "everyone who names the Lord's name should depart from wickedness." 20In a great household there are not only gold and silver utensils, but also wooden ones and clay. Some are for noble use, some for ignoble. 21If therefore one cleanses oneself from these, that one will be a vessel ready for noble use, consecrated, useful to the master, prepared for every good work.

Notes on Translation

There are remarkably few textual variations in this section. Most are understandably found in 2:14, for the transition to this new section of the letter is not smooth. Some MSS have either "Christ" or "Lord" in place of "God" in the phrase "before God," probably because scribes felt these terms would connect better to the concept of witnessing to Jesus (see 1:8). The evidence is well distributed, but "God" is the hardest reading, since it is the least likely to have been a correction. Other MSS contain two further corrections in the same verse: one making *logomachein* an imperative rather than an infinitive and the other replacing the preposition *ep'* with the more familiar *eis* to express result. Other textual variants are insignificant.

The number of hapax legomena dramatically increases in the passage. In vv. 14–18, we find eleven terms that do not appear in the undisputed letters or in the NT at all: *logomachein, chrēsimos, katastrophē, anepaischynton, orthotomein, bebēlos, kenophōnia, periistēmi, gangraina, nomē, anatrepein.* All of these terms pertain specifically to the subject of false teaching, and their presence is, therefore, not so startling. There are two names in v. 17 that are also unattested either in the undisputed letters or in Acts. Philetos appears nowhere else, while Hymenaios is mentioned in the company of Alexander in 1 Timothy 1:20.

The diction of vv. 19–21, in contrast, is much closer to that of the larger Pauline corpus, with only four terms (*mentoi, stereos, xylina,* and *despotēs*) not appearing there. In fact, much of the diction is strikingly Pauline in character. We note expressions used in the same way as in the larger corpus: "admonishing" (*diamartyrein,* v. 14; see 1 Thess. 4:6), "before God" (*enōpion tou theou,* v. 14; see Rom. 14:22; 1 Cor. 1:29; 2 Cor. 4:2; 7:12; Gal. 1:20), "to present oneself" (*parastēsai,* v. 15; see Rom. 12:1; 14:10; 1 Cor. 8:8; Col. 1:22, 28), "approved" (*dokimos,* v. 15; see Rom. 14:18; 2 Cor. 10:18; 1 Cor. 11:19), "workman" (*ergatēs,* see 2 Cor. 11:13; Phil. 3:2), the "word of truth" (*logos tēs alētheias,* v. 15; see Col. 1:5; Eph. 1:13), "foundation" (*themelios,* v. 19; see 1 Cor. 3:10; Rom. 15:20), "great household" (*megalē oikia,* v. 20; see Rom. 9:2), gold and silver vessels for honorable and dishonorable uses (v. 20; see Rom. 9:21), "being cleansed from" (*ekkathairein,* v. 20; see 1 Cor. 5:7), "consecrated" (*hēgiasmenos,* v. 21; see 1 Cor. 1:2), "useful" (*euchrēstos,* v. 21; see Philem. 11), "toward every good work" (*eis pan ergon agathon,* v. 21; see 2 Cor. 9:8; Rom. 13:3). These observations tend to confirm that when 2 Timothy speaks of matters found in the undisputed letters, its language resembles theirs, and when it speaks of different subjects, its diction changes.

Literary Observations

Precisely as in the paraenetic work *To Demonicus,* this next section of 2 Timothy, extending from 2:14–4:5, shifts attention
from the memory and imitation of models to the communication of maxims. In the present case, sometimes these take the
form of maxims properly so called, and sometimes the form of
specific instruction. Two things, however, are constant. First, the
imperatives are singular: it is the character and practice of Timothy as teacher which is in view, and only by extension that of
the "faithful men" he is to recruit (2:2). Second, the imperatives
alternate antithetically with descriptions of the "false teachers"
or their adherents. This antithetic arrangement of maxims is also
classically paraenetic: "Do good and avoid evil."

As mentioned in the introduction to the letter, it is in this
section that the influence of the protreptic discourses used by
philosophers is most evident. As such works present the positive image of the true philosopher (often by use of memory,
model, and imitation), they also spell out the specific demands
of the sage's life by means of maxims or commandments similar to those in 2 Timothy. And it is here that we find such
protreptic discourses employing stereotypical polemic, not as a
direct attack against opponents, but as a negative foil to the
positive portrait of the teacher they are inculcating. Note the
way Epictetus exhorts to a proper understanding of the Cynic's
calling:

> So do you also think about the matter carefully; it is not
> what you think it is. "I wear a rough cloak even as it is, and
> I shall have one then...I shall take to myself a wallet and
> staff, and I shall begin to walk around and beg from those
> I meet and revile them...." If you fancy the affair to be
> something like this, give it a wide berth; don't come near
> it, it is nothing for you. (*Discourse* III, 22, 9–13)

Here also the statements concerning what "they" are doing function as contrast to what Timothy should do, as Paul returns
time after time, "but you...." This pattern continues until Paul
returns to the presentation of himself as a model again in 4:6.

In 2:19, we also find 2 Timothy's closest thing to a scriptural citation. It is actually a composite allusion, with several texts from Torah serving as possible referents. The author speaks of the foundation (of the building first mentioned in 2:20) as having "this seal" (or "sign," *sphragis*) and follows with two statements joined by "and." The first, "the Lord has known his own," (*egnō kyrios tous ontas autou*) echoes part of the LXX of Numbers 16:5 *(egnō ho theos tous ontas autou)*. The second statement in v. 19, "everyone who names the Lord's name should depart from wickedness," is harder to locate. The phrase "should depart from wickedness" echoes such passages as Sirach 17:26, 35:3 and Job 36:10, while not matching any of them precisely. The phrase "names the Lord's name" (*onomazōn to onoma kyriou*) is perhaps an allusion to Isaiah 26:13. The phrase also resembles "calling on the name of the Lord" in LXX Joel 3:5, which we find also in Acts 2:21, Romans 10:13, and 1 Corinthians 1:2 and which appears immediately below in 2:22.

Comment

Having stirred Timothy to a renewed commitment to his calling as a teacher of the good news, Paul turns his attention to the manner of his teaching, using the antithetical pattern familiar to us from paraenetic and protreptic discourses. This middle section of 2 Timothy is best understood when placed in the context of ancient moral philosophy. Four observations from research into hellenistic moral teaching are particularly helpful for understanding this passage.

Identification difficult. Because of the stereotypical character of the polemic used in debates between schools, and because of the literary function to which this polemic is put in protreptic discourses, the precise identification of the "opponents" in any specific situation is difficult. Certain standard charges were levelled against opponents on either side of interschool rivalries, such as those between Epicureans and Stoics or between Stoics and Cynics. Indeed, just as one can speak of a certain idealized picture of the "true philosopher" (see Lucian of Samosata *Demonax* and Julian *Oration* 6-7), so is there a standard portrait of the "false philosopher." The false teacher is dismissed as a "sophist" or a "charlatan," whose teaching is characterized as filled with quibbles or contentious wranglings over words or obscure technical jargon (see Lucian *Timon* 9; *Zeus Rants* 27; Epictetus *Discourse* II, 1, 31; II, 17, 26); sometimes the opposite is the case: the false teacher seeks to win adherents by flattering them shamelessly and pandering to their vices (Dio Chrysostom *Oration* 32.11, 29). The false teacher is almost always accused of hypocrisy, that is, of preaching virtue in public while practicing vice in private (Philostratus *Life of Apollonius of Tyana* 2.29; Julian *Oration* 7.225A; Lucian *Timon* 54). These vices can easily be placed into three standard categories: love of pleasure (*philēdonē;* see Julian *Oration* 6.198B; Dio *Oration* 33.13; Epictetus *Discourse* III, 22, 93); love of money (*philarguria;* see Philostratus, *Life of Apollonius of Tyana* 1.34; Julian *Oration* 6.181C; Lucian *The Runaways* 14); and love of glory (*philodoxia;* see Dio *Oration* 32.10; Julian *Oration* 6.190D; Epictetus *Discourse* I, 21, 34; Lucian *Peregrinus* 38). When, therefore, the opponents in the Pastorals are accused of "word chopping" (2:14, 24) or "vain and uninstructed debates" (2:23) or "profane chatter" (2:16) or "having the form of godliness but not its power" (3:5), we recognize in such charges standard polemic and are unable to conclude with certainty that these were the actual characteristics of the people so being charged (see Johnson, "II Timothy and the Polemic").

There are some specific charges that fall outside this stereotyped polemic. The warning about those "who sneak into houses" (3:6), for example, may be based on an actual practice. Likewise, in the present section, the claim that Hymenaios and Philetos are saying the resurrection already happened (2:18) may be similarly based. This last charge clearly identifies the opposition as Christian. But what do Hymenaios and Philetos mean? They cannot be referring to the resurrection of Jesus, since all would agree that he was raised already. They must be referring to the future, general resurrection of all believers. What does it mean to say of that event, "It has already happened"? The oddest version is found in the *Acts of Paul and Thecla.* In that writing, Paul teaches a future resurrection that is dependent on physical asceticism, specifically virginity, in the present life (*Acts of Paul and Thecla* 5–6); his opponents teach that the resurrection has already happened, but what they mean is, "It has already taken place in the children whom we have, and that we are risen again in that we have come to know the true God" (*Acts of Paul and Thecla* 14). It is very unlikely that this is the view Paul opposes in 2 Timothy. To the contrary, the view is one of the surest signs that the *Acts of Paul and Thecla* is aware of and creatively adapts 2 Timothy.

The most logical possibility is that Hymenaios and Philetos were teaching what is sometimes called an *acute realized eschatology*, that is, an understanding of Christian existence as already in some sense participating in eternal life, with the result that future eschatological expectation is either implicitly denied or denigrated. The clearest statement of this sort of position is found in some of the Gnostic writings from Nag-Hammadi, such as the *Treatise on Resurrection* 49 and the *Gospel of Philip* 56. The Gnostic perception of evil as associated with the body made a purely spiritual interpretation of resurrection logical.

Such tendencies within the Christian movement are attested even earlier. The Gospel of John, for example, seems to emphasize the reality of eternal life in the here and now, with only a very weak sense of future eschatology (see 3:18-21; 5:24-29). In 1 Corinthians, furthermore, Paul's criticism of those who "say there is no resurrection of the dead" (15:12) actually seems directed at a denial of a bodily resurrection because of the conviction that the power of new life enjoyed by the believers was already the final stage: they were already filled, already rich, already ruling (4:8). This acute realized eschatology manifest in Corinth also appears to be attached to an interpretation of moral behavior that was so "strong" it verged on actual immorality and social disruption (see Thiselton, "Realized Eschatology in Corinth"). Paul finds it necessary to rein in members of the community who disregard basic morality (1 Cor. 15:32-34), practice incest (5:1-5), and frequent prostitutes (6:12-20). Some such combination also seems likely in the case of 2 Timothy, for Paul's comments suggest that the teaching on the resurrection is connected to "youthful passions" (2 Tim. 2:22) and the disruption of households by the seduction of women driven by impulses (3:6). In short, the realized resurrection life is celebrated not by asceticism (as at Nag Hammadi), nor by biological childbearing (as in the *Acts of Paul and Thecla*), but by neglect of basic morality.

Morality and medicine. One of the master metaphors for moral teaching in the hellenistic world was the practice of medicine (see Nussbaum, *The Therapy of Desire*). The philosopher was regarded as the "physician of the soul" (see, e.g., Epictetus *Discourse* III, 22, 72-73; Dio *Oration* 32.10; 77/78.43-45; Lucian *Demonax* 7, 10; *Nigrinus* 38). Virtue was a matter of health, vice a matter of sickness. Moral teaching, therefore, was to make someone "well." Indeed, Epictetus calls his philosophical classroom a hospital: "Men, the lecture room of the philosopher is a hospital; you ought not to walk out of it in pleasure, but in pain" (*Discourse* III, 23, 30). It should come as no surprise, then, that in this protreptic discourse directed at a moral teacher such as Timothy, medical language is pervasive (see Malherbe, "Medical Imagery in the Pastorals"). Thus, we have already seen that Paul provides Timothy with an example of "healthy" teaching (*hygiainontōn logōn*, 1:13). In the present passage, likewise, the teaching of the opponents is characterized as "gangrene" (*gangraina*) that (in a distinctive medical usage) "will spread" (*nomēn hexei*, 2:17). Finally, Paul uses a term with medical connotations, which are camouflaged by translation. He wants his delegate to "rightly delineate the word of truth" (2:15). I translated the term this way to catch something of the etymology of *orthotomein*, "cutting straight." Especially when used in combination with "gangrene," *orthotomein* likely has something of the sense of "practice surgery."

Teaching style. Despite widespread similarity in the overall image of "the philosopher," there were also marked differences between individuals — which accounts in part for the polemics they used against each other! Some of these differences were doctrinal and involved diverse conceptions of how to achieve real "spiritual health." One of the commonest charges against philosophers, indeed, was that they all promised the truth but did not agree on what it was (see Lucian *The Parasite* 27; *Hermotimus* 15-16). Other differences were stylistic. There was disagreement, for example, on the issue of payment for teaching (see Hock, *Social Context of Paul's Ministry*). Some differences also arose concerning the degree of severity that should be used in teaching. Healing people of vice obviously required confrontation (Epictetus *Discourse* III, 22, 26-30) and some severity: "A good prince is marked by compassion, a bad philosopher by lack of severity" (Dio *Oration* 32.18). Certainly rebuke was more appropriate than flattery (Dio *Oration* 33.13). But how much severity? Within the Cynic tradition, there developed two approaches, each of which could be understood in medical terms (see Malherbe, *Paul and the Popular Philosophers*, 11-24). The first emphasized rebuke and abuse, the rough and harsh treatment of the surgeon (see Dio *Oration* 77/78.45). The second emphasized the need for gentleness and encouragement, the approach of the nurse (see Epictetus *Discourse* III, 22, 90; Dio *Oration* 4.19; Lucian *Demonax* 12-67). In the next passage, we will see how the opponents are characterized in terms of their disputatiousness and harshness (2:23), whereas Timothy is to conduct himself without "polemics" (v. 14), and with gentleness (vv. 24-25). This second image, by the way, is the one Paul uses when, in a passage full of language associated with hellenistic moral discourse, he refers to himself: "We were gentle among you, like a nurse taking care of her children" (1 Thess. 2:7; see Malherbe, *Paul and the Popular Philosophers*, 35-48).

Images of conversion. The turning away from vice to virtue was a form of conversion (see Lucian *Nigrinus* 38). The philosopher himself needed to be a person of proven virtue, not governed by love of pleasure (Epictetus *Discourse* III, 22, 13) or love of money (III, 22, 26-30) or love of glory (III, 22, 83-86). And his speech must be directed to the healing of others, "in the hope that he may thereby rescue somebody from folly" (Dio *Oration* 77/78.38). In 2:19-21 of the present passage, we see the first emphasis; in 2:25-26 (discussed on pp. 79-86), we shall see the second.

The statement about the household in 2:19-21 combines two metaphors that are found in slightly different form elsewhere in Paul. The "house" or "household" as metaphor for the community is worked out most elaborately in 1 Corinthians 3:9-4:2, in Paul's discussion of the mutual ministries of himself and Apollo. In that passage, we find the apostle laying a foundation (*themelios*) on which another builds (1 Cor. 3:10), the foundation being Jesus Christ (3:11), on which others might build with materials made of gold, silver, precious stones, wood, hay, or straw (3:12). Within the household, the ministers are "stewards" who dispense the mysteries of God (4:1). Paul extends the metaphor by calling the community the temple of God: "God's temple is holy and that temple you are" (3:17). The metaphor of "household utensils" for people destined for certain tasks is found in Romans 9:21. There, in response to the charge that God is unfair, he compares God to a potter: "Has the potter no right over the clay, to make out of the same lump one vessel for beauty (*timē*) and another for menial use (*atimia*)?

In the present passage, the "firm foundation of God" (*stereos themelios tou theou*, 2 Tim. 2:19) is in contrast to the faith of some that is being overturned by false teachers (v. 18). The foundation itself has a sign or seal on it, making two points also familiar in Paul. The first, "the Lord knows his own," points to the fact that God will sort out truth and falsehood in the judgment, when "God judges the secrets of men" (Rom. 2:16). The second points to the necessity of separation from wickedness in order to belong to the holy people (cf. esp. 1 Cor. 5:1-8; 2 Cor. 6:14-18).

Within the "great household" of v. 20, there are vessels of various worth, to be used for noble purposes (*timē*) or menial (*atimia*). In this application of the metaphor, however, the emphasis is put, not on the predestined use of the vessels, but on their capacity to become something more through a process of change, which is here called a purification: "if therefore one cleanses oneself from these" (v. 21). Who or what is intended by "from these" (*apo toutōn*)? Presumably, Paul could mean the opponents themselves, but since "from all wickedness" in v. 19 is the immediate antecedent, it is more likely that he refers to the teachings and practices of the opponents. It is indeed striking that the only other use of the term *ekkathairein* (cleanse from) is in 1 Corinthians 5:7, a passage demanding a similar sort of separation. The "temple" aspect of the household image that was explicit in 1 Corinthians 3 is here intimated by this use of purification language and by the statement that the person thus purified then becomes "consecrated/sanctified" (*hēgiasmenon*, v. 21). Timothy, then, can become a "proven and unashamed workman" (v. 15, note the repetition of "shame" from 1:8, 11, 16) by such a moral conversion, which begins with the avoidance of evil things. Then he will be "useful for the master of the household (*despotēs*) and prepared for every good work" (v. 21).

The Servant of the Lord — 2:22-3:9

2:22Flee cravings for novelty. Instead pursue righteousness, faithfulness, love, and peace, with those who call on the Lord's name from a pure heart. 23Avoid senseless and uneducated disputes. You know that they generate conflicts. 24God's servant, in contrast, must not engage in battles, but must be gentle toward all, an apt teacher and long-suffering. 25He must teach with mildness those who oppose him. Perhaps God will give them a change of heart so that they recognize the truth. 26And perhaps they will regain their senses, once they have been snatched alive by God from the devil's snare, so that they can do God's will. 3:1But know this: difficult times are approaching in the last days. 2People will be selfish, greedy, boastful, arrogant, blasphemers. They will not be loyal to their parents. They will be ungrateful, unholy, 3unaffectionate, intractable. They will be slanderers, out of control, wild. They will not care about doing good. 4They will be traitors, rash and crazed. They will love pleasure more than they love God. 5They will have the appearance of piety while denying its power. Avoid these people especially. 6Now from among them are the ones who sneak into households and capture silly women who are beset by sins and driven by various passions, 7women who are always learning but are never capable of reaching the recognition of truth. 8In the very way that Jannes and Jambres opposed Moses, so also these men oppose the truth. They are corrupted in mind, untested concerning the faith. 9But they will not progress much further, for just as it happened with those men, their stupidity will become obvious to everyone.

Notes on Translation

This section of text has a number of fascinating textual variants. In 2:22, many MSS add "all" to the phrase "those who call on the name of the Lord with a pure heart," no doubt influenced by the presence of the fuller phrase in Romans 10:12 and 1 Corinthians 1:2. In 2:24, there is considerable evidence to support the reading *nēpion* (like a child) rather than *ēpion* (mild/gentle), much as in 1 Thessalonians 2:7 where the same options exist. Here, as there, *ēpios* is the preferred reading because it better fits the context of moral discourse we discussed in the previous section. MSS evidence is also split between the subjunctive *dǭ* in 2:25 and the optative *dǭē;* the optative better expresses the indefiniteness of the statement and is found also in 1:16 and 1:18, which of course can also be argued as a reason why it should be regarded as a logical correction for a scribe to make!

A few witnesses (especially in the Latin) read *Mambres* for one of Moses' opponents in 3:8, rather than the *Iambres* read by most MSS. Speaking of these names, which appear nowhere else in the Bible, Paul assigns them to the biblical account's "wise men, sorcerers and magicians" of Pharaoh's court. In Exodus 7:11, when Aaron's rod turns into a serpent, the magicians turn theirs into serpents as well (although Aaron's serpent eats theirs); in Exodus 7:22, the magicians match the trick of turning the water of the Nile into blood. They do not appear for the later signs worked by Moses and Aaron. The names "Jannes" and "Jambres" appear to have been given to the magicians by the Jewish haggadic tradition (they are mentioned by the second-century writer Numenius of Apamea, according to Eusebius *Praeparatio Evangelii* 9. 8.1), and there seems to have been an apocalyptic work containing both names, which is not extant (see *CD* 5:18). The appearance of the names in *Targum Pseudo-Jonathan* may or may not offer further evidence for the pre-Christian Jewish tradition concerning the magicians (see Grabbe, "The Jannes/Jambres Tradition").

The most striking variants throughout the passage are offered by the fifth-century Uncial Alexandrinus (A). In 2:22, it reads, "all those who love the Lord" (influenced by James 1:12?); in 3:1, it has the plural *ginōskete* (know ye) rather than the singular; in 3:6, it adds "and pleasures" (*kai hēdonais*) to the desires of women; and in 3:9, it replaces *anoia autōn* (their stupidity) with *dianoia autōn* (their purpose); a busy and inventive scribe, indeed, perhaps during a long afternoon of copying!

The diction in this section reflects the distinctive subject matter and has a high number of NT hapax legomena (eighteen) and Pauline hapax legomena (fifteen). A large number of these are contained in the vice list of 3:2-4. Among its nineteen items are seven NT hapax and five Pauline hapax; four of the terms are in the undisputed letters, and two are found only in the Pastorals. Before we draw rash inferences, it is helpful to make a comparison to Paul's vice list in Romans 1:29-31. Its twenty-two items contain seven NT hapax (same as 2 Timothy), one Pauline hapax (four less than 2 Timothy), and fourteen terms found elsewhere in the undisputed letters (versus four in 2 Timothy).

One hapax legomenon offers particular translation difficulties. In 2:22, the word for the desires, "cravings," Timothy is warned away from is modified by the adjective *neōterikos,* which usually means "pertaining to youth" (see Polybius *Histories* 10.21.7). Thus, the phrase is often translated "youthful desires." For those seeking biographical verisimilitude, the phrase would appear to support the perception of Timothy as youthful. A second meaning, attested in some papyri, is "modern in style," or "novel." The cognate verb *neōterizein,* on the other hand, has the sense of "making innovations," often with a connotation of violence or revolution (see Isocrates, *Letter* 7.9). Josephus combines *neōterikos* with *authadeia* (boldness/rashness) in *Antiquities* 16.11.8. I have chosen to translate the phrase as "cravings for novelty," a rendering which seeks a middle ground.

In 2:23, the adjective I have translated as "uneducated" is *apaideutos.* It can also bear the connotation of "rude" or "boorish" (Plato *Gorgias* 510B). If that coloration is adopted, the harshness of the opponents is again underscored.

Translation decisions: As in previous sections, the main problem is turning long Greek sentences into shorter and more idiomatic English ones. The vice list in 3:2-4 presents a special challenge. The Greek achieves its rhetorical impact by the piling up of words. In English, this begins to sound silly. It is necessary to find sentences with equivalent rhetorical effect.

The translation decision that most affects meaning is posed by 2:26. The RSV has, "They may escape from the snare of the devil, after being captured by him to do his will." This is a possible translation but seems to miss the point of the argument.

At issue is the identity of the one who captures alive and whose will gets done. The verb *zōgrein* (here in the perfect passive participle) means literally to "capture alive," as one does in fishing (see Luke 5:10). Note that in LXX Joshua 2:13 and 6:24, the verb is used for the rescuing of Rahab and her family from the destruction of Jericho. It seems better, then, to take the "capturing alive" as God's action: he has plucked them from the trap of the devil. And since the topic *is* conversion (*metanoia*), it follows that "so they can do his will" applies also to God rather than to the devil (for the "snare of the devil," see also 1 Tim. 3:6–7).

Literary Observations

We note immediately that the antithetical pattern of instruction continues. Paul alternates positive and negative commands to his delegate Timothy (all in the second-person singular; 2:22, 23, 24; 3:1, 5) and juxtaposes these to descriptions of the practices of those opposing him (usually in the third-person plural; 2:23, 25; 3:2–5, 6, 8–9).

The characterization of the opponents is enriched in 3:2–5 by the use of a vice list, a regular feature of a catalogue-happy hellenistic moral discourse (see Fitzgerald, "Virtue/Vice Lists"). The proper way to read such lists is not to obsess over their individual elements but to assess their overall impact. Such lists were based on the premise that wicked people tended to practice all the vices, just as good people practiced all the virtues. The longest vice list on record is that produced by Philo Judaeus, which consists of some 140 elements (*Sacrifices of Cain and Abel* 32)! The rhetorical impact of such lists depended on the internal rhymes and rhythms created by the individual elements. Remember that all ancient reading was done out loud, so such lists could have a great impact through oral delivery. In the present list, for example, note the repetition of the *ph* sound in *philautoi, philargyroi, . . . hyperēphanoi, blasphēmoi,* not to mention the effect created by the *oi* endings. Note also the combination of alpha-privative beginnings and *oi* endings in this sequence: *acharistoi, anosioi, astorgoi, aspondoi.* In the present case, of course, the general moral vacuity of the population in the eschaton is specified in terms of the opponents: "Now from among them are the ones..." (v. 6).

Finally, we can note the brief allusion to the magicians of Pharaoh's court who opposed Moses and Aaron (3:8–9). The puzzle posed by the names *Iannēs* and *Iambrēs* should not distract us from how thoroughly characteristic a Pauline move this scriptural example is. Paul adverts to the exodus story in 1 Corinthians 10:1–11 as an example for the Corinthian congregation: "These things happened to them as a warning, but they were written down for our instruction, upon whom the end of the ages has come" (v. 11). The apostle also implies that in the present age he plays the role that Moses played in the time of the exodus (see Rom. 9:3 and 2 Cor. 3:12–18). It should come as no shock, then, to see the exodus story yield one more lesson for his delegate. It is a particularly appropriate one: Timothy stands to Paul, after all, much as Aaron did to Moses. Now, as then, the opponents are the more spectacular and are enjoying success. Their having been called "sophists, magicians, and sorcerers" by the LXX fits perfectly the polemic of Paul's time, in which charges of "charlatan" and "magician" could be tossed around at will (see the *Letters of Apollonius of Tyana* 1–2, 5, 8, 16–17). Paul holds out the hope that in the present case, as in the ancient one, "their stupidity will become obvious to everyone" (2 Tim. 3:9). This scriptural exemplum should be borne in mind when we analyze Paul's statement about the functions of Scripture in the next section.

Comment

The portrait of the opponents that emerges is clearly not a flattering one. They reveal in their character and practice all the negative traits that Timothy is to avoid. As in the earlier section, much of this is standard polemic: they are stupid (3:9) and foolish (2:23), engage in uneducated debates (2:23), and seek after novelty (2:22). They oppose the truth (3:8) and are corrupted in mind (3:8). More distinctive to the polemic within a religious movement is the statement in v. 8 that they are "untested (*adokimos*) with regard to the faith"; contrast this with Paul's desire in 2:15 that Timothy present himself as a "tested (*dokimos*) workman." The hellenistic commonplace that false philosophers teach but don't practice is given in 3:5 a specifically religious turn: they have the form of godliness (or piety) but not its power (*dynamis;* again, see the contrast with Paul and Timothy in 1:7–8, 12; 2:1).

Beneath the stereotyped polemic, however, we may get a glimpse of the actual practice of the opponents. In 3:6, they are said to "sneak into" households — in the sense of "insinuate themselves" — and make captives of *gynaikaria.* The translations (like mine) that render this as "silly women" or "weak women" are not far off the mark, for the term bears something of the male condescension found in the English expression "little woman" (see Epictetus *Encheiridion* 7). Because the Pastorals are so regularly charged with sexism, it may be worth briefly considering this particular passage, for 2 Timothy has a distinctive perspective on the gender issue not found in 1 Timothy. It is abundantly clear, first of all, that Paul (or the author of this letter) is not sexist in the proper sense. We have learned before this that Timothy's faith was anticipated by that of his grandmother and mother; they stand as models for him to imitate. Later, in 3:14–15, Paul will remind Timothy to remain in what he has come to know, aware of "from whom" (plural) he had learned it, since from his childhood he had been aware of the Scriptures. The allusion here surely must be to Lois and Eunice, the maternal forebears who taught Timothy in the faith of Judaism and in discipleship. The greetings at the end of the letter, furthermore, include Priscilla, Pudens, and Claudia (4:19–21). The author of this letter would not say that women as such are silly or incapable of arriving at the knowledge of the truth.

The author's description of the particular women of 3:6–7, that they are "beset by sins and driven by various passions... always learning but are never capable of reaching the recognition of truth," points, not to the nature of women as such, but to the problems of women in the ancient world possessed of a certain wealth and social class. The closest contemporary analogue would be those women of a certain age and class so gently parodied by Helen Hokinson's *New Yorker* cartoons. They are women of means and mobility, but without real education and real power in the world. Therefore, no matter how much they take themselves and their projects seriously, they always appear to male observers as "silly." We meet in 2 Timothy 3:6–7, I think, the wealthy leisured women (in a "household," after all), who have time for the pursuit of philosophy, but whose training does not enable them to distinguish the authentic from the counterfeit. These women are, therefore, the perpetual students of wisdom, ready prey for charlatans who go from house to house, eager to be persuaded by the charlatans' impressive appearance and swayed by their rigorous message. Women of position and means have often been seduced in this way, never more clearly than in the twentieth century when the czarina of Russia was infatuated with the severe monk Rasputin. Paul is here not a sexist, but an acute social observer.

Let's push this analysis one step further and ask what appeal the proclamation of a realized resurrection would have had for such women. I have already suggested that such an understanding of the resurrection could lead either to sexual promiscuity (since "we" are already in the kingdom and are not subject to rules) or to sexual rigor (since "we" are leading the life of the angels). Thus, it was possible for some at Corinth to have as their slogan, "It is good not to touch a woman" (1 Cor. 7:1). Paul, as we have seen, rejected the option of sexual promiscuity altogether, but he also carefully qualified a commitment to celibacy, allowing it for the freedom it gave "for the Lord" while also insisting that marriage was indissoluble except under the most extraordinary conditions (1 Cor. 7:10–11).

Could either of these options have had particular appeal to the leisured women of households who were chronically seeking wisdom? Paul's phrase "driven by various passions" in 3:6 has a definite sexual connotation, and it is easy to imagine something more than spiritual seduction taking place. But he also lists "beset [or burdened] by sins." It would appear that a version of realized eschatology that made celibacy the norm for the Christian life could have a strong appeal for such women. It would offer them two things: freedom from the guilt and desires associated with sexual life and also, perhaps, freedom from the obligations of the household. This precise combination, it should be noted, is found in the career of Thecla in the *Acts of*

Paul and Thecla, but there it is stimulated not by the opponents but by Paul himself!

The purpose of this paraenetic/protreptic letter, however, is not the identification of the opponents or their victims but rather the character and practice of Timothy, who as Paul's delegate is called to the role of moral teacher in the communities where he represents Paul (see 1 Cor. 4:17). Two things in particular stand out in this portion of Paul's portrait of the "servant of the Lord" (2:24). The first is the emphasis on his personal virtue — he is to pursue righteousness, faithfulness, love, and peace (v. 23) — and the second is the way those personal qualities are translated into a teaching practice that is remarkable for its gentleness (vv. 24-25). Timothy is to be "gentle toward all" and "long-suffering," a term that suggests the willingness to endure the hardship of being an "apt teacher" (v. 24). He is not to get into wrangles with his opponents, but teach/instruct them with mildness (v. 25). This point needs to be stressed because the tone in both 1 Timothy and Titus is much more severe.

Paul connects the emphasis on gentleness in teaching to an optimism concerning the results of such behavior (vv. 25-26). The apostle holds out the hope (even if expressed as a velleity, in the optative mood) that "perhaps" God will give even such as these opponents a change of mind (*metanoia*) enabling them to have a recognition of the truth (v. 25), so that, freed by God from the devil's snare, they might do God's will (v. 26). This hope for repentance among the opponents is, like the gentleness and persuasiveness recommended to the teacher, a distinctive trait of 2 Timothy among the Pastoral letters.

Remaining in a Living Tradition — 3:10-17

3:10 But you have carefully followed my teaching, my practice, my purpose, faith, forbearance, love, and endurance, **11**through the persecutions and sufferings that came to me when I was in Antioch, Iconium, and Lystra. I bore such persecutions and the Lord delivered me from them all. **12**And indeed all those who wish to live piously in Christ Jesus will be persecuted. **13**Evil men and charlatans will make progress in wickedness. They are deceivers and are themselves deceived. **14**But you, remain in those things which you learned and of which you have been convinced. You are aware from whom you learned them. **15**And you have known the sacred writings since you were a child. They are capable of making you wise concerning salvation through faith in Christ Jesus. **16**Every scripture is God-inspired and useful for teaching, reproving, correcting, toward an education in righteousness, **17**in order that the man of God might be mature, fitted for every good work.

Notes on Translation

Two textual variants in the passage are of interest for demonstrating scribal tendencies rather than affecting the meaning. In 3:11, some MSS have a gloss (that is, a marginal comment made by a scribe as he copied from one MS to another) that explicates Paul's adventures in Antioch, Iconium, and Lystra by a combination of information from the Acts of the Apostles and the *Acts of Paul and Thecla*, writing, "that is, those [persecutions] that were afflicted on account of Thecla from Jews on those believing in Christ." The gloss shows at least that these scribes were familiar with the apocryphal work. The "persecutions and sufferings" mentioned in v. 11 took place, according to Acts, in the period before Paul's recruitment of Timothy as his companion (Acts 16:1-3), during his first missionary trip with Barnabas through Antioch of Pisidia (Acts 13:49-52), Iconium (14:4-6), and Lystra (14:19-22). Iconium is also the setting for Paul's activities in the *Acts of Paul and Thecla* 1-2, immediately after his departure from Antioch. Readers must decide, as they must with the names of characters, the question of literary dependence: Do Luke-Acts and 2 Timothy represent separate historical sources, or does 2 Timothy depend on Luke-Acts? Does the *Acts of Paul and Thecla* derive from Luke-Acts and 2 Timothy together or separately, or does it have its own source of oral tradition?

The second variant has the singular *para tinos* in 3:14 rather than the plural *para tinōn* (from whom). The singular would make the statement logically refer to Paul himself, whereas the plural would logically refer to the maternal forebears Eunice and Lois, from whom Timothy learned how to be faithful (see 1:5). In this case, the scribe probably "corrected" to the singular in order to make the whole passage work as a presentation of Paul as the model for Timothy to imitate.

The diction of the passage is for the most part recognizably Pauline. There are seven NT hapax legomena in the eight verses, five Pauline hapax legomena, and two words found only in the Pastorals (*ōphelimos* in v. 16 and *eusebōs* in v. 12). Of the terms not otherwise found in the undisputed Pauline letters, six are peculiar to the subject matter of moral teaching and correction (*ōphelimos, elegmon, epanorthōsis, sophisai, goēs, agōgē*).

The term that has attracted the most attention by translators is another NT hapax legomenon, *theopneustos* in 3:16. As the etymology of the word suggests, it is appropriately rendered as "God-inspired" or "God-breathed" or "divinely inspired." The debate has to do with whether it should be taken as an attributive or predicative adjective. Is it "Every God-inspired scripture is..." or "Every scripture is God-inspired and..."? The debate is much less about Paul's point, which is clear enough, but about the doctrine of the inspiration of Scripture. As a theological debate centered on the literalistic reading of a single verse, it lies outside the province of this commentary.

Much more pertinent to the meaning of the passage as a whole is the difficulty of translating *parēkolouthēsas* in 3:10 (some MSS, influenced by 1 Tim. 4:6, have *parēkolouthēkas*). Built on the root verb *akolouthein* (to follow), the verb can range in meaning from literally "walking behind someone" to "following with the mind," as in the case of an argument at a lecture (see Epictetus *Discourse* I, 6, 13). It is something close to this meaning that seems to prevail in Luke 1:3 and here as well. The RSV translation "you have observed" is misleading if it is taken as a visual observation when Timothy was in Paul's presence (which would in any case contradict the sequence of events in Acts 13-16). The verb here suggests rather that Timothy has paid attention to what he has learned of Paul's experiences and the manner in which he endured them. The note of imitation lies just below the surface, as indeed the very next verse shows.

Literary Observations

The pattern of antitheses continues into this passage, but here the entire focus is on Timothy himself: note the repetition of "but you" in 3:10 and 3:14. Whereas the opponents have been characterized in terms of progress and movement (see 2:16–17; 3:6, 9), Timothy has been told to "shun," "avoid," "flee," and "turn away from" them and their practices (see 2:16, 22–23; 3:5). Now, Timothy is told that he "has followed" Paul's own way (3:10) and is commanded to "remain" in what he has been taught (v. 14). In contrast to progressive novelty going nowhere, Timothy is exhorted to be as stable as "God's firm foundation" (2:19).

The section also represents a partial, implicit return to the presentation of Paul as a model of endurance in suffering that was so critical to the first part of this personal paraenetic/ protreptic letter (cf. 1:6–14). Thus, the statement in 3:12 that "all those who wish to live piously in Christ Jesus will be persecuted" serves as the link between the fact that Paul had endured sufferings and had been rescued by the Lord and the implication that Timothy also is following closely in the same path.

Finally, I offer a word about the literary function of 3:16–17, a passage that has been unduly tortured in theological debates of the fundamentalist/modernist variety in which the inspiration of Scripture — and therefore, it is erroneously thought, its authority — is the issue. Paul's purpose here is, not to make a statement about the ontological status of scripture (which for him, as we know, could mean only Torah, since there was yet no New Testament), but rather to make a statement about its *usefulness*. Therefore, the statement in 3:16–17 is a functional statement. In Romans 15:3–4 Paul concluded an application of LXX Psalm 68:9 to Jesus, and therefore to the present circumstances of the Roman community, by stating, "Whatever was written in former days was written for our instruction, that by steadfastness and by the encouragement of the scriptures, we might have hope." Likewise, he concluded his application of the story of the wilderness to the Corinthian congregation by affirming, "These things happened to them as a warning, but they were written down for our instruction, upon whom the end of the ages has come" (1 Cor.

10:11). In the same way, the application of the exodus story to
the situation of Timothy and the opponents — particularly the
way Timothy should respond to them (see 2:19 and 3:8) — is supported by *this* statement concerning the function and efficacy
of these God-inspired writings.

Comment

As Paul works toward the end of his exhortation, the real contrast between Timothy and his opponents emerges more clearly.
The opponents are those who are eager for novelty, who engage
in disputes precisely to generate conflicts. Timothy is to stand
fast within that which has come from the past: the heritage of
Torah which he learned as a child from his maternal forebears
who had the same faith dwelling in them as Timothy does in
him. The false teachers' profane chatter is just for show, but the
words of Torah are "useful" (*ōphelimos,* one of the central criteria
for authentic moral teaching in the hellenistic world) for the correction and instruction of others, a true *paideia* of righteousness
(3:16).

The false teachers are evil people and charlatans whose influence over others is like the spread of gangrene. Timothy is
a "servant of the Lord" and a "man of God" whose equipment
is the doing of every good work. The false teachers enter into
households in order to disrupt them. The opponents upset the
faith of some people and make captives of women who, eager
for the novelties they offer, never come to a secure recognition of the truth. In contrast, Timothy dwells within the "firm
foundation" of the community of faith, a network of those who
nurture faith even in children (real or fictive). In this community, women are not the weak and silly captives of charlatans,
but are themselves those who can hand on the true faith to
children and raise them within the symbolic world of Torah.

The opponents have the form of piety but not its power. Their
teaching of a realized eschatology is a way of bypassing the suffering of the cross. Paul and Timothy have been given the gift
of power that enables them to endure the suffering and persecution that comes with a life dedicated to God. The malicious vices
in which the opponents share are a sign that the "last days" are

here; Paul and Timothy await the reward that will come to them as to all those who love God on "that day."

Does this contrasting pattern place stability, peace, continuity, tradition, and the household in a positive place over against insurrection, conflict, discontinuity, innovation, and a disruption of the household? Yes. But it is up to the reader to decide whether such a contrast is compatible only with a later "domesticated" Paul or whether it corresponds perfectly with the Paul of 1 Corinthians, who declared in his discussion of charismatic gifts, "God is a God not of confusion but of peace... did the word of God originate with you, or are you the only ones it reached?... all things should be done decently and in order" (1 Cor. 14:33, 36, 40).

A Final Exhortation — 4:1–8

4:1I exhort you in the presence of God and of Christ Jesus, who is coming to judge the living and the dead, and in view of his appearance and his kingdom: **2**Preach the word! Apply yourself to it in good times and bad. Refute and rebuke! Give comfort with every sort of long suffering and teaching. **3**For there will be a time when, because they have itchy ears, they will not put up with healthy teaching, but will multiply teachers fashioned to their passions. **4**They will stop listening to the truth. They will turn aside to myths. **5**But you, stay sober in all matters. Endure the hard things. Do the work of a minister of the good news. Fulfill your ministry. **6**For I am already being offered up as a sacrifice, and the time for my death is near. **7**I have fought the noble battle, finished the race, held tight to the faith. **8**There is already waiting for me the crown given to the righteous, which the Lord, the righteous judge, will award me on that day. It will be given not only to me but also to all those who have loved his coming.

Notes on Translation

Although the passage has several small textual variants, none affects the meaning to a significant degree. One that could is the elimination of *kakopathēson* (endure the hard things) by some MSS in 4:5, for that would mean the passage less obviously recapitulates the themes of 1:6–14. The majority of the best witnesses, however, contain this verb. Indeed, one goes further and adds "as a good soldier of Christ Jesus." This longer reading is undoubtedly erroneous because it is found in only one witness, Alexandrinus, which has already shown itself erratic in this composition, and because it clearly is entered under the influence of 2:3.

The diction throughout these eight verses is, as in other places where the subject is largely biographical, impressively Pauline. There are four NT hapax legomena and seven Pauline hapax legomena. As before, several of these are rooted in the specific subject matter of moral teaching and polemic (*epitimōn, hygiasynē, knēthian, ektrapein*). One expression in particular represents a commonplace in hellenistic moral literature, even though it is not attested in the undisputed Pauline letters: the combination *eukairōs akairōs*, which is often translated as "in season and out of season" and which I have rendered "in good times and bad," is, with some variations, widely attested (see Malherbe, " 'In Season and Out of Season' ").

Translation decisions: The opening exhortation in 4:1 (*diamartyrein*, also in 2:14) is very solemn, made "in the presence of God and of Christ Jesus"; all this is straightforward. More difficult is the double phrase in the accusative case, "his appearance and his kingdom." After the verb *diamartyrein*, the accusative stands for the thing sworn upon, thus "by his appearance" or, as I have rendered it, "in view of his appearance" (see Zerwick and Grosvener, *Grammatical Analysis,* 2:644). The second, co-ordinated phrase may have been in the accusative to avoid a series of dependent genitives (thus, Blass, Debrunner, and Funk, *Greek Grammar,* 442, par. 16). It could, therefore, be read as "the appearance of his kingdom."

I have translated the aorist imperative of *ephistēmi* in 4:2 as "apply yourself to it" (cf. "be urgent" in the RSV). The verb means literally "to stand by" something or "to take one's stand on" something (see Acts 10:17; 12:7; 1 Thess. 5:3). But the verb can also mean to "fix one's mind on" or "pay attention to" (see Aristotle *Metaphysics* 1090A; *Politics* 1335B). In context, that meaning seemed to me to be more appropriate.

In 4:3, the translation "itchy ears" is almost unavoidable for *knēthomenoi tēn akoēn,* although the expression means literally "being itchy with respect to hearing." The traditional translation is useful because its metonymy enables the medical imagery to work; note that this restlessness is combined with the hearers' inability to "bear with (*anexontai*) healthy teaching (*hygiainousēs didaskalias*)." The addition of "because" in this clause strengthens the causative implication of the participle.

My translation of 4:6 is fairly free, since I try to make the allusive language more precise. The verb *spendomai,* for example, means literally "to pour out as a drink offering" — the cultic implication is unavoidable (see Homer *Iliad* 9.177). Here, the verb is in the passive, with the "pouring out" standing metaphorically for the offering of the person as a dedication (cf. esp. Phil. 2:17). Likewise, the noun *analysis* can mean a deliverance, as from evils (Sophocles *Electra* 142), or a departure (Josephus *Antiquities* 19.4.1). The phrase "dissolution of the body" appears in the *Sentences of Secundus* 19. It is, therefore, possible to argue that the author might have intended something other than Paul's death by the use of *analysis* (see Prior, *Paul the Letter Writer,* 98–113), but the context strongly suggests this meaning, and I have translated it accordingly. Note in Philippians 1:23 Paul's use of the verb *analysai,* which can only be read as a reference to the apostle's death.

Literary Observations

Rhetorically, the protreptic argument of 2 Timothy comes to a satisfying conclusion in this passage, even though the remaining verses of the letter are not devoid of paraenetic purpose. There is a solemn and resumptive quality to Paul's words in this section, conveying a very real sense of commission from the apostle to his delegate at the time of the apostle's imminent death. Until the end, Paul presents himself as a model of those qualities that Timothy is to emulate.

The passage is particularly rich in eschatological language and imagery. Christ Jesus is coming to judge the living and the dead, and this is connected to "his appearance and his kingdom" (4:1). Paul is to receive the crown of righteousness, which is to be

given also to all those who love "his coming" (*epiphaneia*, appearance). It is not simply that Paul's life is approaching its end;
an ending of a more drastic and cosmic sort seems intimated as
well. We are invited by this language to consider the eschatology of 2 Timothy more closely. Does the letter present itself as
responding to a situation of a delayed parousia, in which there
is a diminished expectation of Jesus' return in judgment? Is its
eschatology reduced to the private realm of individual reward
or punishment, with no element yet of the apocalyptic battle
between good and evil leading to God's triumph?

Before looking at the evidence presented by the letter, we
should remember that the eschatology in the undisputed letters of Paul is scarcely uniform or consistent. It is, rather, made
up of several not easily reconcilable elements that exist side by
side rather than in a linear development. Thus, while in 1 and
2 Thessalonians the dominance of a future, cosmic eschatology
is obvious, it is less certain that it dominates Paul's thinking as
much as it does that of his readers. Indeed a fair reading of those
compositions might suggest that Paul takes it as his duty to re-
tard too vivid a sense of expectation in those congregations (see
1 Thess. 4:13–5:3; 2 Thess. 2:1–12). In contrast, he emphasizes
the reality of future eschatology to those Corinthians whose appreciation of their present power leads them to neglect the need
for future transformation (1 Cor. 7:29–31; 15:35–58). In 2 Corinthians 5:1, Paul's language suggests that at the time of death
"we have a dwelling from God," without reference to a future
cosmic event. He speaks of standing before the judgment seat of
Christ and being judged by what each one has done "whether
good or bad" (2 Cor. 5:10). The eschatology here is far more
private and platonic than that suggested by the Thessalonian correspondence. In Philippians, finally, Paul combines both streams.
He says "the Lord is near" (4:5), suggesting a future expectation,
but at the same time he speaks of "dying and being with Christ"
as something that would happen right after death (1:23).

Even this short survey shows the complexity of eschatology
in the indisputably Pauline letters (see Dupont, *syn christō*). Indeed, that complexity includes the designations Paul uses for the
future event. He can speak of "that day" (*hēmera ekeinē*, 2 Thess.
1:10), of "the day" (Rom. 2:16), of the "day of Christ Jesus" (Phil.

1:6), of "the day of Christ" (Phil. 2:16), of "the day of the Lord"
(1 Thess. 5:2), and "the day of our Lord Jesus Christ" (1 Cor.
1:8). Paul's apocalyptic viewpoint is more consistent in his perception of inimical spiritual forces at work just outside the realm
of the community: demons inhabit places of idolatrous worship
(1 Cor. 10:20–21), and Satan stands as a present threat and opponent (Rom 16:20; 1 Cor. 5:5; 7:5; 2 Cor. 2:11; 12:7; 1 Thess.
2:18; 2 Thess. 2:9).

In 2 Timothy, Paul uses the phrase "that day" (*hēmera ekeinē*)
three times, each time with reference to the judgment of humans by God that will lead to their punishment or reward. Thus,
God will preserve Paul's *parathēkē* until "that day" (1:12) and
will reward Onesiphorus with mercy on "that day" (1:18). Finally, in 4:8, "that day" is when Paul will receive the crown of
righteousness together with all those who have loved "his appearance" or the coming of the one who is "righteous judge."
The connection of "the day" with the parousia here seems
unavoidable, especially since in 4:1 "appearance" is explicitly attached both to Jesus' judging of the living and the dead and
his "kingdom." The sense of a future, communal, eschatological
event is found also in the lines of 2:11–12: "If we have died with
him, we shall live with him; if we endure, we shall also reign
with him (*symbasileusomen*)."

The apocalyptic tone of 2 Timothy is evident in chapter 3 in
the description of "the last days" (*eschatais hēmerais*) as filled
with harsh times and evil people. The author uses the future
tense, it is true, but it is also the case that his application of the
evil qualities to the present-day opponents (*ek toutōn gar eisin
hoi*) in 3:16 collapses the horizon between the present and the
eschatological period, leaving the impression that "the last days"
are in fact the present ones. The same can be said of the present
passage. "There will be a time when they will not put up with
healthy teaching" (4:3) is not so much a prediction of the future
as a statement of the audience Timothy can expect to face. And
as in the undisputed letters, the activity of human opponents
is connected to the opposition posed by cosmic powers, such as
"the trap of the devil" in 2:26. Whether real or fictive, therefore, the eschatology of 2 Timothy is at least as future oriented,
communal, and apocalyptic as that found in the recognized cor-

pus. There is nothing in 2 Timothy to suggest a diminished eschatological expectation (see Towner, "The Present Age").

The point of the perception of the days as evil and the listeners as restless cravers after novelty is to emphasize the seriousness and the difficulty of the charge taken up by Paul's delegate. Therefore, just as Timothy is to "exhort in the presence of God" those whom he has chosen as teachers (2:14), so does Paul even more solemnly "exhort in the presence of God" his representative (4:1). Once more, we see the contrast between the fickleness and superficiality of the audience and the need for Timothy to be steady. He is to apply himself to the task "in good times and in bad" (4:2), and because they will frequently be bad, he needs above all those qualities of long-suffering (*makrothymia,* v.2) and sobriety (v. 5). Note that Paul's charge, "But you, stay sober in all matters" (*nēphe en pasin*) echoes the advice given to the Thessalonians in their apocalyptic context (1 Thess. 5:6, 8). The final three clauses of the charge (4:5) are mutually interpretive. To do the work of an evangelist in such a hostile and unwelcoming environment is, inevitably, to "endure the hard things" (*kakopathēson,* see 1:8, 12; 2:9), and to so endure is to "fulfill one's ministry," as Paul shows by his own recital of the effort he has now expended: "I have fought the noble battle, finished the race, held tight to the faith" (4:7).

The Pauline Network of Communication — 4:9–22

4:9 Make an effort to come to me quickly, **10**for Demas, having fallen in love with this world, has left me and gone to Thessalonika. Crescas has gone to Galatia, Titus to Dalmatia. **11**Only Luke is with me. When you have picked up Mark, bring him along with you, for he is useful to me in service. **12**And I sent Tychichos to Ephesus. **13**When you come, bring along the cloak I left behind at Carpus's place in Troas. Bring also the books and especially the parchments. **14**The coppersmith Alexander has acted badly toward me in many ways. The Lord will repay him according to his deeds. **15**You keep away from him also. He has greatly opposed our words. **16**No one was beside me at my first defense presentation. Instead they all

abandoned me. May it not be counted against them! ¹⁷The
Lord, on the other hand, stood by me and gave me strength,
so that through me the proclamation might be fulfilled and
that all nations might hear. And I was delivered from the
mouth of the lion. ¹⁸The Lord will deliver me from every evil
deed, and he will save me for his heavenly kingdom. To him
be glory for ever and ever. Amen. ¹⁹Greet Prisca and Aquila
and the household of Onesiphorus. ²⁰Erastus has remained in
Corinth. But I left Trophimus ill in Miletus. ²¹Try to get here before winter. Eubulus and Pudens and Linus and Claudia, and all
the brethren, greet you. ²²The Lord be with your spirit. Grace
be with you.

Notes on Translation

For reasons that are not at all clear, one group of MSS (F, G, L, P)
reads the imperfect rather than the aorist for the various verbs
involving the *leip/lip* endings in 4:10, 13, 16, and 20. The textual
variants otherwise are few and insignificant In 4:19, the same
MS (181) that added a gloss from the *Acts of Paul and Thecla*
in 3:11 contributes another: after the name Aquila, the MS adds
"Lectra his wife [presumably Aquila's?] and Zimmia and Zenon
his children" (see *Acts of Paul and Thecla* 2). The only other
noteworthy variation concerns the final prayer, which appears
in longer or shorter versions, according to which other letters of
Paul might have influenced different scribes.

The diction in this passage is, as in other places where Paul's
own situation is described, close to that in the undisputed letters. In the fourteen verses, there are twelve NT hapax legomena
and two Pauline hapax legomena, but eight of these are personal
names, and two are place names. Nine other personal names in
the passage are known to us from other NT sources.

Demas is mentioned with Luke as "coworkers of mine" in
Philemon 24. Luke is mentioned also in Colossians 4:10 (and
possibly in Rom. 16:21). Titus, as we have seen, plays an important role in Paul's ministry as a delegate (see 2 Cor. 2:13; 7:6,
13-14; 8:6, 16, 23; 12:18; Gal. 2:1, 3; Titus 1:4). Mark appears as
"John Mark" in Acts 12:12, 25 and 15:37, 39 as a companion of
Paul and Barnabas, holding the position that Timothy was to as-

sume in 16:3. He is located with Paul in prison by Philemon 24 and is identified as the nephew of Barnabas by Colossians 4:10. Someone named Mark is also mentioned in 1 Peter 5:13. Tychichos is mentioned with Trophimus as "Asians" associated with Paul by Acts 20:4. In Colossians 4:7 and Ephesians 6:21, Tychichos serves as the messenger who delivers letters to communities as well as personal news concerning Paul, who is in prison. In Titus 3:12, the author expresses the intention to send his delegate "Artemas or Tychichos." Trophimus is mentioned only once more, in Acts 21:29. Prisca and Aquila are fellow workers with Paul in Acts 18:2, 18, and 26, as well as in 1 Corinthians 16:9 and Romans 16:3. Erastus is named in Acts 19:22 with Timothy as one of those ministering to Paul, and in Romans 16:23, an Erastus is identified as the treasurer (*oikonomos*) of the city (presumably Corinth).

The percentage of known personal names to unknown is remarkably high. Compare Philippians, where Paul names Timothy, but then also four other personal names (plus the "members of Caesar's household") otherwise unattested in the NT. In Romans 16, as well, only six of the many names mentioned by Paul are known to us from other sources, while some twenty-seven are otherwise not found in the NT.

Translation decisions: I have translated *spoudason* in 4:9 as "make an effort" (cf. the use in Gal. 2:10; 2 Tim. 1:17; 2:15) because in the context there is the suggestion that Timothy must overcome a certain reluctance. The adverb *tacheōs* (quickly) in v. 9 is used in just this way by Paul in 1 Corinthians 4:19. In 4:11, the reference to Mark as "useful (*euchrēstos*) to me in service" is ambiguous. The term *diakonia* could refer to "ministry," as in 4:5, "fulfill your ministry." But it could also refer to the "personal service" that Mark could render to Paul as his assistant (cf. Philem. 13).

The translation of 4:14 is difficult, although the meaning is clear. The Greek is literally, "Alexander the coppersmith showed me many bad things." The verb *endeiknymi* means "to show forth" or "demonstrate"; here it has the sense of "exhibited toward me." My loose translation seeks the sense in appropriate English. Finally, the exact sense of *eis tēn basileian autou* in 4:18 is unclear. Is it simply elliptical, so that the full sentence should read, "he will save me [so that I can enter into] his heavenly kingdom"? Or does the construction (*eis* plus the accusative) denote purpose: "he will save me [so that I can work for] his heavenly kingdom"?

Literary Observations

Paul's undisputed letters sometimes, but not always, end with just such a flurry of personal news, greetings, and directions (see Rom. 16:1–23; 1 Cor. 16:1–23; Col. 4:7–18), as does 2 Timothy. The Pastorals show the same diversity, with 2 Timothy having this long section devoted to personal matters, Titus only four verses (3:12–15), and 1 Timothy nothing. In the Pauline letters that do have this element, we can observe three functions. The first is simply to take care of the practical concerns of the complex Pauline mission, particularly the movement of persons. The second is to reinforce networks of communication. This function is most obvious in the case of Romans, where, despite writing to a church that he has never met, Paul can greet many in the community by name, thus reinforcing his own credibility by invoking their recognition of him. The third function is to reinforce some of the points made in the earlier argument. In Romans, for example, the identification of some in the Roman church as Paul's "kinsmen" helps reinforce his argument concerning the place of Jew and Gentile in God's plan. In 1 Corinthians, the request that the community be submissive to the household of Stephanas (16:15–18) reinforces Paul's concern for good order in that church, just as his news about Apollos confirms his earlier argument that this missionary was a cooperative colleague rather than a rival (16:12).

The literary functions of the ending in 2 Timothy are basically the same: Paul touches on the movements of delegates, communicates greetings, and reinforces his main argument. He does this last by continuing to present himself as a model for Timothy. Paul faced opposition in Alexander (4:14); so also Timothy is to beware of him. Paul was abandoned by all at his first defense, but the Lord strengthened (*endynamōsen*) him (vv. 16–17), just as Timothy is to be "empowered" (*endynamou*) by the grace in Christ Jesus to carry out his mission (2:1). Paul was rescued and saved for the heavenly kingdom (4:18), just as Timothy will reign, if he will but endure (2:12), and share in the crown of righteousness laid up for all who have loved his appearance (4:8).

Comment

This final passage in 2 Timothy can once more be read from two very different perspectives. From the perspective of pseudonymity, these closing remarks serve two functions. First, the network of names and the personal business are the fictional accoutrements of pseudepigraphic literature. The author has available to him some traditional elements concerning Paul (from Acts and such letters as Romans and Philippians) and uses such traditions together with the elaboration of new characters (Crescas, Carpus, Alexander, Onesiphorus, Eubulus, Pudens, Linus, Claudia) to present a picture of Paul that is at once familiar and yet showing a "new stage" in his life. The effect of such details as the abandonment at Paul's first defense, his desire for company, and his wish for a cloak and materials for study is the poignant portrait of an aging apostle facing death with discomfort yet dignity.

Second, the emphasis on Paul's solitary struggle and his expectation of human defeat and death serves the function of setting up the generational transition that the Pastoral letters have been written to ensure. Having Paul at the point of death, prescient about the continuation of present opposition into the future, is the classic setting for the farewell discourse, or testament. The fact that he is now about to die means that his tradition, if it is to survive, must be carried on by his "delegates," that is, those committed to this form of Christianity in the succeeding generations.

Such a reading almost demands that 2 Timothy be read as a single literary composition with 1 Timothy and Titus, for without those compositions, the purpose for writing would be reduced to the level of entertainment or hagiography. But even as the "cover" for the other two letters, 2 Timothy serves only this very narrow function of legitimating the sort of domesticated Paulinism they purvey. It goes without saying that, if this perspective is correct, 2 Timothy offers us no real information about the Pauline mission or the character of Paul.

Reading this passage within the context of Paul's life and ministry, the second perspective finds what is said about the apostle's situation, the attitude he expresses, and the movements of his associates both credible and instructive. The network of names, for example, does not appear random or arbitrary. We can take Trophimus as a test case. As noted earlier, Trophimus is mentioned in the NT only here and in two passages of Acts. In Acts 20:4, he is called an "Asian," and in Acts 21:29, he is called an Ephesian. Ephesus, it will be recalled, is in the neighborhood of Miletus (Acts 20:17).

By saying that "I left Trophimus in Miletus sick" (2 Tim. 4:20), the "pseudepigrapher" is thought by some to be making an error, since Acts 21:29 places Trophimus in Jerusalem with Paul. Thus, the textual conjecture *melitē* has been suggested in place of Miletus in 4:20 to relieve Paul of what appears to be a chronological error. But such a position demands that the author was both dependent on Acts for knowing about Trophimus (he appears nowhere else) and getting his home base correct and yet also careless about the further narrative development in Acts. By no means, however, does the verb *apoleipein* (to leave) require a physical leave-taking. One can also "leave one in place," in the sense of an appointment. Such is exactly the sense in Titus 1:5. Read this way, Paul can simply be stating that Trophimus has been left in position in Miletus despite his being ill.

Another name that appears also in Acts is that of Alexander (4:14). In Acts 19:33, a certain Alexander appears momentarily during the riot at Ephesus but plays no major role. Did the author of 2 Timothy get this name from Acts, yet also confuse Alexander with Demetrius the craftsman in silver (Acts 19:24), thus getting both his trade and his function confused? Another Alexander appears in the *Acts of Paul and Thecla*, but he is explicitly designated a Syrian, and his plot function is to accost Thecla on the street and get soundly humiliated by her in turn (*Acts of Paul and Thecla* 26). Finally, an Alexander also shows up in 1 Timothy 1:20 together with Hymenaios as people Paul has consigned to Satan so they will learn not to blaspheme. In a case like this, it is necessary simply to acknowledge our inability to sort out the confused data.

Other bits of information in the passage find impressive, if indirect, confirmation. What is said about Mark, that he is "useful to me in service," has just the same ambiguity concerning Mark's role in Paul's mission (part missionary, part personal assistant) that the brief account in Acts (*and* 1 Pet. 5:13) suggests. Likewise, the note that Titus has gone to Dalmatia is confirmed by Paul's reference to his mission extending to Illyricum in Romans 15:19, and nowhere else. Similarly, the connection of Erastus to Corinth is certainly suggested by Romans 16:23, but 2 Timothy does not exploit the legendary possibilities that would be offered by his being "the treasurer of the city," which is also stated in Romans.

As for the depiction of Paul, this second perspective readily allows that something like a "generational transition" is taking place here, especially if one takes seriously that Paul sees himself as facing death! But this transition is a matter of continuing in the path already begun during Paul's lifetime by his trusted delegate. Yes, Paul is concerned about the courage of his emissary. Yes, he feels abandoned and desolate as he suffers as a prisoner. Indeed, so true to life is this portrayal that the most plausible interpretation is that it comes from one facing the situation he describes.

I have already noted the many resemblances between 2 Timothy and Philippians in setting, style, and mode of argumentation. But it is in the finely shaded nuances of mood that the comparison is most striking, a shift in the author's own perspective that is best accounted for by a change in circumstances. Written to a community that is particularly dear to him and on which he has been financially dependent, Philippians is fundamentally positive about Paul's situation and prospects. His chains serve to advance the mission (Phil. 1:12-13); although he is ready to die, he is confident that he will remain with them (1:21-26); he is convinced in the Lord that he will see them soon (2:24); he has the sense of not yet having reached his goal (3:12-16). In 2 Timothy, all these perceptions have shifted: his first defense was not successful, he feels abandoned, and false teachers are making great progress. The sense of finality and resignation is unmistakable. He is sure that the word of God cannot be chained (2:9), but he is not certain that he himself will ever escape imprisonment in this life. Paul is now ready to receive the crown for which he has been striving. Are these words from the heart, or the work of great art? Let the reader decide. But in the case of 2 Timothy, it must be said, there is as much to be said in favor of reading it as an authentic composition written by Paul, as there is in favor of regarding it as a second-century pseudonymous production (see Prior, *Paul the Letter Writer*).

Works Cited in 2 Timothy

Allen, J. A. "The 'In Christ' Formula in the Pastoral Epistles." *NTS* 10 (1963): 115–21.

Blass, F., A. Debrunner, and R. Funk. *A Greek Grammar of the New Testament.* Chicago: University of Chicago Press, 1961.

Dahl, N. A. "Form-Critical Observations on Early Christian Preaching." In *Jesus in the Memory of the Early Church*, 30–36. Minneapolis: Augsburg, 1976.

Duncan, J. G. *"Pistos ho logos." ExpT* 35 (1923–24): 124.

Dupont, J. *syn Christō: l'union avec le Christ suivant St. Paul.* Bruges: Editions de l'Abbé St. Andre, 1952.

Fitzgerald, J. T. "Virtue/Vice Lists." In *The Anchor Bible Dictionary.* 6:857–59. New York: Doubleday, 1992.

Grabbe, L. L. "The Jannes/Jambres Tradition in Targum Pseudo-Jonathan and Its Date." *JBL* 98 (1979): 393–401.

Hock, R. E. *The Social Context of Paul's Ministry: Tentmaking and Apostleship.* Philadelphia: Fortress Press, 1980.

Johnson, L. T. "The New Testament's Anti-Jewish Slander and the Conventions of Ancient Polemic." *JBL* 109 (1989): 419–441.

———. "II Timothy and the Polemic against False Teachers: A Reexamination." *JRS* 6/7 (1978–79): 1–26.

Karris, R. J. "The Background and Significance of the Polemic of the Pastoral Epistles." *JBL* 92 (1973): 549–64.

Käsemann, E. "Sätze heiligen Rechts im Neuen Testament." *NTS* 1 (1954–55): 248–60.

Kurz, W. *Farewell Addresses in the New Testament.* Collegeville, Minn.: Liturgical Press, 1990.

MacDonald, D. R. *The Legend and the Apostle: The Battle for Paul in Story and Canon.* Philadelphia: Westminster Press, 1983.

Malherbe, A. J. "Ancient Epistolary Theory." *Ohio Journal of Religious Studies* 5 (1977): 3–77.

———." 'In Season and Out of Season': 2 Timothy 4:2." *JBL* 103 (1982): 23–41.

———. "Medical Imagery in the Pastorals." In *Texts and Testaments,* edited by W. E. March, 19–35. San Antonio: Trinity University Press, 1980.

———. *Moral Exhortation: A Greco-Roman Handbook.* Philadelphia: Westminster Press, 1986.

———. *Paul and the Popular Philosophers.* Minneapolis: Fortress Press, 1989.

Meeks, W. A. *The First Urban Christians: The Social World of the Apostle Paul.* New Haven: Yale University Press, 1982.

Moule, C. F. D. *Idiom Book of New Testament Greek.* 2d ed. Cambridge: Cambridge University Press, 1959.

Nussbaum, M. C. *The Therapy of Desire: Theory and Practice in Hellenistic Ethics.* Princeton: Princeton University Press, 1994.

O'Brien, P. T. *Introductory Thanksgivings in the Letters of Paul.* Leiden: E. J. Brill, 1977.

Prior, M. *Paul the Letter Writer and Second Timothy.* Journal for the Study of the New Testament–Supplement Series 23. Sheffield: JSOT, 1989.

Redalié, Y. *Paul après Paul: le temps, le salut, le morale selon les epîtres à Timothée et à Tite.* Geneva: Labor et Fides, 1994.

Schubert, P. *The Form and Function of the Pauline Thanksgiving.* Berlin: A. Topelmann, 1939.

Stowers, S. K. "Social Typification and the Classification of Ancient Letters." In *The Social World of Formative Christianity and Judaism,* edited by J. Neusner, et. al., 78–89. Philadelphia: Fortress Press, 1988.

Thiselton, A. C. "Realized Eschatology in Corinth" *NTS* 24 (1977–78): 520–26.

Towner, P. H. "The Present Age in the Eschatology of the Pastoral Epistles." *NTS* 32 (1986): 427–48.

Wolter, M. *Die Pastoralbriefe als Paulustradition.* Forschungen zur Religion und Literatur des Alten und Neuen Testaments. Göttingen: Vandenhoeck & Ruprecht, 1988).

Zerwick, M., and M. Grosvener. *A Grammatical Analysis of the Greek New Testament.* Vol. 2. Rome: Biblical Institute Press, 1974.

Chapter Two

1 Timothy

First Timothy comes closest to the stereotypical picture of the Pastorals. It contains elements, to be sure, of the personal paraenetic letter: Paul is once again a model, though this time of God's mercy to sinners (1:16), and Timothy is to be a model to the church (4:12). As in 2 Timothy, moreover, the instructions concerning Timothy's attitudes and actions are contrasted antithetically to those of the opponents (1:3–20; 4:1–16; 6:2b–16, 20–21). The letter, however, has less obvious literary coherence than we found in 2 Timothy.

The letter also gives little information concerning Paul and his delegate, who is now stationed in Ephesus. Paul has left for Macedonia (1:3) but hopes to return soon (3:14). Ostensibly, he is writing to give instructions for Timothy in his absence (4:13), "so that you may know how it is necessary to behave in the household of God, which is the church of the living God—a pillar and support for the truth" (3:15). For those convinced that the Pastorals as a whole are pseudonymous, this entire scenario is fictitious. For those who wish to place 1 Timothy in Paul's lifetime, his extensive period of ministry in Ephesus and Asia minor (Acts 19:10; 20:17–38) and his frequent trips from that center (Acts 19:21–22; 20:1; 2 Cor. 1:16; 7:5) make the situation envisaged by the letter at least possible, if not plausible.

The instructions or commandments (*parangeliai*) are what give 1 Timothy its distinctive character. They deal with the respective roles of men and women in the liturgical context (2:1–15); the qualifications for bishops or overseers (*episkopoi*, 3:1–7), deacons (3:8–13), and women deacons (3:11); the care of widows (5:3–16); the resolution of charges against elders (5:19–22); and the attitudes of slaves (6:1–2) and the wealthy (6:17–19). Two things in particular are striking about these directives. The first is their consistently *ad hoc* and nonsystematic character. The second is the way they alternate with the paraenetic sections of the letter. If one pulled out all these concrete commandments and left only the materials dealing with Timothy and the opponents, we would have a letter that looked much more like 2 Timothy. It is almost as though the paraenetic/protreptic material functions as a framework within which the instructions have been placed somewhat haphazardly.

If 1 Timothy were to be judged pseudonymous — and I think it is the most difficult of the three letters to defend as authentic — then it could easily have been constructed on the basis of 2 Timothy. The author could have inserted the instructional material — of the sort that some scholars identify as a step on the road to the Christian church orders (see Dibelius and Conzelmann, *The Pastoral Epistles*, 5–7) into the seams of the paraenetic/protreptic prototype offered by 2 Timothy. This hypothesis has become less necessary, however, in the light of more recent epistolary research, which has provided evidence for letters dating from Paul's time and earlier that exhibit precisely the same combination of characteristics found in 1 Timothy and, to some extent, in Titus as well (see Fiore, *The Function of Personal Example*, and Wolter, *Die Pastoralbriefe als Paulustradition*). Such letters carry the *mandata principis* (commandments of the ruler) to a newly appointed delegate in a district or province. Although addressed to an individual (namely, the delegate in question), these directives (or *entolai*) have a quasi-public character; they are intended to be read by others as well as by the addressee.

An almost perfect example is the Tebtunis Papyrus 703, in which an Egyptian senior official instructs a subordinate in some of his responsibilities. Much of the letter is taken up by specific tasks that the delegate is to undertake. But these alternate with passages that are broader and more general in character and that focus on the character of the delegate and his manner of conducting himself in this new position. The delegate is to exhibit himself as a model of the behavior desired among the populace and can find in his own superior an example that he might also imitate (see Fiore, *The Function of Personal Example*, 81–83).

According to Dio Cassius *Roman History* 53.15.4, such letters were routinely sent to Roman proconsuls and prefects as early as the first century B.C.E. In Philo Judaeus's *Adversus Flaccum* 74, there is an example of the sort of instructions that Augustus sent to Magius Maximus, his prefect in Egypt (see Wolter, *Die Pastoralbriefe als Paulustradition,* 164–65, for these and other examples).

If a delegate carried with him such a letter and had it read in the assembly when he took up his post (even for such a short period as is envisaged by 1 Timothy), two things would be accomplished. First, the practical instructions would be publicly proclaimed as the will of the chief administrator, and not simply as the whim of the delegate. The effect of this would be to legitimate the practical measures proposed by the delegate. Second, the hortatory sections emphasizing the good personal qualities that the delegate should demonstrate would also make his subsequent behavior measurable by a norm set out by the ruler. Thus, the populace would have reason for appeal if the delegate failed to live up to the standards set out in the letter.

Such *mandata principis* letters provide the perfect literary antecedent for 1 Timothy and Titus. They fit the situation proposed by these Pastoral Letters: Timothy and Titus are sent by Paul to communities as his representative with specific tasks to carry out. They also help account for the odd joining of personal and public topics in 1 Timothy and Titus, for such a combination was a standard feature of such letters. Finally, the *mandata principis* letters explain the otherwise oddly detached tone of 1 Timothy and Titus, which are so much less personal and intense than 2 Timothy: the letters are not really private. Although addressed to an individual, they are intended for public consumption, not only for the support of the delegate, but also for the setting of a standard by which his performance could be measured.

Does the discovery of such a literary precedent prove 1 Timothy to be authentic? By no means. Certainly a pseudepigrapher could have made use of this literary form as easily as could Paul himself. But it does increase the probability that 1 Timothy was written by Paul during his lifetime. Its strange combination of elements may be due, not to the clumsy inefficiency of someone trying to imitate his other letters, but to the conventions of an

epistolary form that Paul himself used as freely as he did others
in the amazing range of letters found in the Pauline collection.

The delegate is expected to attend to the problematic aspects
of the Ephesian church. A precise reconstruction of the situation
in Ephesus — as portrayed by the letter, whatever its historical
accuracy — is difficult. The reader gains the distinct impression
that this church, in sharp contrast to the one portrayed in Titus,
is already well established. It had the basic structures of organization in place long enough to make realistic a caution against a
"new convert" becoming bishop (1 Tim. 3:6). How long would a
community need to exist before such a distinction applied? According to Acts, there was a foundation in Ephesus even before
Paul became involved in the community there (see Acts 18:24–
28), and his own sojourn lasted two years before the time of
the riot (19:10). Certainly this is sufficient time for a local community, not only to have well-established structures, but also to
face some difficulties with them.

Some of the difficulties appear to be generated by deviant
teachers. The names Hymenaios and Alexander occur as they did
in 2 Timothy, only this time in combination (1 Tim. 1:20; cf.
2 Tim. 2:17; 4:14). We are told little about them except that they
"have spurned a good conscience. They have suffered shipwreck
concerning the faith," so that Paul was forced to hand them
over to Satan (1:19–20). They are, then, either present or former members of the community and, therefore, themselves also
Christian. Apart from these names, Paul refers only generally to
"certain ones" (*tines,* 1:3, 6; 6:21).

Timothy is to charge these certain ones not to teach "other
doctrines" (*heterodidaskalein,* 1:3). What these doctrines might
be is not clear. Some wanted to be considered "teachers of the
law" (1:7) and are preoccupied with "myths and endless genealogies" (1:4). Some "liars whose consciences are seared" are against
marriage for Christians and advocate dietary restrictions (4:2–3)
and possibly other forms of asceticism (4:7–8). Some may seek
money for their teaching, although this charge is also frequently
part of conventional polemic (6:5). Paul's final characterization
is that they are involved with "godless chatter and contradictions
of what is falsely called knowledge" (*gnōsis,* 6:20). The profile
here is distinctive; note that there is no reference to the res-

urrection already having happened (as in 2 Timothy), nor any implication of the need for circumcision (such as we find in Titus). When all the conventional slander is peeled away, we find a coherent profile of those who demand performance ruled by law and asceticism, rather than by conscience.

First Timothy can be distinguished from 2 Timothy on several counts in the matter of false teachers. First, this letter makes no reference to the aggressive missionary tactics of the opponents or the progress they are making. Second, the opponents in 1 Timothy appear not so much to be rival teachers outside the Pauline circle as they do ambitious and elitist members of the community itself. Third, in contrast to 2 Timothy, this letter does not emphasize the correction of the troublemakers. They are simply to be commanded. Fourth, this letter has neither the note of gentleness nor the hope for conversion that we noted in 2 Timothy. Fifth, on several occasions, this letter does more than dismiss the opponents with polemic. Their theological position is engaged and refuted (see 1:8–10; 4:3–5, 7–8; 6:5–10).

In the course of the commentary, we shall ask whether there is any direct connection between the positions held by the opponents, or the disruptions they are causing, and Paul's specific directives to Timothy. That some connection can be made seems clear. The emphasis on certain qualities desired in supervisors and elders correlates with problems such as disruption and quarreling in worship and charges being brought against elders. In particular, we may wonder whether this letter's concern for young women becoming gadabouts and gossips (5:13) and its sharp refusal of any teaching role to women (2:8–15) may not be connected to the positions or practices of the opponents. Certainly we can detect a link between this composition's wholehearted affirmation of the order of creation and its deeply conservative position regarding the "natural" roles of the genders.

Finally, we can note that 1 Timothy contains some striking allusions to familiar Pauline teaching, above all in its insistence on God's salvific will for all humanity (see 1:15–16; 2:3–6; 4:9–10; 6:13–16). The letter also contains a fascinating version of Paul's conversion — now portrayed as an example of God's mercy to sinners (1:12–16), allusions to the trial and testimony of Jesus

(2:6; 6:13), and to one of Jesus' sayings (5:18). These elements, however, are dominated by the practical instructions within the context of moral exhortation, with its "sound teaching" (1:10; 6:3), "training in godliness" (1:4; 4:7), and "good conscience" (1:5, 19; 3:9) contrasted to a "seared conscience" (4:2).

The Opening Commission — 1:1-11

1:1 From Paul, an apostle of Christ Jesus by the command of God our savior and of Christ Jesus our hope, **2**to Timothy, my genuine child in the faith. Grace, mercy, and peace from God Father and from Christ Jesus our Lord. **3**As I exhorted you when I left for Macedonia: stay in Ephesus so that you can command certain people **4**not to teach different doctrines or devote themselves to myths and endless genealogies. These stimulate conflicts more than faithful household management for God. **5**The goal of the commandment is love from a pure heart and a good conscience and a sincere faith. **6**Some people have missed these. They have turned aside to foolish chatter. **7**They want to be teachers of law, without understanding what it is they are talking about or the things to which they are so committed. **8**We, in contrast, know that the law is good if it is used appropriately, **9**knowing this, that it is not laid down for a righteous person, but for the lawless, and those who are insubordinate, the godless and irreligious and unholy and profane: people who kill fathers, who kill mothers, who are murderers; **10**people who are fornicators, sodomites, slave-dealers; people who take false oaths, and do anything else that is opposed to the healthy teaching **11**that accords with the glorious good news from the blessed God, the good news with which I have been entrusted.

Notes on Translation

There are only a handful of textual variants to consider. Codex Sinaiticus has *epangelian* in 1:1, rather than *epitagēn,* to make the text read "according to the promise of God," rather than "according to the commandment of God." But the former reading is influenced by 2 Timothy 1:1. The use of *epitagē* is especially appropriate in a *mandata principis* letter: Paul's authority is also "according to command" (see also Titus 1:3). In 1:4, a majority of MSS have *zētēsis* (dispute) rather than *ekzētēsis*, which means "investigation" or "inquiry" (see LXX 2 Kings 4:11). Despite going with the "harder" reading (that is, the one that creates problems for readers), we still translate the term as "dispute," since that is clearly what is meant in context. Another decision in 1:4 is much easier. Only a handful of witnesses have *oikodomē* (edification) rather than *oikonomia* (household management), and the former would be the easier reading as a familiar Pauline concept. The use of *oikonomia* is pertinent in a letter whose expressed concern is how one should behave in the *oikos theou* (3:15).

The diction in this opening passage of 1 Timothy is mixed in a way that persists throughout the letter. On the one hand, all of the terms in the greeting are found in Paul's undisputed letters, even the phrase *kat' epitagēn* ("according to the command"; see Rom. 16:26; 1 Cor. 7:6) and the term *sōtēr* (savior), which is applied to Jesus in Philippians 3:20 and Ephesians 5:23. For the use of "genuine" (*gnēsios*) in v. 2, compare 2 Corinthians 8:8 and Philippians 4:3, and for Jesus as "our hope" in v. 1, compare Colossians 1:27. In 1:3–11, on the other hand, we find a large number of NT and Pauline hapax legomena. As in 2 Timothy, many of these occur in the context of polemic against opponents (see *heterodidaskalein, prosechein, mythoi, genealogia, aperantos, ekzētēsis, astochein, ektrapein, mataiologia, nomodidaskaloi* — all in vv. 3–7!). The other place dominated by strange vocabulary is the vice list in 1:9–10. In its fourteen terms, we find five NT hapax, three Pauline hapax, and one word shared by the Pastorals alone. This can be compared to the vice list in 2 Timothy 3:2–5, whose nineteen terms include seven NT hapax and five Pauline hapax, and the one in Romans 1:29–31, whose twenty-two terms include seven NT hapax and one Pauline hapax.

Two phrases in 1:11 illustrate the mixed diction I have mentioned. When Paul refers to the good news "with which I have been entrusted" (*ho episteuthēn egō*), the construction at first appears suspiciously "pastoral" (appearing also in Titus 1:3) and un-Pauline. In fact, however, the idiom is one used by Paul.

In Romans 3:2, he says of the Jews, *hoti episteuthēsan ta logia tou theou* ("they have been entrusted with the words of God"), and, even more strikingly, he declares in Galatians 2:7 that the Jerusalem leadership *idontes hoti pepisteumai to euangelion tēs akrobystias* ("saw that I had been entrusted with the gospel of uncircumcision"; see also 2 Thess. 1:10). The epithet "blessed God" (*makarios theos*), in contrast, is never found in Paul, nor in the entire NT apart from this letter (see also 6:15). It is, however, an epithet frequently applied to God by hellenistic authors (see Aristotle *Nicomachean Ethics* 1178B; Diogenes Laertius *Lives of Eminent Philosophers* 10.123), including hellenistic Jewish writers (Philo *On the Cherubim* 86; *On the Immutability of God* 26; Josephus *Against Apion* 2.190). The phrase is the perfect example of the slightly more "hellenistic" tone that we find in 1 Timothy. Please note, however, that such language was available in the first century and did not require a further "hellenization" of Christianity to be employed.

Translation decisions: The sentence beginning in 1:3 is anacoluthic, that is, it starts with one sort of syntactical construction but does not follow through on it. I have chosen to treat the accusative-plus-infinitive construction following "as I exhorted you" as the equivalent of a direct command, thus: "stay in Ephesus."

The precise rendering of *oikonomia theou* in 1:4 is difficult. The RSV, for example, offers "divine training," with the marginal alternatives "stewardship" and "order." The NRSV also has "divine training," but offers "divine plan" as a marginal alternative (see also the NAB). In ordinary Greek usage, *oikonomia* simply means "household management" (see Xenophon *Oecumenicus* 1.1; Aristotle *Politics* 1253B), and that is the sense intended here. Timothy is to focus on the orderly functioning of the *oikos theou* (household of God, 3:15). For *oikonomia* elsewhere in Paul, see 1 Corinthians 4:1, 9:17, and Colossians 1:25. More difficult still is deciding how the prepositional phrase *en pistei* should be translated. I have chosen "faithful" as an adjective qualifying "household management," but I recognize the rendering "which consists in faith" may be equally valid and may perhaps be an even better way to establish the important theme of faith in this letter.

In the vice list of 1:9–10, most of the terms are straight-forward. Two are perhaps deserving of special note. The noun *arsenokoitēs* means, literally, "one who sleeps with a man." It is used in the vice list of 1 Corinthians 6:9 as well. The translation "sodomite" is certainly not politically correct by to-day's standards, but a translation such as "gay males" would be both inaccurate and anachronistic. The term I have translated "slave-dealers" (*andrapodistai*) has the specific sense of "sell-ing into slavery free men who had been captured in war" (see Herodotus *Persian War* 1.151; Plato *Republic* 344B). It can some-times also be used for "kidnapper" (see Xenophon *Memorabilia* 4.2.14).

The presence of wordplay in 1:8–10 makes the translation of some terms and phrases difficult. Paul says in 1:8 that "we know the law (*nomos*) is good (*kalos*) if anyone uses it *nomimōs*." The first part of the sentiment is Pauline enough. Paul says in Romans 7:12, "the law (*nomos*) is holy and the commandment (*entolē*) is holy and righteous and good." He further says in Romans 7:14, "the law (*nomos*) is spiritual (*pneumatikos*)," and in Romans 7:16, "I agree that the law (*nomos*) is good (*kalos*)." The second part of the statement in 1:8 is more difficult. What does Paul mean by "use *nomimōs*"? The adverb literally means "lawfully," but it ap-pears nowhere else in the NT apart from 2 Timothy 2:5, where I translated it "by the rules." In Plato's *Symposium* 182A, it has the sense of "naturally" or "appropriately." In the present composi-tion, Paul's objection is to those who seek to make law replace conscience as a guide for behavior; therefore, it makes sense to translate it here as "appropriately," the meaning of which is spelled out in the subsequent verses.

Equally problematic is the second wordplay. Paul contrasts the law which "is not laid down for a righteous person" (*diakiō ou keitai*, 1:9) and the vices of the wicked which "is opposed to" (*an-tikeitai*, 1:10) the healthy teaching contained in the good news. The word in v. 10 clearly means "oppose/stand in opposition to," so there is a simple contrast between the sickness of these vices and the health of the gospel. The translation of the phrase in v. 9, however, is trickier. The verb *keimai* means literally "to be laid/lie" (Homer *Odyssey* 11.577) and from there comes to mean "to be situated" (see Herodotus *Persian War* 5.49). It is also used explicitly for "established laws" (see Euripides *Hecuba* 292; Xenophon *Memorabilia* 4.4.21). In the NT, the verb bears its literal sense in Matthew 3:10, 28:6, and Luke 2:12, but is used metaphorically in 1 Corinthians 3:11, 2 Corinthians 3:15, Philippians 1:16, and 1 Thessalonians 3:3. We shall consider further in the Comment what Paul might mean by stating that the law is not "established for/laid against" the righteous person.

Literary Observations

The greeting fits the standard form (see the observations on 2 Tim. 1:1–2 on pp. 43–45). I have already mentioned that the phrase *kat' epitagēn* (by the command) is appropriate for a *mandata principis* letter. The designation in v. 2 of Timothy as "genuine child in the faith," likewise, is less personal than the "beloved child" in 2 Timothy 1:2 and more fitting to the semipublic character of this letter. That Paul truly considered Timothy to be "genuine" is confirmed by Philippians 2:20: "I have no one like him, who will be genuinely (*gnēsiōs*) anxious for your welfare." The combination of "God our savior" and "Christ Jesus our hope" in v. 1 seems to deliberately anticipate themes in the letter. God is characterized as "savior" twice more (2:3; 4:10), and three times Paul stresses the need for hope in the living God (4:10; 5:5; 6:15).

It is customary for Paul immediately to follow the greeting with a thanksgiving, such as we saw in 2 Timothy 1:3–5. In one of the undisputed letters (Galatians), however, Paul eliminates the thanksgiving altogether and plunges directly into the business that preoccupies him. In that case, in fact, the opening statement resembles a set of curses much more than a blessing (Gal. 1:6–9). Titus also lacks a thanksgiving entirely, moving directly to the business at hand with the phrase *toutou charin* (Titus 1:5). In 1 Timothy, there is a delayed thanksgiving in 1:12–17, whose special character will be noted in the commentary on that section.

Two further literary aspects of 2 Timothy 1:11 can be noted. First, we see that Paul uses conventional polemic against the agitators within the community. For the problems in cutting through this rhetoric to find the specific qualities of opponents, see the comments on 2 Timothy (cf. pp. 73–78). In the present instance, for example, the charge that the false teachers give themselves to "myths and endless genealogies" (1:4) might simply be another way of stating that they have given themselves to "foolish chatter" (*mataiologia,* 1:6), or it might have some specific reference to their teaching: are these, perhaps, devotees of proto-Gnostic speculation about the *pleroma,* or are they amateur rabbis, obsessed with *haggadoth* (myths) and the chain of tradition ("genealogies")? Both are possible, neither is necessary (see, e.g., Colson, "Myths and Genealogies").

Second, we observe another function of that favorite device of hellenistic moral discourse, the vice list. In 2 Timothy 3:2–5, it was used to describe the character of people in the "last days." In the present passage, the vices serve as a catalogue, a sampling, of the sorts of behaviors that contradict the healthy teaching that derives from the good news. As in the 2 Timothy list, we find the use of sound as important as sense, with many of the terms beginning with alpha-privatives and with the dative-plural endings creating a pleasing assonance. The suggestive quality of the list is shown by the conclusion "and anything else" (v. 10, see McEleney, "Vice-Lists of the Pastoral Epistles").

Comment

The interpreter who adopts the position that 1 Timothy is a real letter written by Paul during his lifetime to his delegate, left for a time in Ephesus to attend to matters in that local church, is obliged to seek connections between the ideas expressed in the composition in a way not required of those holding to the hypothesis of pseudonymity, who regard the characterization of the opponents much like the details about Paul's own life, as the stuff of fiction. In this opening section of the letter, then, it is important to take seriously the precise language used by the author concerning his charge to the delegate and the situation faced by Timothy. In other words, this opening foray, urgent enough to delay the typical Pauline thanksgiving, may be fundamentally more programmatic than we might assume and might set the basic framework and motivation for the rest of the instructions.

We see, then, that Timothy's first charge is to instruct certain people "not to teach different doctrines" (1 Tim. 1:4).
Since they are purportedly within Timothy's jurisdiction and
since (as 1:20 indicates) they can even be excommunicated, we
are justified in assuming that they are not agitators from the
outside, but are members of the local community. Paul does
not actually call them "teachers of the law" (*nomodidaskaloi*,
v. 7; a term otherwise found only in Luke 5:17 and Acts 5:34,
referring to Jewish teachers), but says they "wish" to be so,
suggesting an intellectual ambition unmatched by skill or training. Indeed, he says clearly that they are ignorant of what
they say or the things they profess (v. 7). Their foolish chatter
and endless disquisitions, we are to suppose, are the fustian of
pseudointellectuals.

But what is it that these people are trying to accomplish by
"teaching different doctrines" centered in the law? Presumably
they are claiming that the observance of Torah is necessary for
the virtuous life. In order to understand Paul's punning response
("the law is good if used lawfully") in v. 8, we need to grasp
that he is stating a slightly different version of the argument in
Romans 6–8. The Christian life based in the good news is a matter of faith (1 Tim. 1:4), and the goal of "the commandment"
(*parangelia*) is love. This love, in turn, finds its source in internal
qualities of character: a pure heart, a good conscience, sincere
faith (v. 5). This is the healthy teaching connected to the "good
news" Paul preaches (v. 11). It is by such faith and love that
a person is a "righteous person" (*dikaios*). As Paul will shortly
make clear, all of this life and virtue derives from the merciful
gift of God.

What, then, of the law? It "lies against" (1:9) all those wicked
human activities that "oppose" this healthy teaching (v. 10).
But it does not by itself make one righteous, give one faith,
enable love, or make the conscience good. Paul is in effect distinguishing between a heteronomous and autonomous norm for
life. The norm of Christian righteousness is found, not in a law
that stands outside the person, but in the commandment of love
which is rooted in internal dispositions.

The law that these people are pushing is, for Paul's readers,
not necessary. In fact, by suggesting that it is necessary, they

are generating conflicts that disturb the "household manage-ment for God," which is all about faith. Here, the other nuance of *oikonomia* in v. 4 is important. I mentioned above several of the translations used to capture this elusive phrase. One of the most interesting in light of the present discussion is that found in the NIV, which renders it as "God's work." As a literal trans-lation, it is misleading, and it misses the nuance of "household management," which is thematic. But it is right on target for the fundamental contrast between the standards set by these elitists and the way in which God has been and is working in the com-munity. Paul's subsequent thanksgiving will make that contrast more explicit.

Recalling the Basis of Hope — 1:12–20

1:12I give thanks to the one who has empowered me, Christ Jesus our Lord, for he has considered me faithful by putting me into service. **13**Earlier I was a blasphemer. I was a persecu-tor. I was an insolent person. But I was shown mercy because in ignorance I acted with faithlessness. **14**And the gift of our Lord with the faith and love that are in Christ Jesus was extrav-agant. **15**This saying is reliable and worthy of all acceptance, that Christ Jesus came into the world to save sinners. I am the first among them! **16**But I was shown mercy for this reason, that Christ Jesus might demonstrate all possible patience in me first, as an example for those who would come to believe in him unto eternal life. **17**To the king of the ages, to the immor-tal, invisible, only God, be praise and glory for ever and ever. Amen. **18**My child Timothy, I entrust this commandment to you according to the earlier prophecies made concerning you, so that you might continue fighting the noble battle by means of them, **19**having faith and a good conscience. Some people have spurned a good conscience. They have suffered ship-wreck concerning the faith! **20**Among them are Hymenaios and Alexander. I have handed them over to Satan, so that they may be taught not to blaspheme.

Notes on Translation

The textual variants in this passage are not extensive, but do offer some insight into the problems that scribes saw in the text and tried to correct. In 1:12 and 1:18, for example, some MSS offer a different tense of the verb. In the first case, they have the present participle *endynamounti* rather than the aorist *endynamōsanti* found in the Nestle-Aland 27th edition. What is at stake? Perhaps it is a different perception of Paul's relationship to Christ. Was Paul empowered in the past, or is he continuing to be empowered in the present? By far the better MS evidence supports the past tense, but it is also the easier reading, since the tense of the main verbs is also past. In 1:18, the choice is again between the aorist and present tenses in the subjunctive mood: does Paul want Timothy to "fight the noble battle" (as the aorist would have it) or "continue fighting the noble battle" (as the present tense signifies)? I have followed Nestle-Aland in choosing the present tense, even though the external support for the aorist is not insignificant. In this case, the "continuous action" is the easier reading, for it corresponds to the "keep at it" tone of the protreptic.

Some scribes sought to improve on the awkwardness of *to proteron onta* in 1:13. As it stands, the neuter relative adjective is used adverbially, "at an earlier time." Some MSS add the personal pronoun *me* and change the neuter to the masculine accusative to yield, "I was formerly." No big difference in meaning occurs, only a concern for proper grammar on the part of MS copiers. An idiosyncratic opinion found its way into some Latin MSS, which read *anthrōpinos ho logos* in 1:15 rather than *pistos ho logos,* thus yielding "it is a human word" rather than "it is a faithful word." Finally, in 1:17, we see a variety of modifiers for God in Paul's doxology: some MSS read "deathless, invisible," others "incorruptible, invisible, deathless," while still others add "wise" to "only God." Such alterations reflect, in all likelihood, the language of worship.

In 1:20 the names Hymenaios and Alexander appear as among the "certain ones" who have abandoned conscience in order to push doctrines concerning the law. Apart from Timothy and Paul himself, these are the only personal names mentioned in

the letter. Both names are found also in 2 Timothy, but separately. In 2 Timothy 2:17, Hymenaios is teamed with Philetos as
a charlatan whose speech spreads like gangrene. And in 2 Timothy 4:14, Alexander "the coppersmith" is named as one who
has done Paul considerable harm. Why should names linked to-   ⁊
gether here appear separately in 2 Timothy? We simply have
insufficient evidence to pursue the matter further.

If we merely engage in word counting, the diction of this
passage is among the most thoroughly Pauline in the Pastorals,
containing only two Pauline hapax legomena (*blasphēmos* in
v. 13, *proagein* in v. 18) and two NT hapax legomena (*diōktēs*
in v. 13, *hyperpleonazein* in v. 14), in addition to the names Hymenaios and Alexander. The fact that these particular words do
not appear in the rest of the Pauline corpus seems largely a matter of chance: Paul uses the verb *pleonazein* frequently (e.g., Rom.
5:20; 6:1; 2 Cor. 4:15; 8:15) and is particularly fond of *hyper*-
constructions (see, e.g., 1 Thess. 3:10; 4:6; 2 Cor. 3:10; 10:14;
Rom. 7:13; 8:26; 8:37). Likewise, though he never calls himself a
diōktēs, he is candid about the fact that he persecuted (*diōkein*)
the church (Gal. 1:13; Phil. 3:6).

On the other hand (and with the Pastorals there is always another hand), the passage contains phrases which, while made
up of Pauline words, are not typically Pauline expressions. Although the term *basileus* (king) occurs in 2 Corinthians 11:32,
only in this letter is God called "king" (1:17, see also 6:15). Sim-   ✓
ilarly, the phrase *charin echō* for "I give thanks" is found only
here in v. 12 and in 2 Timothy 1:3. As we saw in 2 Timothy,
the phrase *pistos ho logos* (v. 15) is distinctive to the Pastorals,   ✓
and the verb *paratithēmi* in v. 18 is used differently than in
1 Corinthians 10:27.

Still other constructions are remarkably like those in the undisputed letters. Compare, "I give thanks to the one who has
empowered me (*endynamōsanti me*)" in v. 12 to "I am able to
do all things by the one empowering me (*endynamounti me*)"
in Philippians 4:13. Similarly, the use of the participle *themenos*
in v. 12 for "putting me into service" is precisely the same as
Paul's use of *themenos* in conjunction with "the word of reconciliation" in 2 Corinthians 5:19. Finally, the expression "I have
handed over to Satan" (*paredōka tō Satana*) in v. 20 is remarkably

close to Paul's own *paradounai ton toiouton tǭ Satanǎ* ("hand over such a one to Satan") in 1 Corinthians 5:5.

Two conclusions are confirmed by these observations. First, the analysis of vocabulary is of limited use in determining authorship because there are so many variables to consider. Second, one of the most important variables is subject matter. Here, where the topic is Paul's former life, the diction is recognizably more Pauline than in the discussion of other subjects.

Literary Observations

Although we speak of the "Pauline thanksgiving" as though it were a single thing, the form and placement of these prayers in the Pauline letters varies considerably. In the case of 1 Timothy, as we have seen, Paul's initial instruction to Timothy displaces the thanksgiving, which as a result, and probably intentionally, becomes part of the argument of the letter. Paul's thanksgiving here is self-referential, recounting his turn from persecutor to believer in Christ Jesus, one to whom the good news had been entrusted. In its focus on his own experience and mission, it resembles the thanksgivings in Romans 1:8–15 and 2 Corinthians 1:3–7 rather than those that focus on the experience of the addressees (e.g., 1 Cor. 1:4–9; Phil. 1:3–11; Col. 1:3–8).

The phrase "this commandment" in 1:18 forms an *inclusio* (literary bracket) with "in order that you might command" in 1:3. As a result, we find that attention to the false teachers in 1:4–10 and 1:18–20 brackets Paul's presentation of himself as a model of the sinner who has been saved by Christ Jesus (1:12–17). The rhetorical function of this placement is to reinforce the contrast between "the healthy teaching" of the good news and the legalism of the false teachers by showing the *experiential* basis for authentic Christian faith. Paul's former life, in this account, reveals the misanthropic tendencies that no law could rectify. He can testify, from his own experience of having been empowered, that salvation came to him by the gift of Christ Jesus, and not by the keeping of the law.

Comment

In the previous passage, we saw that Paul established a contrast between the commandment that had love as its goal, derived from a pure heart and good conscience and sincere faith (1:5), and the propagation of the law as a heteronomous norm for behavior. The same contrast continues in the present passage. Hymenaios and Alexander, we notice, having rejected a good conscience, have thus shipwrecked their faith (1:19), whereas Timothy is to carry on the noble battle with the very qualities that the opponents have rejected. The present passage intensifies the contrast by emphasizing the role of spiritual power on the side of conscience: faith is a matter not of external observance but of internal transformation. Thus, Timothy's teaching has been prepared for by prophetic utterances (v. 18), perhaps those proclaimed in the assembly at the time when hands were laid on him by the *presbyterion,* or board of elders (4:14). At that occasion prophecy played a role, as Timothy was given the spiritual gift required for his ministry (4:14).

The role of transforming power is even more emphatically portrayed in Paul's account of his conversion (1:12–16), which serves as an elaboration of his statement in 1:11 that he was entrusted with the "glorious good news of the blessed God." Thus, Paul thanks Christ Jesus for counting him faithful enough to be placed in service, despite his prior behavior (v. 12). But what is most striking is his gratitude for being "empowered": the overflowing gift of our Lord cited in v. 14 was an empowerment and a transformation. The mercy shown Paul (vv. 13, 16) was not simply forgiveness of past behavior, but the gift of power that enables him to live in a new way.

Paul's experience serves to demonstrate two points. The first is the truth of the proposition that "Christ Jesus came into the world to save sinners" (1:15). Once more we meet *pistos ho logos* as the introduction to a fragment of tradition, this time from the sayings tradition of the gospel. This is not a direct citation, but seems to echo the conviction expressed by Luke 19:10, "The Son of Man came to seek out and save that which was lost." For a statement of the same sentiment by Paul, see Romans 5:8–9: "What recommends God's love to us is that while we were still

sinners Christ died for us; how much more, therefore, since we
have been made righteous by his blood, shall we be saved by
him from the wrath?" God's will to save will be made even more
explicit in the following passage (1 Tim. 2:4).

The second point Paul's experience demonstrates is how God
works for all. Just as Paul was "first of sinners," so is he the
model (*hypotyōposis*, v. 16) of all those who would come to faith
in Christ. Here is quite a different use of the model motif. In
2 Timothy, Paul presented himself to his delegate in paraenetic
fashion as an exemplar of teaching, character, and suffering.
Here it is not Paul's behavior that is exemplary, but rather God's
mercy. Most important, the same is true for all those in the Ephesian church. Not their own efforts or their own debates over
law but the merciful power of God saves them "unto eternal
life" (1:16, cf. Rom. 2:7; 5:21; 6:22–23 as well as 1 Tim. 6:12;
Titus 1:2; 3:7). It is God's work rather than human intelligence
or effort that saved Paul and that saves others.

How shall we assess the Pauline character of this account? It
might at first be thought that Paul's characterization of himself
in v. 13 as a blasphemer, persecutor, and insolent person conflicts with Paul's other versions of his precall life. In Galatians
1:13–14, for example, Paul emphasizes his way of life as a Jew
as well as his zeal for his ancestral traditions. And in Philippians 3:5–6, he declares that he was a Pharisee and, "according
to righteousness in the law, blameless." But in both passages, he
also declares that he was a persecutor of the church.

The fact that he was blameless under the law, furthermore,
does not in the least mean that he was not a "blasphemer"
against the name of Jesus and an "insolent person" by seeking
to be the defender of Torah who would extirpate the Christian
movement. Indeed, it is precisely Paul's point in this passage
that being a sinner is not mitigated by allegiance to law but
only by personal transformation. Paul had been acting in *apis-
tia* (faithlessness, v. 13) when he persecuted the church, out of
his "ignorance" (*agnoōn*, v. 13). In other words, he was like those
fellow Jews he characterizes in Romans 10:2 as "having zeal for
God but not according to recognition (*kat' epignōsin*)." As for
the role of God's mercy in Paul's transformation in v. 16, compare such passages as Romans 9:15–16, 18, 23, 11:30–32, 15:9,

and 2 Corinthians 4:1. There is nothing in this passage, in short, that could not have come from the "real Paul," and much that accords well with his statements elsewhere.

The same can be said concerning Paul's statement that he had handed over Hymenaios and Alexander to Satan so that they could learn not to blaspheme (1:20). The resemblance to Paul's recommendation to the Corinthian church in the matter of the brother living in incest is obvious; there too, the excommunication has a salvific purpose, "so that his spirit might be saved in the day of the Lord" (1 Cor. 5:5). What is even more significant is the typical way in which Paul deals with severe deviance (cf. Gal. 4:30; 2 Thess. 3:10–14). In the present case, having so briskly addressed the pretensions of the false teachers, Paul is able to turn to the specific tasks he wants Timothy to perform. The opponents will appear hereafter only as the shadow of the positive qualities of Paul's delegate and in a final exhortation to avoidance at the end of the letter (6:20–21).

Instruction on Prayer — 2:1–7

2:1I am requesting first of all, therefore, that entreaties, prayers, petitions, and thanksgivings be made in behalf of all human beings, 2for kings and all those who are in positions of authority, so that we might lead a peaceful and quiet life in complete piety and dignity. 3This is a noble thing to do, and acceptable in the sight of our savior God, 4who wants all human beings to be saved and to come to the recognition of truth. 5For God is one. One also is the mediator between God and humans, the human being Christ Jesus. 6He gave himself as a ransom in behalf of all. The testimony was given at the right time. 7I have been appointed its herald and apostle — I speak the truth and do not lie — a teacher of the nations in faith and truth.

Notes on Translation

To the translator, this passage presents some challenges, which are reflected as well in a number of textual variants. The Western textual tradition in particular (represented by D and the Latin

versions) seemed to have tried to rectify what they saw as a defective text. For example, rather than the first-person singular "I
am requesting" (*parakalō*) in 2:1, some of these MSS read the
imperative "exhort that" (*parakalei*), which has a certain logic
in view of the entrusting of the *parangelian* to Timothy in 1:18.
Similarly, many of these same MSS inserted in 2:3 a *gar* into
the phrase "this is a noble thing to do," marking more clearly
the explanatory character of the statement: "*for* this is a noble
thing."

The most difficult phrase to translate in the passage also
shows the most scribal ingenuity. In 2:6, the phrase *to martyrion
kairois idiois* is simply problematic, both in terms of its meaning
and how it connects to the phrases before and after it. The noun
martyrion means "that which stands as evidence or proof" (see,
e.g., Herodotus *Persian War* 2.22; 8.120; Plato *Laws* 943C). It can,
therefore, refer to a fact or deed or statement (see Aristotle *Rhetoric* 1376A). In the Gospels, a healing "stands as evidence" to the
priests (Matt. 8:4; Mark 1:44; Luke 5:14). In Paul, the term can
be used loosely, as roughly equivalent to "witness" (see 1 Cor.
2:1; 2 Cor. 1:12; 2 Thess. 1:10), which is the meaning in 2 Timothy 1:8, where Paul told Timothy, "Do not be ashamed of *to
martyrion* of our Lord," which in context could only mean "of
bearing witness to our Lord." The phrase *kairois idiois* (literally,
"in its own times/seasons") is also difficult. The idiom appears
in Diodorus Siculus (*Roman History* 1.50.7) with the meaning
"the proper time" (see also Josephus *Antiquities* 11.5.7). But how
do these phrases go together and how to they connect to their
context?

The textual variants show the scribes' struggle with the lap-
idary and asyndetic character of the phrase. Some add the word
kai (and), which makes the "witness" part of what Christ "gave."
Other MSS add a relative pronoun and a verb to make a full
clause that comments on Christ's giving of himself as a ransom:
"to which testimony was given at the proper time." These corrections show what kinds of adjustments must be made to yield
any satisfactory sense. Since I have followed the harder reading
adopted by the Nestle-Aland text (27th ed.), I have had to am-
plify the phrase: "The testimony was given at the right time." By
no means, however, does this resolve the problem of meaning!

There is a great deal of scribal "traffic" on 2:7 as well, although the motivation for it is more obscure. The addition of "in Christ" by many MSS after the phrase "I am speaking the truth" is easily explicable because of the parallel expression in Romans 9:1, "I am telling the truth in Christ, I am not lying." The witnesses that replace the word "faith" (*pistei*) with "knowledge" (*gnōsei*) must have been influenced by the foregoing phrase "recognition of the truth" in 2:4; those that replace it with "spirit" (*pneumati*) may have been influenced by the Johannine combination "spirit and truth" (see John 4:24).

An analysis of the diction in the passage yields a typical pattern. For the most part, the vocabulary is Pauline, especially in 2:4–7, where we find only one NT hapax legomenon, namely, *antilytron* (ransom, v. 6), the occurrence of which is less striking since Paul uses *apolytrōsis* with much the same meaning in Romans 3:24, 8:23, 1 Corinthians 1:30, and Colossians 1:4. First Timothy 2:1–3 at first sight seems much less Pauline, with three NT hapax legomena (*enteuxis, ēremos, apodekton*), three terms that occur elsewhere in the NT but not in the undisputed letters (*hēsychios, bios, eusebeia*), and two terms that are found only in the Pastorals (*diagein, semnotēs*). This last term, *semnotēs*, denotes "gravity," "dignity," even "solemnity." It is found only in 1 Timothy 2:2, 3:4, and Titus 2:7, while the adjective *semnos* is found in 1 Timothy 3:8, 11 and Titus 2:2. Here it appears with *eusebeia* (godliness/piety), which is (with its cognates) another favorite term in these letters (see 1 Tim. 2:2; 3:16; 4:7, 8; 5:4; 6:3, 5, 6, 11; 2 Tim. 3:5; Titus 1:1). Closer analysis, however, shows that the occurrence of terms is more a question of emphasis than of utter difference. Although the undisputed letters do not use *eusebeia*, for example, the word was scarcely outside Paul's vocabulary, since he uses its antonyms, *asebeia* (ungodliness/impiety) in Romans 1:18 and 11:26 and *asebēs* in Romans 4:5 and 5:6. Likewise, although the undisputed letters do not have *semnotēs*, Paul does use the adjective *semnos* in Philippians 4:8. Similarly, although he does not use *bios*, he does use *biotika* (see 1 Cor. 6:3). He does not use *apodektos*, but he does use *dektos* with the same meaning (2 Cor. 6:2; Phil. 4:8). Most significantly, although Paul does not use the term *hēsychia* elsewhere, the use of its cognates in 1 Thessalonians 4:11, and 2 Thessalonians 3:12

points to the same ideal of a quiet life, removed from public turmoil.

The most difficult translation decision in this section involves the phrase discussed above, *to martyrion kairois idiois*. The presence of the same idiom, *kairois idiois*, in Titus 1:3 confirms that the translation here is on the right track, but its precise significance is equally ambiguous. Paul himself uses the singular *kairō idiō* to mean "in the appropriate season" in Galatians 6:9. But what "right time" is meant in 1 Timothy? Does the author mean something like Paul's expression *en tō nyn kairō* ("in the now time"; Rom. 3:26; 11:5) to signify the present time of God's revelation through Christ? And if (as in my translation) the verb "was given" is supplied, then does the statement suggest that this time of revelation was in the past and, if so, how much in the past? Or should we read the phrase, not with what precedes it, but with what follows? Then it would read something like this: "The evidence for this is being given at the appropriate time, for which I have been appointed as herald and apostle." The syntax would, I think, just allow such a construal, and it might work better than the alternative, even though the usage here would then be different from that in Titus 1:3. Perhaps the biggest puzzle is why the phrase is used at all; it adds little to the statement but seems rather to obfuscate it.

Literary Observations

Analysis of the form of Paul's letters (esp. by Bjerkland, *Parakalō*) has shown that the transition to the business portion is often marked by the use of the verb *parakalō* (see 1 Cor. 1:10; 2 Cor. 2:8; 6:1; Eph. 4:8; Phil. 4:1; 1 Thess. 4:1; Philem. 10). The verb itself has a range of meaning from "comfort" to "exhort." Here, I translate it as "I am requesting." Paul uses *oun* (therefore) to indicate that this request/exhortation is based on what has gone before; we are invited to look back to 1:3 where Paul also uses the term *parakalein* (as I exhorted you) and to 1:4 where he mentions the *oikonomia theou en pistei* (faithful household management concerning God). The phrase *prōton pantōn* (first of all) means, in this context, simply the first thing in a series, not necessarily the most important thing to be considered (cf. 1 Cor. 15:3; James 5:12).

As it did with 2 Timothy 1:9–10 and 2:11–13, the Nestle-Aland text (27th ed.) indents 1 Timothy 2:5–6, thus indicating the editors' judgment that the words are poetic or hymnic and/or traditional. The same procedure is followed in passages such as Philippians 2:5–11 and Colossians 1:15–20. But in the case of 1 Timothy, we find such indentation in 2:5–6, 3:16, and 6:6–8, 11–12, and 15–16. Apart from the issue of the appositeness of such literary judgments, it should be recognized that the procedure only exacerbates the impression that the Pastorals are a rough pastiche of traditional materials. In the case of 1 Timothy 2:5–6, there is no reason to consider Paul's statement either as hymnic/poetic or as traditional. It is, however, one of his typically compressed christological, soteriological statements, such as can be found also in Romans 3:21–26, 5:8–10, 1 Corinthians 8:6, 2 Corinthians 5:19–21, 8:9, Galatians 1:4, 2:20, Ephesians 5:?, Philippians 2:5–11, Colossians 1:15–20, and 1 Thessalonians 5:9–10.

The only part of 1 Timothy 2:5–6 that does not find a parallel elsewhere in the undisputed letters is the characterization of Jesus as the *mesitēs* between God and human beings (*anthrōpoi* must be translated as "human beings" throughout the passage for the theological point to be clear). In Galatians 3:19–20, Paul spoke of the law being delivered through angels "by the hand of a mediator" (*en cheiri mesitou*), concluding that this meant the law was not given directly by God, since "a mediator is not for one person, and God is one." It is striking that the affirmation "God is one" (*heis gar theos*) occurs also in the present passage, but the view of the mediator is quite different. Here it is not a case of lesser spiritual powers below God that would seem to diminish the unity of God (Paul's point in Galatians), but rather a "human being Christ Jesus" who serves as the *mesitēs*.

The mediator, as the term suggests, is the one who acts as a go-between, or negotiator, between two parties (see Josephus *Antiquities* 7.8.5). The word is used for the relation between God and humans in LXX Job 9:33 and *Testament of Dan* 6:2 and for the role of Christ in Hebrews 8:6, 9:15, and 12:24. Quite apart from the word used, the perception that Jesus was the agent who effected reconciliation between God and humans is, of course, absolutely central to Paul's theology (see, e.g., 2 Cor. 5:16–21). The other parts of the statement in vv. 5–6 are instantly recognizable as Pauline: For "God is one," see Galatians 3:20, Romans 3:30, and 1 Corinthians 8:6. For "the human being Christ Jesus," see Philippians 2:7 and especially Romans 5:12–21. For Jesus' death as a "ransom" (*antilytron*), see Romans 3:24. For "he gave himself" (*ho dous heauton*), see Galatians 1:4 (*tou dontos heauton*), 2:20 (*paradontos heauton hyper emou*), and Ephesians 5:2 (*paredōken heauton hyper hēmōn*).

Comment

It should not surprise us that Paul's first directives should concern the liturgical practice of the community, for it is in worship that the *ekklēsia* actually becomes "convocation," that is, a gathered people. Such face-to-face gatherings also tend to reveal in acute form the underlying tensions that persist chronically in less intense expressions of community existence. In 1 Corinthians, it will be remembered, Paul devoted considerable attention to the practices of the community gathered for worship (1 Cor. 11–14). By no means, however, does Paul provide the Ephesian community with an order of worship. He gives no instructions concerning the time of worship, its place, or its arrangement. These are all presupposed. Only two topics are considered: the saying of prayers for others (2:1-7) and appropriate behavior for men and women (2:8–15).

Paul's instruction on prayer is brief but leads us into a symbolic world that, however much presupposed by him and his readers, remains alien to our own. He takes it for granted that "entreaties, prayers, petitions, and thanksgivings" should be part of worship (2:1), as he did also in telling the Philippians, "by prayer and supplication with thanksgiving make your requests known to God" (Phil. 4:6). But Paul also indicates in two ways the range of interest included by their prayer. He wants them to pray for "all human beings" and also for "kings and all those who are in positions of authority." We can consider them in reverse order.

The prayer for rulers is the Jewish and Christian way of combining a refusal to acknowledge earthly princes as divine (no matter what they claimed for themselves) and the duties of good citizens of the world. The king, or emperor, was regarded as the head of the entire household that was the civilized world (*oikoumenē*). Among the household duties of all peoples, therefore, were respect and obedience to the emperor and his delegates. Visions of alternative societies were not entirely unknown in the ancient Mediterranean; Plato's *Republic* and *Laws,* after all, were thoroughly reformist if not utopian. But under the empire, which by Paul's time had been the only real political fact in the Mediterranean for over three hundred years, such alternatives were not seriously entertained. The most obvious social fact was this: that a single hierarchical order reached from the top to the bottom of the human family, an order in which authority moved downward and submission moved upward. Moralists further solidified this order by viewing it as "natural" and asking only "what are the duties" (*ta kathēkonta*) of each member of society within this given structure (see, e.g., Hierocles *On Duties* 3.39.34–36 and Arius Didymus *Epitome* in Malherbe, *Moral Exhortation,* 89–90, 145–47).

Those who today live in the fragile and fragmented social worlds after the ages of renaissance and revolution may find it difficult to appreciate the sheer facticity of the ancient social order. It was generally regarded, indeed, as part of the *oikonomia theou,* the very ordering of reality by God. Nature and society were part of the same continuum, governed by God's will, or "providence." Deviation from the social order meant also going against nature and God's *oikonomia.* It is important for present-day readers to grasp that the idea of a Jeffersonian democracy was as far from Paul's imagination as the concept of a nuclear suburban family with dual-career spouses. His instructions were aimed at a world different from our own, not only in structure, but above all in conception. Fundamental to the contemporary "symbolic world," is the understanding that the social world is one that can be changed. That precise perception would not have been shared by Paul or his readers. There might be good emperors and bad, but there would always be an empire!

These understandings are critical to the proper appreciation of this entire chapter of 1 Timothy. By praying for kings and rulers, Jews and Christians could express their deep solidarity with their own cultural world, without committing themselves to any form of idolatrous acknowledgment. It took the hard experience of persecution at the hands of the state itself for Christians to perceive that the empire could make unacceptable demands of allegiance and even appear as demonic (see Rev. 17:1–18). Outside of that experience, it was possible for Paul to be affirmative of the given social order (see esp. Rom. 13:1–7), to see the emperor's authority as coming from God (Rom. 13:1), to perceive rulers "not as a terror to good conduct but to bad" (Rom. 13:3), and to call for obedience to the ruling powers as a matter of "conscience" (Rom. 13:5).

The position toward the state taken in 1 Timothy is actually less conservative than in Romans 13, for by "praying for kings and those in positions of authority," there is an implicit critique of any claims they might put forward concerning their absolute authority. By placing them in God's hands, their power is clearly subordinated to God's. Yet praying for them also expresses a fundamental recognition of them *as* kings and rulers, without questioning their legitimate right to rule. First Timothy evidences a delicate compromise, one that later Christian apologists would further develop from the lead provided by Paul.

The motivation for so praying, as I noted above, is also a familiar Pauline theme: "that we might lead a peaceful and quiet life in complete piety and dignity" (2:2). The same sentiment is expressed in other letters (1 Thess. 4:11–12; 2 Thess. 3:12; Col. 4:5–6; 1 Cor. 14:23). A quiet and orderly life not only nurtured the work of the Holy Spirit (see 1 Cor. 14:33), it also earned the respect of outsiders. A community deviant enough in other ways did not need to draw attention to itself within an empire that tended to be suspicious of groups meeting regularly in convocation.

More striking and original is Paul's instruction to pray "for all human beings" (2:1), a request that he goes on to support theologically in v. 3. It is important to avoid an androcentric translation here. The RSV, for example, translates *anthrōpos* in 2:1 as "all men," in 2:4 as God wills the salvation of "all men," and in 2:5 as Jesus the mediator, "the one man." Such translations are inaccurate and misleading (and avoided by the NRSV).

In each case the noun is *anthrōpos,* not *anēr.* It is not males for whom the community is to pray but for all people; God desires the salvation of all human beings. It is not the maleness of Jesus that makes him mediator but his humanity. Exclusive translations in this instance would be misleading by themselves. But in a passage where Paul proceeds to make distinctions between male and female, they are intolerable.

Paul's extension of community prayer to "all human beings" is a leap forward in early Christian consciousness. For the most part, the NT writings confine their concern to intracommunity relations, expressed succinctly as "love of the brethren" (1 Thess. 4:9). Outreach beyond the community was limited: "so then, as we have opportunity, let us do good to all [people], and especially to those who are of the household of the faith" (Gal. 6:10). But here in 1 Timothy they are to pray for all people because "God wants all human beings to be saved and to come to the recognition of truth" (2:4). In as radical a fashion as in Romans 3:29–30, Paul grounds this universal salvific will in the *oneness* of God: "God is one" (v. 5). If God is to be more than a tribal deity, then God must be one for all humans, and if God is to be righteous (fair), then there must be some mode of access to God for all humans. It is as a witness to this truth that Paul has been made a herald and apostle and teacher *of the nations* (or Gentiles, v. 7). There is a possible edge here against any who would propose the keeping of the law as a necessary regimen for access to God, for the law is a code that is available only to some, whereas the one God wills the salvation of all humans.

To this principle, Paul adds a more paradoxical one: "One also is the mediator between God and humans, the human being Christ Jesus" (2:5). This at first appears contradictory to the prior statement, for it reintroduces an element of particularity. That is why it is important to note (as in Rom. 5) that Jesus is not the mediator on the basis of his teachings or deeds, or even as an object of belief, but on the basis of his very humanity: Jesus is the representative human before the one God. His mediation is found first in his common humanity and second in his "giving himself as a ransom in behalf of all" (v. 6). Jesus' gift of self was for all other human beings.

Certainly, an element of particularity remains. Paul is convinced that it is through the gift of Christ Jesus that humans are "to come to the recognition of truth" (v. 4). That is why Paul is a herald and an apostle! But this particularity is itself rooted, not in an ethnic or a cultic difference, but in a shared humanity through which God wills the salvation of all. Nowhere in the NT is there such an inclusive statement of hope concerning all humanity. It is particularly important to recognize its presence here, since the sentences that follow retreat from this functional equivalent to the statement in Galatians 3:28, "There is neither Jew nor Greek, there is neither slave nor free, there is neither male nor female, for you are all one in Christ Jesus."

Gender Roles in Worship — 2:8–15

2:8 Therefore I want the men in every place to pray with their hands lifted up with piety, removed from anger and argument. **9**Likewise women should adorn themselves in appropriate dress with modesty and discretion, not in braids or gold or pearls or costly apparel, **10**but in a way fitting to women dedicated to the service of God, through good works. **11**Let a woman learn quietly in complete submission. **12**I do not entrust teaching to a woman, nor authority over a man. She is to stay quiet. **13**For Adam was made first, then Eve. **14**Also, Adam was not deceived, but the woman, once she was deceived, fell into transgression. **15**Yet she will be saved through childbearing, if they remain in faith and love and holiness with self-control. This is a reliable opinion.

Notes on Translation

For a passage with such potential for misunderstanding, the text is remarkably stable, with no critically significant variants in 2:8–14. A very real problem in establishing the text — and the meaning — comes at the end of v. 15. Should the phrase *pistos ho logos* be read with 2:15 or as the introduction to 3:1? As noted earlier, the phrase is peculiar to the Pastorals, but its precise function is not always clear. I argued that in 2 Timothy 2:11 it be read, not as an introduction to a citation, but rather as a comment on "the word of God is not enchained" in 2:9. In Titus 3:8, the only occurrence of the term seems to point backwards to the soteriological statement in 3:4–7. In 1 Timothy 1:15, the phrase clearly and obviously points forward. In 4:9, it could point either way, though it more likely refers to the foregoing proverbial statement. In short, there are precedents for taking it either with what precedes or what follows! In the present case, 3:1 is sufficiently gnomic to deserve such an introduction. On the other hand, all the other occurrences of *pistos ho logos* are connected to statements concerning salvation (in 1 Tim. 4:9 in either direction!). The statement in 2:15 certainly qualifies for that category, while the one in 3:1 certainly does not. With the 27th edition of Nestle-Aland, then, I view the phrase as commenting on 2:15. Some of the Western textual witnesses modify the phrase to *anthrōpinos ho logos* ("this is a human opinion") as they did also in 1:15. We cannot know whether this was a case of a scribe's disapproving the statement on women in 2:15 or clarifying the status of the sentiment about bishops in 3:1.

As might be expected for a topic so little discussed elsewhere (but see 1 Pet. 3:3–6), 2:8–10 contains a large number of terms not found elsewhere in the Pauline corpus (*hosios, sōphrosynē, kosmein, margaritai, himatismos, polytelēs*) as well as some not found in the rest of the NT (*katastolē, kosmios, aidos, plegma, theosebeia*). But 2:11–15 is thoroughly Pauline in its diction. No matter how much the sentiments expressed may dismay readers, there are only two NT hapax legomena (*authentein* in v. 12, *teknogonia* in v. 15).

First Timothy 2:15 presents two real and difficult problems in translation (and interpretation). The first is determining the subject of the two clauses. Grammatically, "she will be saved" is in the singular, and "if they remain" is in the plural. Does the first clause refer to women in general (note the collective sense of *hē gynē* in 2:14), and the second simply make the implied plural explicit: "Women will be saved through childbearing if they [the women] remain in faith"? Or is there a shift in subject from "the woman/women" to their children (picking up from *teknogonia*): "She [the woman] will be saved through her bearing of children, if they remain in faith"? Both these options take the term "saved" as referring to salvation, that is, being in a right relationship with God. The first option makes the woman's own faith response the critical element in her vocation of child rearing; the second makes her success in having her children remain in the faith the condition for her own salvation! Another possibility, though less likely, is to take "be saved" as "surviving," so that the sentence would read, "But she will be brought safely through childbirth, if they remain in faith." None of the options is entirely satisfactory, but I am inclined to think that Paul is thinking in terms of the woman's raising her children, for in 5:4, the children's responsibilities to mothers are also touched on.

Literary Observations

The tone of command dominates this section of the letter. In 2:1, we saw *parakalō* (I am requesting); in 2:8, we find *boulomai* (I desire/will); in 2:12, *ouk epitrepō* (I do not entrust/allow); in 3:14, *tauta soi graphō* (I am writing these things to you). Commands concerning separate groups are joined by "likewise" (*hōsautōs*) in 2:9, 3:8, and 3:11. Paul uses the impersonal verb *dei* (must) in 3:2 and 3:7. The commander is laying out directives. We can note also the use of antithesis, with the characteristic "not this but that" in 2:9–10, 2:12, 2:14, and more extended antithetical contrast developed in 3:2–7.

The sociohistorical context for these directions seems to be that of first-century synagogue worship, in which men took the public role of prayer and teaching, while women remained silent in the assembly and played a leadership role in the domestic sphere. Recent analysis of archaeological evidence suggests that women played more of a leadership role in the diaspora synagogue than had formerly been supposed, but the very little evidence we have concerning the actual practice of worship still, with some intriguing exceptions, supports the view that males played the more active and public role (see Chesnutt, "Jewish Women"). Remember that the synagogue (or *beth ha kenesset*) also functioned as the place for the study of Torah (as *beth ha midrash*), with the two activities flowing one into the other. Paul's instructions concerning the prayer of males "removed from anger and argument" may be connected precisely to the agitation caused by those who wished to be *nomodidaskaloi*

(teachers of law). Paul's concern is consistently for good order and peace within the context of worship, "for God is not a God of confusion [*akatastasia,* literally "social upheaval"] but of peace" (1 Cor. 14:33).

Despite the deeply problematic character of Paul's directions concerning women for present-day readers, the sociohistorical context in which they make the most sense is once more in the first-generation Pauline churches. The insistence that women dress modestly and display their good deeds rather than their finery is a commonplace topic for moralists, both Greco-Roman and Jewish (see Phyntis *On the Temperance of a Woman* 153.15– 28; Perictione *On the Harmony of a Woman* 143.26–28; Philo *Special Laws* 3.169–71). First Peter 3:1–7 offers a good parallel (see Balch, *Let Wives Be Submissive*).

As for the command that women keep silence in the assembly (v. 12), it fits Paul's cultural perceptions perfectly. Some scholars find this position uncomfortable. They argue that the "authentic Paul" is one deeply committed to the sort of gender equality expressed in Galatians 3:28, and that it is the "Paul of the Pastorals" who suppresses the active and public role of women in the assembly (see, e.g., Scroggs, "Paul and the Eschatological Woman"). This is too simple a solution. I would not by any means deny that Paul had deeply egalitarian instincts in the matter of gender and social class. But Paul was a human being also formed by the cultural perceptions of his world, and those instincts did not infiltrate his perceptions of every social situation.

One social setting that both Jew and Greek agreed belonged to males was the public assembly, which encompassed the role of proclamation or teaching (see Sterling, "Women in the Hellenistic and Roman Worlds"). Even an educational progressive like Musonius Rufus, who argued that women were as capable as men of learning philosophy, advocated their education so that they could better fulfill their *domestic* roles (see *Oration III: That Women Too Should Study Philosophy* 10.2–4, 11–14). In Judaism, the study of Torah (and therefore the activity of teaching in the assembly) was an exclusively male preserve. In rabbinic literature, women are largely seen as temptation and distraction from study (see *Pirke Aboth* 1.5; *Aboth de Rabbi Nathan* 2). In-

deed, this is a place where Paul's Pharisaism may have been
the dominant influence on him. But everywhere in this male-
defined Mediterranean world, the submission of women to men
was the basic cultural assumption (see Josephus *Against Apion*
2.199; Philo *Apology for the Jews* 7.3, 5). Deviation from that
norm was actively resisted (see Juvenal *Satire* 6). In Romans 7:2,
for example, Paul states as a universal given: "A married woman
[literally, "an under-a-man-woman," *gynē hypandros*] is bound by
law to her man while he is alive" (see also 1 Cor. 7:39).

A collection of such cultural assumptions concerning the
place of women is found in 1 Corinthians 11:3-16, where Paul
discusses whether women who are prophesying or praying in the
assembly can do so with their heads unveiled. To support his
position that they should stay veiled, Paul says: the man is the
"head of the woman" (*kephalē gynaikos ho anēr*); the woman is
the "glory of the man" (*gynē doxa andros*, v. 7); and, relying on
the Genesis account, "man is not from woman but woman from
man" (v. 8). Now, in that passage, we see how such cultural perceptions come into conflict with the egalitarian impulses of the
new resurrection life, so that these assumptions are countered
by Paul himself (see 1 Cor. 11:11-12). He can find, therefore, no
real theological warrant. So he falls back on what "nature itself
teaches" (v. 14) and, ultimately, on the custom of the churches,
"we recognize no other practice, nor do the churches of God"
(v. 16). Nevertheless, Paul does not challenge in this passage the
fact that women do pray or prophesy: these are gifts given by
the Spirit. His concern is with the manner of their doing so.

In 1 Corinthians 14:33b-36, on the other hand, Paul's directions are far clearer. At the end of a discussion of spiritual gifts
and their exercise, he declares,

> As in all the churches of the saints, let women keep silence
> (*sigatōsan*) in the assemblies (*en tais ekklēsiais*). It is not al-
> lowed (*ou gar epitrepetai*) for them to speak (*lalein*). Rather,
> let them be subject, as the law declares. But if they wish to
> learn, let them ask their own husbands in the household.
> For it is a shameful thing (*aischron gar estin*) for a woman
> to speak in an assembly. Or did the word of God start with
> you, or are you the only ones it has come to?

This passage from 1 Corinthians 14 is even stronger in its emphasis on the "shameful" character of women speaking in assemblies than is 1 Timothy 2:11-15, but in the passage is an important interpretive clue: Notice the distinction between "assemblies" (the public forum) and "household" (the domestic forum). Notice further that the issue is one of learning/teaching and of "speaking/declaiming" (*lalein*). The matter for Paul in 1 Corinthians is not that of ecstatic speech controlled by the Spirit but of public teaching in the assembly. As in 1 Corinthians 11:3-16, Paul invokes both Torah and the custom of all the churches to resist this infringement of the cultural norm.

Finding these passages to be so contrary to what Paul "really thought," some scholars argue that they are later interpolations by the author/editor of the Pastorals, who thereby "found" in the authentic Paul the same sexist perspective that was being advanced a hundred years later by 1 Timothy (see, e.g., Murphy-O'Connor, "The Non-Pauline Character," and Conzelmann, *Commentary on First Corinthians*, 246). The fact that some Western witnesses place 1 Corinthians 14:34-35 after 14:40 seems to them to support the possibility of an interpolation (see Fee, *First Epistle to the Corinthians*, 699-702). The textual evidence, however, is overwhelmingly in favor of seeing vv. 34-35 as part of the original text written by Paul (see the discussion in Wire, *The Corinthian Women Prophets*, 149-52). The statement on women not only accords with the other cultural perceptions of Paul that we have listed, but the specific support offered for the regulation accords with Paul's rhetorical strategy in other parts of this letter: for the normative force of *nomos*, see 1 Corinthians 4:6, 9:8-9, and 10:1-11; for an appeal to the broader custom of the churches, see 1 Corinthians 1:2, 4:17, and 11:16 (cf. Osburn, "The Interpretation of 1 Cor 14:34-35"). And if 1 Corinthians 14:33b-36 is authentically Pauline, then there is no statement closer to the one we find in 1 Timothy 2:11-15. The details are different, but the sensibility and the mode of argument are familiar.

Certainly 1 Timothy 2:11-15 is closer to 1 Corinthians than it is to second-century writings. *First Clement* 1:3 (written ca. 95) praises the Corinthian church for teaching wives to "remain in the rule of obedience and to manage their household with seemliness, in all circumspection," but does not address speech in the assembly. *First Clement* 21:7 has, "Let us lead our wives to that which is good. Let them exhibit the lovely habit of purity, let them show forth the innocent will of meekness, let them make the gentleness of their tongue manifest by their silence (*sigēs*), let them not give their affection by factious preference, but in all holiness to all equally who fear God."

In Polycarp's *Letter to the Philippians* (Pol. *Phil.*, written some-time between 117 and 155), we find only two comments perti-nent to the issue of women. In the first, Polycarp writes, "Next teach our wives to remain in the faith given to them, and in love and purity, tenderly loving their husbands in all truth, and loving all others equally in all chastity, and to educate their chil-dren in the fear of God" (4.2). In the second, he says, "Let us teach the widows to be discreet in the faith of the Lord, praying ceaselessly for all men, being far from all slander, evil speaking, false witness, love of money, and all evil, knowing that they are an altar of God, and that all offerings are tested, and that nothing escapes him of reasoning or thoughts, or of the secret things of the heart" (4.3). There is simply no resemblance be-tween these directives and the sharp command found both in 1 Corinthians 14:34–35 and here in 1 Timothy 2:11–15.

Comment

The purpose of the present commentary is to understand, so far as we are able, the language used in this composition within the literary and sociohistorical contexts out of which it emerges. The hermeneutical issue — the question of what to think or do about what the composition says — is not our present task, even though it has colored the reading of this passage for all those concerned about women's role in the world, from the nineteenth-century *Women's Bible* to the present. I consider some aspects of the nor-mative issue in a pastoral treatment of these letters and will not repeat those comments here (see Johnson, *1 Timothy, 2 Timothy, Titus,* 67–74).

After issuing the request that prayers be said for all people, including rulers, since God wills the salvation of all human be-ings, Paul issues specific directions concerning the *behavior* of people at worship, directions that are gender specific. The points made to each gender are different; the point of making them is the same: worship is to exemplify the "quiet and peaceful life" (1 Tim. 2:2) that is the goal of a people dedicated to God. The behavior singled out in each instance is, in the eyes of the author, disruptive of that tranquillity.

The first set of instructions are even handed and well balanced; the command to the men is joined (*hōsautōs*) to that for women. In each case, the behavior is typically associated with the respective genders. Thus, in a cultural context in which men are the public speakers in *ekklēsia* (assembly) and specifically in a tradition in which the practice of prayer and the study of Torah meld one into the other and particularly in the community where some of the men have set themselves up as "teachers of law," we can easily imagine that "anger and argument" could prove disruptive of worship (1 Tim. 2:8). Similarly, in a world in which women who dressed in extravagant finery were widely perceived as disreputable and in a tradition in which women's roles were defined in terms of the domestic sphere, the instruction against elaborate hairdos and glamorous clothing and jewelry makes sense. This, too, is provocative and disruptive behavior. We meet here for the first time the suggestion that the Ephesian church was wealthy enough for such extravagance to be on display, a social fact to be kept in mind also in the interpretation of 5:3–16 (see Padgett, "Wealthy Women at Ephesus").

The third instruction is the most extended, consisting not only of a repeated command ("Let a woman learn quietly in complete submission [*hypotagē*]," 2:11, and "She is to stay quiet," v. 12), but also of a generalized opinion ("I do not entrust teaching to a woman, nor authority over a man," v. 12) and two theological warrants, the first from the order of creation (v. 13) and the second from women's greater susceptibility to deception (v. 14). The instruction ends in v. 15 with an exceptive clause that defines women's role domestically. The explicitness, fullness, and weightiness of the injunction requires us to ask first what could have motivated it. Is Paul acting out of an instinctive androcentric bias, adding this rider to his instructions as a prophylactic against any future "abuse"? Or is he actively suppressing a nascent feminist movement in the Ephesian community, in which some women are seeking to exercise authority and to teach in the assembly? The concern expressed about "younger widows" in 5:6 and 11:9-15 suggests that some such activity was at work, especially since women there are described as "learning in idleness" and "speaking things they ought not to" (5:13). The likeliest scenario is a situation like that in Corinth, where Paul finds that the freedom given by the Spirit pushes past the boundaries of cultural norms — especially among those with sufficient wealth to be relatively free of the harsher domestic constraints imposed on the poor by economic need — in a way that threatens his sense of orderliness, and, like most men in similar situations, Paul moves to defend male prerogatives.

The social setting of teaching and learning is even more obvious here than in the parallel passage of 1 Corinthians 14:34-35, but teaching is here further connected explicitly to "authority over a man." Paul moves to define gender roles according to public and domestic spaces and activities. In public, the woman is to be *en pasē hypotagē* (in all submission/in all subordination, v. 11) and is to be a learner, not a teacher. The passivity of her role is expressed by her silence/quiet (the term *hēsychia* in vv. 11-12 is broader than the *sigē* in 1 Cor. 14). The exceptive statement in v. 15 defines her way to salvation through childrearing and a virtuous life (see "through good works" in v. 10), whether of herself or of her children (see discussion on p. 133).

None of this is particularly new or shocking. What does strike many readers as excessive is the theological warrants that Paul adduces. In 1 Corinthians 14:34, he had appealed to the authority of Torah for women's being in submission. The most obvious text in support of this is Genesis 3:16, where the woman is told, "Your desire shall be for your husband, and he shall rule over you." In the present text, Paul again turns to the Genesis account for support of his position. There is no surprise in this either, for Paul refers to the story of Adam when speaking of Jesus in 1 Corinthians 15:22, 45 and Romans 5:14-21. In those passages, the apostle plays on the fact that Adam is a "type" of the "man from heaven," and he contrasts the disobedience of Adam to the obedience of Jesus. Paul also makes a negative reference to Eve in 2 Corinthians 11:3 — "as the serpent deceived/

seduced Eve by his cleverness" — using the same term *exapatan* as he does in 1 Timothy 2:14 (for a full discussion, of the passage, see Greer, "Admonitions to Women in 1 Tim 2:8-15").

Paul's first argument is from the order of creation: Adam was made first, then Eve (v. 13). As we have seen, Paul tried the same approach in 1 Corinthians 11:8-9, but there he immediately qualified it by the recognition that "in the Lord" men and women are bound together and that men also derive from women (11:11-12). There is no such qualification of the order of creation by the order of resurrection life "in the Lord" in the present passage. Paul's use of Genesis 2:18-24 is also unfortunate since the sequence-of-creation argument actually works against him: the creatures God created first were always inferior to those created later. The logic would imply that women, created later, are actually superior.

The apostle draws his second argument from the account of the temptation and transgression of the Lord God's command in Genesis 3:1-7. As in 2 Corinthians 11:3, Paul plays on the fact that the serpent deceived Eve rather than Adam. Presumably this is to show that women are less capable of distinguishing truth from falsehood or are too driven by their passions to be reliable leaders and teachers. Once more, of course, the logic is flawed. The woman, after all, was won over by "the most subtle creature that the Lord God had made" (Gen. 3:1). But all the woman had to do was offer the fruit to the man, and he ate it (3:6)! We note that in Genesis 3:17, it is not the woman who is blamed for the eating, but the man. It is obvious, however, that Paul is not doing sober exegesis of the Genesis account. He is rather supporting his own culturally conservative position on the basis of texts that seem to him to support the greater dignity and intelligence of the male and, therefore, the need for women to be subordinate to men at public functions.

Qualifications of the Supervisor — 3:1-7

3:1If anyone seeks to be a supervisor, it is a noble role that he desires. 2The supervisor must therefore be blameless, the husband of one wife, sober, prudent, well-balanced, hospitable, an apt teacher. [3]He must not be addicted to wine, nor a violent person, but should be reasonable, neither a lover of battle nor a lover of money. [4]He should be ruling well over his own household, with his children in submission with complete reverence. [5]For if someone does not know how to rule his own household, how can he take charge of God's assembly? [6]He should not be a recent convert, so that he does not become deluded and fall into the judgment reserved for the devil. [7]And he should also have the commendation of outsiders, so that he does not fall into reviling and the trap of the devil.

Notes on Translation

The only significant textual variant is found in 3:3, where a few witnesses add *aischrokerdē* (fond of dishonest gain). It is clearly added by some scribes under the influence of Titus 1:7 and would repeat the same idea as *aphilargyros* found just a few words later. This passage is one of those in 1 Timothy whose diction is furthest from that familiar to us in the undisputed Pauline letters. It contains a number of NT hapax legomena (*anepilēmptos, kosmios, neophytos*), but an even larger number of Pauline hapax legomena (*episkopē, oregomai, philoxenos, aphilargyros, epimelomai, empiptō*) and words that are found only in the Pastorals (*nēphalios, sōphronos, didaktikos, paroinos, plēktēs, amachos, semnotēs, typhoō*). The majority of these terms occur in the list of qualities that the supervisor should adhere to or avoid.

Three translation difficulties present themselves. The most obvious is the decision concerning the administrative position Paul addresses. The verb *episkopein*, as the etymology suggests, means simply "to overlook, oversee, supervise" (see, e.g., Plato *Republic* 506A; Philo *Decalogue* 98). One who carries out that function for a group, whether it be a club or cult or community, is an *episkopos*, that is, a "supervisor/superintendent/overseer" (see Josephus *Antiquities* 10.4.1). The office of "superintendent/overseer/supervisor" is *episkopē*: thus in LXX Numbers 4:16, the *episkopos* is to have the office of *episkopē*. In 1 Timothy 3:1, it is this "position of supervisor" (*episkopē*) that a person seeks, and the *episkopos* should be blameless (v. 2).

The larger issue, of course, has to do with the character of this office within the nascent Christian movement. This is the only passage in the NT where *episkopē* appears with reference to a position within the community, and the term *episkopos* in this sense appears only here and in Titus 1:7, Acts 20:28 (where Paul addresses the "elders of the church of Ephesus," Acts 20:17), and in Philippians 1:1 in Paul's greeting (where it appears, as here, in combination with *diakonos*). In Acts 20:28, Titus 1:7, and here (4:14), the term *episkopos* occurs also in combination with *presbyteros/presbyterion* (elder/board of elders). Apart from this (broadly) Pauline evidence, we find the combination of *episkopos/diakonos* in *Didache* 15:1; *1 Clement* 42:4–5 has *episkopoi* and *diakonoi,* as well as *presbyteroi* in 44:5, 47:6, 54:2, and 57:1. In Ignatius of Antioch, the threefold combination is everywhere (see only Ign. *Eph.* 1.3; 2.1–2; 4.1); perhaps surprisingly, Polycarp's *Letter to the Philippians* mentions only *presbyteroi* (in the greeting; 6.1; 11.1) and *diakonoi* (5.2).

The question of the origin and interrelationship of these positions will be treated below. The first decision, however, is the actual translation. In my judgment, translating the term as "bishop" is distorting. The later development of the office of bishop, and in particular its theological legitimation in authors like Ignatius, has little resemblance to the position Paul describes in 1 Timothy. The use of a different term is truer to the historical functions that the text suggests and avoids the confusion caused by anachronistic inferences. I have therefore chosen to translate *episkopos* as "supervisor."

The supervisor, says Paul, is to be *mias gynaikos anēr,* literally "a man of one woman" (3:2). Does he mean monogamous rather than polygamous? Does he mean married only once, and if widowed, not remarried? Does he mean faithful to a wife and without a mistress? All are possible. The decision matters only if later communities seek normative guidance from it. Preceded by "blameless," the phrase points to the avoidance of the appearance of immorality. The value Paul seeks is that of fidelity and respectability, so I have translated the phrase according to the most universal norm of respectability in that world.

In 3:6–7, Paul adds a purpose clause to his statements of what the supervisor should and should not be: "so that he not." In each case, the *diabolos* (devil) is involved. The difficulty is whether to translate the genitive constructions as subjective or objective. The first I have decided to translate objectively: "the judgment reserved for the devil," since the subjective ("the judgment rendered by the devil") seems impossible. The second is more difficult, since the objective, "the trap set for the devil," is possible. In this case, the parallel in 2 Timothy 2:26, where the "trap of the devil" (that is, "set by the devil") is certain, has weighed heavily in my translating it subjectively. To some extent, the decision also rests on whether the association of the supervisor with "reviling" (*oneidismos*) in v. 7 is itself subjective or objective: does he revile or is he reviled?

Literary Observations

The mandates concerning community order in 1 Timothy are of a very mixed character. Only these in chapter 3 properly take up the issue of qualifications for positions of supervisors, helpers (as I will translate *diakonoi*), and (possibly) women helpers. The discussion of widows in 5:3–16 and the directions concerning elders in 5:17–25 address problems in administration rather than the qualities of those filling positions. The instructions concerning slaves and the wealthy (6:1–2, 17–19) deal with roles within the individual household rather than the *ekklēsia theou*.

We meet here once more the lists so typical of Greco-Roman moral discourse. Lists appear in inventories of vices and virtues, in polemic, in catalogues of suffering. More pertinent to the present passage are extant lists of qualities desired of those in various offices (see the text of Onosander's *De Imperatoris Officio* in Dibelius and Conzelmann, *The Pastoral Epistles,* 158–60). In 1 Timothy 3:1-7, the list of qualities desired in a supervisor of the community are laid our antithetically (he should be this, not that). The same sort of arrangement used for the instruction of Timothy, in other words, is here applied to the supervisor within the local community. There is really no parallel to such a description in the authentic Pauline letters, which may be due, at least partly, to the circumstance that Paul nowhere else addresses the issue. The most striking parallel to the arrangement here is found in Polycarp's *Letter to the Philippians,* in which the moral characteristics desirable in wives, widows, deacons, younger men, and elders are presented *seriatim* (4.2–6.1).

Comment

The first question this passage raises has already been dealt with to some extent in the introduction to the commentary, namely, the question of the kind of church order we find in 1 Timothy and its proper placement in the development of early Christianity. I remind the reader that "the church order of 1 Timothy" is the proper characterization, since Titus has only one line devoted to the qualities of the supervisor/elder and 2 Timothy has nothing at all about community organization. I also note again that, in line with other recent scholarship on this subject, I reject the theologically motivated view that earliest Pauline Christianity was devoid of structure (see, e.g., Burtchaell, *From Synagogue to Church,* and Campbell, *The Elders*).

The structure revealed in 1 Timothy is simple. The leadership of the group is held by the *episkopos,* who seems to be part of a "board of elders" (*presbyterion,* 4:14). The most important clues about the functions of the board are found in 5:17: "Elders who govern well should be considered worthy of double compensation, especially those who labor in speech and in teaching." What this suggests is that the basic function of the *presbyterion* as a whole was to govern, and that additional duties were added on (see the discussion in Meier, "*presbyteros* in the Pastoral Epistles"). Perhaps the office of supervisor was a revolving one, according to gifts and abilities. Not all elders "labor in the word and in teaching," that is, apparently not all preach and teach. Yet the supervisor should have among his qualities the ability to teach (*didaktikos*).

Such a collegial leadership with a single figure as the coordinator is the basic structure of intentional groups in the first-century Mediterranean world. At Qumran, for example, we find a "council of holiness" (*1QS* 8:6–8; 9:3–11) as well as an officer called the *mebeqqer,* whose title and duties seem purely administrative and similar to those envisaged for the *episkopos* here (see *1QS* 6:12, 20; *CD* 9:18–19, 22; 13:6–7). We also find various *collegia* and cults within Greco-Roman culture to have

just such structures, whose main functions were administrative:
raising funds (from dues) and distributing them (for group functions). Sometimes various cultic activities were added to these
functions. The most obvious example is the Roman senate combined with the consulship. The office of consul was rotated
by members of the larger *collegium,* which was the senate (see
Campbell, *The Elders,* 67–96).

The structure of the diaspora synagogue, so far as we can
reconstruct it, followed the same lines. The *gerousia* (board of
old men, elders) was the basic governing unit that handled
financial affairs, oversaw the community charity, and settled
disputes within the community. Another figure who appears is
the *archisynagōgos,* or "head of the synagogue," sometimes a single figure, sometimes plural. From inscriptionary evidence, we
know that the "head of the synagogue" was often wealthy and
a patron of the community. It makes sense to suppose that the
members of the *gerousia* were also men of property and heads
of households. The synagogue also had an officer known as the
chazzan (server), who appeared to serve more practical functions
at worship (see Burtchaell, *From Synagogue to Church,* 180–271).

In 1 Timothy, we find the board of elders, a leadership position known as the supervisor, and subordinate officials (perhaps
both male and female, see 3:11) literally called "servers" (*diakonoi*). The correlation of office to function is not revealed. But
we know that the community carried out certain activities: public prayer with reading, exhortation, and teaching (4:13; 2:1–3);
charity distribution to widows and probably to orphans (5:3–
16); hospitality (3:2); and the hearing and settling of disputes
(5:19–20). In other words, the offices and functions known to us
in the diaspora synagogue are found here in 1 Timothy.

So little is shown us of the actual ecclesiastical structure in
Polycarp's *Letter to the Philippians, 1 Clement,* and the *Didache*
that it is not difficult to agree that the basic lines of structure
therein resemble those in 1 Timothy. That is, the same titles
appear, although even less is said in those writings about activities and responsibilities. The same can be said about the basic
structure of organization found in the letters of Ignatius of Antioch, although the office of *episkopos* seems, in Ignatius, to be
definitely elevated above that of the presbyters, whereas such

a distinction is impossible to detect in 1 Timothy or Polycarp. There is, however, this critical difference: 1 Timothy lacks entirely the elaborate theological legitimation found in Ignatius. The leadership bears secular titles and is given no priestly or cultic functions.

How does the range of titles and functions regarding the leadership in local congregations that we find in 1 Timothy correspond with what we find in the undisputed letters? The evidence is not overwhelming, but neither is it insignificant. The picture we get from 1 Timothy of the community organization at Ephesus, as well as its characteristic functions of worship, hospitality, charity, teaching, and settling disputes, accords perfectly with the scattered data in the undisputed Pauline letters. In 1 Thessalonians, acknowledged as Paul's earliest extant letter and, more significantly, written to a church that had not been in existence for any length of time, Paul writes, "We beseech you, brethren, to respect those who labor among you and are over you in the Lord and admonish you, and to esteem them very highly in love because of their work" (5:12–13). The phrase "are over you in the Lord" (*proistamenous hymōn en kyriō*) clearly refers to a role in the assembly, and *prohistesthai* is the same term for "presiding/managing" that is used of the supervisor in 1 Timothy 3:4. In 1 Corinthians 6:1–8, Paul shows his disgust at disputes over *ta biotika* (everyday matters) being settled by lawsuits between members before pagan courts rather than by the community itself; in other words, he expects such a decision-making mechanism to be in place. Among the charisms listed by Paul in 1 Corinthians 12:28 are two that point to everyday administrative tasks: *antilēmpsis* (the doing of helpful deeds) and *kybernēsis* (leadership/governing). And in a passage too-seldom noted, Paul tells the Corinthians to "be submissive" to such men as the householder Stephanas "and all those laboring and working with them" (1 Cor. 16:15–16). The exhortation is important above all because the influential role of such patrons within the community (see 16:18) as "elders" fits exactly the picture we get in the case of the diaspora synagogue and also in 1 Timothy 3:4–5, where being an effective "head of household" is a positive criterion for a supervisor.

The list of *charismata* in Romans 12:7–8 is particularly revealing. There we find *diakonia* (service) and *didaskalia* (teaching), and *paraklesis* (exhortation, see 1 Thess. 5:12). But the last three are most striking: two of them concern the sharing of possessions (*ho metadidous* and *ho eleōn*) and the third is, again, "presiding" (*proistamenos*). In Romans 16:1, Paul identifies Phoebe as "deacon of the church at Cenchreae" (a suburb of Corinth) as well as a financial patron (16:3), thus attesting to the presence of at least one female deacon among his churches, as well as the use of that title for "the helping role" in communities other than Philippi. In Galatians 6:6, Paul advises that those who are "instructed in the word should share in all good things with the one instructing them." This confirms the presence of a teaching role that was financially supported in the Galatian churches, as well as Paul's position concerning support for those laboring in the word (1 Cor. 9:3–18). Finally, leaving aside Colossians and Ephesians, we find the explicit greeting to "supervisors and deacons" (*episkopois kai diakonois*) in the church at Philippi (Phil. 1:1).

Two further aspects of 1 Timothy 3:1–7 can be noted more briefly. The first is the way in which the *oikos* functions as point of reference. In 3:15, Paul will refer to the *ekklēsia* itself as the *oikos theou* (household of God). But here the boundaries between the *ekklēsia* and the *oikos* are maintained. We will find this to be the case also in the discussion of 5:3–16. In this reading, I disagree sharply with the position of D. C. Verner (*The Household of God,* esp. 128, 145–47). In the present instance, the ability of a man to manage his own household (particularly the proper social relations within it) is a qualifying sign for a supervisor; the inability so to manage is a definite disqualification.

The notion of "good management" provides our best insight also into the particular virtues that should characterize the supervisor. They are not the virtues of excitement and dynamism, but of steadiness, sobriety, and sanity. It would be a mistake, however, to conclude that the Pastorals are therefore only interested in a "bourgeois morality." As Paul said in another discussion of "stewards of households" (*oikonomoi*) such as himself and Apollos, "It is required of stewards that they be found trustworthy" (1 Cor. 4:2). Fidelity to one spouse, sobriety, and hospitality may seem trivial virtues to those who identify authentic faith with momentary conversion or a single spasm of heroism. But to those who have lived longer and who recognize how the administration of a community can erode even the strongest of characters and the best of intentions, finding a leader who truly is a lover of peace and not a lover of money can be downright exciting.

Behavior in the Household of God — 3:8-15

3:8 Helpers likewise should be dignified. They should not be duplicitous, overfond of wine, or people who do anything for a profit. **9**They should hold on to the mystery of faith with a pure conscience. **10**But these helpers should first be tested, and then, being blameless, they can carry out their service. **11**Women helpers likewise should be dignified, should not be gossipers, should be sober, and should be faithful in every respect. **12**Let the helpers be men who have one wife, who manage their children and their own household affairs well. **13**For those who have served well have gained a good position for themselves and much confidence in the faith that is in Christ Jesus. **14**I am writing these things to you even though I hope to come to you shortly. **15**But if I am delayed, you should know how it is necessary to behave in the household of God, which is the church of the living God — a pillar and support for the truth. **16**The mystery of godliness is — we confess — a great one:

> He was manifested in flesh;
> He was made righteous by spirit;
> He appeared to angels;
> He was preached among nations;
> He was believed in by the world;
> He was taken up in glory.

Notes on Translation

As we might expect, 1 Timothy 3:16 has generated a couple of significant textual variants. The adverbial form *homologoumenōs* seemed to some scribes to be a mistaken contraction, so they put *homologoumen hōs* (we confess as great). My translation comes close to this reading by trying to make more idiomatically English a term that is sometimes rendered "confessedly." The hymnic section in 3:16 begins with the relative pronoun *hos*. Part of the Western textual tradition altered this to the neuter pronoun *ho*, which would agree better with the antecedent *mystērion* (mystery). Still other MSS (including the corrections made to several of the great Uncials) have *theos* (God) rather than *hos* (he). Such a correction reflects a very high, even Monophysite, Christology.

The diction of the passage continues that of the previous section. Most of the vocabulary is Pauline, with a good sprinkling of NT hapax legomena (*dilogos, bathmon, hedraiōma, homologoumenōs*), of words found elsewhere in the NT but not in the undisputed letters (*prosechein, peripoiein, bradynein, eusebeia*), and of words found only in the Pastorals (*aischrokerdēs, diabolos* [with this meaning], *nēphalios*). Of these terms, several present translation difficulties. I have rendered *dilogos* in v. 8 as "duplicitous," taking the etymology (double-worded) as the basic clue. I have been fairly free in the same verse with *aischrokerdēs,* a word that is rich in connotations within the ancient value-system. When translated as "eager for shameful gain," however, it loses its sense for contemporaries. The idea expressed by the term is the one I have aimed for in the translation "people who do anything for a profit," but would be made stronger by adding still another phrase, "they have no shame!"

The presence of such hapax legomena should not obscure the fact that there are many distinctively Pauline turns to the language in this passage. The expression "have much confidence" (*pollē parrēsia*) in 3:13, for example, finds a parallel in 2 Corinthians 3:12 and 7:4, as well as in Philmon 8: *pollēn en christō parrēsian echōn.* The expression "I am writing these things to you" (*tauta soi graphō*) in v. 14 matches exactly 2 Corinthians 13:10 (*dia touto tauta apōn graphō*). Likewise, "how it is necessary to behave in the household of God" (*pōs dei en oikō theou anastrephesthai*) in v. 15 finds a parallel in 1 Thessalonians 4:1: "how it is necessary for you to walk and please God" (*to pōs dei hymas peripatein kai areskein theō*).

In particular, the language of the short hymn is Pauline. Only the use of *analambanein*, which appears in Ephesians 6:13, 16 (although not in the sense of "taken up," see Acts 1:2), is unfamiliar. For "mystery" (*mystērion*), see Romans 11:25 and 16:25, and for the phrase "this is a great mystery" (*to mystērion touto mega estin*), see Ephesians 5:32. For *phaneroun* in the sense of "appear," see Romans 16:26 and Colossians 1:26; for *dikaioun* in the sense of "vindicated," see Romans 4:2; for the passive form *ekēruchthē* (it was proclaimed), see 2 Corinthians 1:19; and for the passive for *episteuthē* (it was believed in), see 2 Thessalonians 1:10.

The hardest decisions for the translator come in 3:8 and 3:11. The first is how to translate *diakonos*. As in the case of *episkopos*, we have a term that later signified, not only an official rank in the church's hierarchy, but eventually one that was a stepping stone to a still higher rank. The translation "deacon," therefore, can be as misleading as "bishop." So I have chosen to use "helper" to correspond with "supervisor." For the range of meanings of the word, see Philippians 1:1, Romans 13:4, 15:8, 16:1, 1 Corinthians 3:5, 2 Corinthians 3:6, 6:4, 11:15, 11:23, Galatians 2:17, Colossians 1:7, and 1 Thessalonians 3:2; it is manifestly a Pauline term. In 3:11, the basic translation difficulty concerns determining what is meant by "women." Are they "women in general" or "wives of the male helpers/supervisors," or are they "women helpers"? The reasons for my translating as "women helpers" are given below.

Translating the words in 3:13 is not itself difficult; making sense of the words is. The first problem is the use of the connective *gar* (for): how does v. 13 illuminate or explain v. 12? It is not clear. The second problem is what Paul means by "a good/noble (*kalos*) position/rank/stage (*bathmos*)." Does this imply that there is a hierarchical system with set ranks that one climbs progressively? Or is it simply that Paul approves of this position as a good one? To some extent, this depends on how we take the final phrase (our third problem). What is meant by having "much confidence" (*pollē parrēsia*), how is it connected to "in the faith that is in Christ Jesus," and how are both linked to the previous clauses? None of this is clear. Is Paul suggesting that the helper who serves well has a sort of career confidence — that is, hope for advancement up the hierarchical ranks? It is possible, but not certain. It might also be that the helper is one who is in a good position and has a secure place within the community of faith.

The translation problem in 3:15 concerns not so much the virtually equivalent terms *stylos* and *hedraiōma,* which are both architectural terms for "supports, stays, or pillars," but rather what or who Paul is referring to by them. Are "pillar and support" to be read in apposition to "church of the living God" or in a delayed apposition to "how one should live," to read "live as a pillar and support of the truth in the church of the living God." This last option is not impossible, and perhaps better accords with the sense of the passage, which emphasizes the effect of individual behavior, and the point of the letter, which concerns the truth and integrity of the *ekklēsia tou theou.* Such a delayed appositional phrase appears elsewhere in the letter (see, e.g., 1:7). Moreover, this application of the terms would also better fit Paul's use of *stylos* in Galatians 2:9 in reference to individual persons (Cephas, James, John) and (using the adjective *hedraios* rather than the noun *hedraiōma*) Paul's plea to his unstable readers in 1 Corinthians 15:58, "Become steady people, not capable of being moved, abounding in the work of the Lord at all times, knowing that your labor in the Lord is not in vain."

Literary Observations

I discussed above my reasons for translating *diakonos* as "helper" in order to designate a subordinate position to the "supervisor" in the Ephesian community. The two offices are found together in Philippians 1:1 and *Didache* 15:1, as well as many places in Ignatius of Antioch (see, e.g., Ign. *Eph.* 1.3; 2.1). The qualities desired in deacons are also listed in Polycarp's *Letter to the Philippians* 5.2. The title can be used for a variety of functions that are joined primarily by their practical character (see the passages listed above). The role of the helpers is not specified in 1 Timothy.

In the diaspora synagogue, we know of a functionary called a *chazzan,* who helped in worship (see the *hypēretēs* in Luke 4:20). No liturgical function is assigned in 1 Timothy. The *chazzan* could also serve in other practical functions (see Burtchaell,

From Synagogue to Church, 246–51). We also know that local synagogues appointed men as collectors and distributors of the community charity (see *bT* Meg. 27a; B. Bat. 8a–b; Rosh. Hash. 4a–5b; Ta'an. 24a; Shabb. 118b). Although the title *diakonoi* is not given them by Luke, the seven appointed by the church to oversee the distribution to the Gentile widows in Acts 6:1–6 clearly fit into this category of helper. A number of times, furthermore, the verb *diakonein* and the noun *diakonia* are used in connection with financial matters such as Paul's collection (see, e.g., Acts 12:25; Rom. 15:25, 31; 2 Cor. 8:4; 9:1). The qualities listed in 1 Timothy 3:8 emphasize honesty—especially a lack of acquisitiveness—and sobriety. Such qualities were desired also in the synagogue workers in charity (see *m.* Shek. 5:2; *bT* 'Abod. Zar. 17b; B. Bat. 8b). We see that the same managerial qualities that are considered valuable for the supervisor also recommend the helper (3:12).

Arguments can and have been made for different understandings of *gynaikes* in 3:11 (see Blackburn, "The Identity of 'the Women' in 1 Tim 3·11"). I have chosen to translate it as "women helpers" for the following reasons:

1. The connective *hōsautōs* seems to differentiate between men and women in the same function (cf. 2:8–9).

2. Although 3:12 mentions that helpers should have one wife, 3:11 does not identify these women as *their* wives.

3. The characteristics desired in the *gynaikes* are strikingly similar to those wanted in a male helper, with "not gossiping" matching "not duplicitous," "dignified" matching "dignified," and "faithful in all matters" equalling "holding the mystery of faith."

4. Paul in Romans 16:1 names Phoebe as a *diakonos* of the church at Cenchreae, so we know that he had no difficulty with a woman holding such a position (also see the argument in Stiefel, "Women Deacons in 1 Timothy").

This being said, we have no more knowledge of what a female helper would do than we have of the male helper. Only one thing is clear: she would not teach in public or have authority over a man (see 2:11–15).

Together with 1:3 and 4:13, 3:14–15 provides the mise-en-scène of this letter: Paul is away, hopes to return soon, but delivers these instructions to his delegate (and over his shoulder, to the church as well) in the apostle's absence. Is this simply a fictional representation? Judgments, we have seen, vary considerably. It must be said, however, that not only are the words recognizably Pauline, but the mode of operation is as well. In 1 Corinthians 4:17, Paul sends Timothy to remind his community "of my ways as I teach them always in every church" while he is absent so that when he arrives, "some of you will not be puffed up about yourselves" (1 Cor. 4:18; see also 16:10–11). Paul sends Timothy to the Philippians in order that he might gain some sense of how that church is doing (Phil. 2:19), even though he hopes himself also to come to them quickly (2:24). When Paul is not able to go himself to the Thessalonians, he sends Timothy in order that they might be "strengthened and comforted/exhorted" in their tribulations (1 Thess. 3:1–6). The sort of *ad hoc* directions we find in 1 Timothy are, in my view, perfectly fitted to the sorts of situations evident from Paul's other letters (see also Mitchell, "New Testament Envoys"). Could a later author, on the basis of just such a literary imitation of the authentic Paul, have created the scenario fictionally? It is possible, of course. But we are working in the realm of probabilities and of moral judgments, not of mathematical certainties.

Earlier in this book, when commenting on 1 Timothy 2:5–6, I objected to the editorial practice of indenting so much of the material in the Pastorals, intimating that it was traditional in character (see p. 127). But in the case of 3:16, Paul's summary of the "great mystery of godliness," the use of such indentation is appropriate, for there is every reason to consider this verse as a hymn-fragment or confessional statement. If the reading of the relative pronoun *hos* at the beginning is correct, the subject is clearly Jesus, as it is in the other christological "hymns" in Paul that start with *hos* (see Phil. 2:6–11; Col. 1:15–20). The verse is also clearly made up of balanced phrases (with only "appeared to angels" breaking the consistent pattern). Finally, these phrases have elements of internal rhyme and assonance.

Comment

This chapter of 1 Timothy provides us with the closest thing in the Pastoral Letters to what could reasonably be called a "church order." In the remarks on supervisors, helpers, and women helpers, we learn about all we are going to about the community structure; Paul's allusion to the "board of elders" in 4:14 and his remarks in 5:1–25 concerning elders and widows are clearly of an *ad hoc* and circumstantial character. It is appropriate, therefore, to pause and consider just what we have learned.

We must be impressed, first, by how little we learn! The treatment of these two (or three) positions is remarkably sparse, consisting in three sentences for the supervisor, one for the women helpers, and four for the male helpers. We learn nothing much, furthermore, about the tasks assigned to these positions, being forced to rely on analogy and inference for the few surmises that might seem plausible. Nor are we told of the relationship between the positions. Second, we must recognize the transparent simplicity of the organization shown us. Perhaps the role of the widows might complicate things a bit, but for the most part, we seem to have the simplest of all collegial governances: older men as a board, a supervisor, and some helpers for practical tasks. Third, we note again that there is no legitimation of these offices: they are not given religious titles; they are granted no particular spiritual power; their tasks seem to be organizational, didactic, and practical, rather than cultic or liturgical. Fourth, we note that the concern of the author is not the description of duties but the recommending of certain moral and managerial qualities.

It remains to ask why these sorts of qualities are regarded so highly and how they might be connected to the christological hymn in 3:16, which to some readers appears as an intrusive bit of evidence for the literary incoherence of 1 Timothy. But if we take the self-presentation of this composition seriously, two issues concerning the leadership in Ephesus — as it existed at the time of writing — emerge forcefully. The first issue is the questionable moral character of some of the leaders. We see in 5:19 that charges are being brought against some elders, and Timothy is warned against appointing leaders hastily or getting caught up in their malfeasances (5:20). Timothy may be tempted to rebuke some of the elders, but is told to exhort them appropriately to their age and position (5:1). The second issue is the competition for leadership among some people whom Paul thinks unworthy and disruptive. These include the women who are going from house to house and saying what they should not (5:13), perhaps even in the assembly asserting authority over men and teaching (2:8–11). And we must count also those whom Paul named as "wanting to be teachers of the law" (1:7) and who hold the opinions he opposes throughout the letter.

In the face of this situation — which can properly be designated a "leadership crisis" — the specific qualities Paul emphasizes here take on a deeper significance. That male supervisors and helpers be "men of one wife" is important in a situation where there is some issue concerning sexual propriety. The same can be said of the other bourgeois qualities of sobriety, steadiness, even dignity. The absence of the vices of "love of money" or "desire for shameful gain" among helpers and supervisors is more than pertinent in a situation where charges are being brought against leaders, perhaps precisely in connection with the distribution of the community's funds (5:3–16). Similarly, the emphasis on consistency and reliability in speech seems suddenly meaningful in such a situation: the supervisor is not to be like those wrangling over the law at worship, but is to be reasonable, an apt teacher, not given to conflict; the male helpers are not to speak out of both sides of their mouths, the female helpers are not to gossip. The quality of being "blameless" and of good reputation with outsiders is now more understandable if the behavior of some in the community endangers the church's stability and safety. The need to "test" helpers in order to show that they are without fault becomes intelligible if those involved in ministry are being brought up on charges. Finally, the capacities to manage a household (*oikos*) well — maintaining its *oikonomia* of wives and children and slaves and funds (3:4, 12) — are of more obvious importance when the disruption of God's assembly threatens the stability and integrity of the *oikos theou* (3:15), when debates and divisions are cultivated rather than the *oikonomia theou* that consists in faith (see 1:4).

This brings us at last to the function of the christological hymn (3:16). I have noted already how its diction is largely Pauline. And with the exception of the two phrases "appeared to angels" and "taken up in glory," its conceptualization is recognizably Pauline as well. The first stanza presents the revelational event: Jesus appeared in the flesh and was vindicated ("made righteous") in the spirit. One can compare the contrast in Romans 1:3–4. The next two stanzas (or four lines) are more difficult to assess. Are they meant to represent a chronological sequence? That would not seem to work, since "was taken up in glory" would not follow "preached among nations." And should "appeared to angels" be better understood as "appeared to messengers," that is, those who proclaimed the resurrected one (cf. Gal. 4:14)? If it is, then perhaps we can view the last four verses as representing separate *aspects* of Christ's being "made righteous by Spirit," that is, four aspects of his resurrection: he appeared to witnesses, he was preached among nations, he was believed in by the world, he was taken up in glory. In this reading, the last four lines form a chiasm, with the appearance and ascension framing the proclamation and belief.

More important than the precise content of the hymn is its overall intent, which is to ground the life of this *oikos theou* in the work of the "living God" (3:15), that is, in the *experience* of the revelation of Jesus Christ, rather than in the lucubrations of human dialectic or the dictates of law. I am returning here to the point argued in the discussion of 1:8–17: this is a community rooted in a revelation that is not simply verbal but experiential (see p. 120). The "mystery of godliness" for this community is a living person, the resurrected Lord Jesus. The leadership of this community, therefore, is to hold *this* mystery as "confessedly great," and make *this* the principle for their *oikonomia,* or administration. Note that the helpers are to "hold on to the mystery of faith with a pure conscience" (3:9) and that the women helpers are also to be "faithful in every respect" (3:11): the reason is that the *oikonomia theou,* as Paul said in 1:4, is "the one in faith" (*en pistei*). The commitment of the leaders and helpers to this mystery is therefore essential.

This brings us finally to the unusual translation of 3:15 that I suggested in the notes above. If we take "pillar and foundation of truth" in the usual way, as an appositional phrase modifying the "church of the living God," we are left with two unfortunate results. The first is a fractured metaphor: the church cannot logically be both house *and* pillar and foundation within a house. The second is the unhappy implication that some ecclesiologies have not been slow to make explicit, which is to equate the church with "the foundation of truth." But if we translate as I have suggested, then all the pieces of the passage come together nicely: if the helpers *are* holders of the mystery of faith and faithful in every respect, then they are also "pillars and supports" for the truth that is the mystery of godliness *within* the "household of God, the church of the living God." Thus they will be precisely the sort of steady and stable leaders that can enable the community to weather its crisis of leadership without betraying the mystery by which it lives.

In Defense of the Noble Teaching — 4:1-7a

4:1 Now the Spirit expressly declares that in later times some people will distance themselves from the faith. They will devote themselves to deceiving spirits and the teachings of demons. **2**They speak falsely with hypocrisy. Their own moral awareness has been cauterized. **3**They forbid marriage, forbid eating foods. These are things that God created to be received with thanksgiving by those who are faithful and have come to a recognition of the truth, **4**because every creature of God is good. Nothing is to be rejected that is received with thanksgiving. **5**For it is made holy by God's word and by prayer. **6**If you propose these things to the brethren, you will be a good helper of Christ Jesus, trained by the words of faith and by the noble teaching which you have followed. **7**But stay away from profane and old-women myths.

Notes on Translation

There are no significant textual variants in this section such as would affect the meaning of the passage; we note only the confusion among scribes concerning *kekaustēriasmenon* (cauterized) in

4:2 and the fact that at least one commentator (Toup) suggested an emendation in 4:3 to relieve an almost intolerable example of asyndeton by supplying "commanding that" in front of "to withdraw from foods."

The diction here is perhaps as "un-Pauline" as in any section of the Pastorals. In these six and a half verses, we find seven NT hapax legomena (*rhētōs, pseudologos, metalēmpsis, apoblētos, enteuxis, entrephesthai, graōdēs*) and an additional seven Pauline hapax (*hysteros, prosechein, ktisma, parakolythein, bebēlos, mythos, paraitesthai*). As so often is the case, we find that such a high concentration of unfamiliar terms is connected to a subject matter that is distinctive — here once more, the use of polemic against opponents.

There are three major problems in translation. All of 4:1–5 is made difficult by the fact that in Greek it forms one long sentence whose syntactical connections are not entirely clear. In order to make sense in English, the translation must break the block into smaller sentences. Unfortunately, this demands some decisions that might otherwise be finessed if the Greek were followed more slavishly. For example, it is not clear from the series of genitive plural endings in *daimoniōn, kekaustēriasmenōn, kōluontōn* (vv. 1–3) whether it is the demons who are cauterized and forbid or the people who get involved in demonic errors. I have decided to make it the people, which seems to be demanded by the content of the strictures. Similarly, the two infinitives *gamein* and *apechesthai* without any linkage between them create an intolerable syntactical strain. The sentence starts with the opponents "forbidding," but that verb cannot command "abstaining" as well. I have simply created consistency by omitting the infinitive "to abstain." Finally, the function of the *hoti* clause beginning v. 4 is not obvious. It can, as in my translation, serve as an explanatory clause. But it can also function as a noun clause supplying the content of "the truth" (v. 3) that believers have come to recognize. This translation would be, "to be received with thanksgiving by faithful people and those who have come to recognize the truth that every creature of God is good."

The second difficulty derives from contemporary sensibilities. How can the adjective *graōdēs* in v. 7a be translated fairly? The cliche "old wives' tales" does not catch the seriousness of the warning. But how seriously should we take the "old woman" part of this? Does it represent the casual sort of sexism that we found in 2 Timothy's *gynaikaria* (little women)? If this were the case, the "endless myths and genealogies" of the male opponents in 1 Timothy 1:4 would be — to our dismay — trivialized by being associated with the stories told by old women around fires. Or does it have more specific reference to the social situation faced by Timothy? Some scholars think that part of the teaching authority asserted by some women (perhaps those wandering widows of 5:13) was to tell the sort of folkloric tales that are found in the *Acts of Paul and Thecla* (see Davies, *The Revolt of the Widows*, 95–129).

The third problem is posed by Paul's application of the term *diakonos* to Timothy himself in 4:6. It is tempting to shift to another translation, such as "minister," in order to distinguish Paul's delegate from the *diakonoi* in the local church the author discussed in 3:8–13. I have retained the term "helper" because I think that a point is being made about the continuity between Timothy's defense of right teaching and that expected of the local helpers.

Literary Observations

The portrayal of false teachers or false prophets as a sign of the last days (here, the "latter days") is not uncommon in apocalyptic literature (see *Sibylline Oracles* 2.154–73; 7.120–38; *Testament of Judah* 23:1–5) and is certainly a constant feature in NT apocalyptic discourse (cf. Matt. 24:24–28; Mark 13:22; 2 Thess. 2:3–4; 2 Pet. 2:1; 1 John 4:1–3; Rev. 13:1–17). The connection between false prophecy and a "spirit of falsehood" (*pneuma planēs*) is found also in 1 John 4:6. The most obvious parallel to the present passage is 2 Timothy 3:1–5, which lacks reference to demonic spirits, but does combine "the last days," evil people, and false teachers.

I mentioned above the difficulty presented by Paul's application of the designation *diakonos* to his delegate Timothy in 4:6 and my decision to render it as "helper." Although Paul uses *diakonia* language freely for himself and his associates (see passages on p. 151), the choice here seems deliberately intended to link the attitudes and actions of Paul's delegate to those of local helpers. Timothy is to exemplify the behavior he enjoins on local leaders. This theme becomes explicit in 4:12, when Paul tells Timothy, "Become a model (*typos*) for believers," but the point is made here already by applying to his delegate the same title as that borne by the lesser leaders in the Ephesian community. The two parts of this chapter, in fact, can be read as paraenesis touching on two aspects of Timothy's presence to that community: first, his defense of the noble teaching (4:1-7a) and, second, his own manner of life (4:7b-16). We are not surprised, therefore, to find once again (in an extremely compressed form) the typical use of polemic as a foil to the positive ideal: just as Timothy is to present the healthy teaching to his people, he is to avoid the teaching of people with cauterized consciences.

Comment

Having sketched the qualities desired in the church's administrators, Paul turns again to the responsibility of his delegate to represent and defend the noble teaching of the gospel. As in 2 Timothy 3:10-17, the ability to carry out this responsibility is connected to the fact that the delegate himself has been reared in the words of faith and has followed that noble teaching (4:6). Opposed to Timothy, once more, are "certain people" (*tines*) who have turned away from faith (v. 1). We see that, as with the helpers of 3:8-13, the criterion of holding on to the mystery of faith that concerns Christ Jesus (3:16; 4:6) is what distinguishes the teaching and practice of those who have "come to a recognition of the truth" (4:3) and those who are involved with "deceiving spirits" (4:1).

We recognize the stereotyped polemic that is conventional in this sort of protreptic contrast between good and bad teachers. We are not, therefore, shocked to see that the noble teaching identified with "godliness" (3:16) is opposed to "profane myths" (*bebēlous mythous,* 4:7). Medical imagery also recurs. In 2 Timothy 2:17, the teaching of opponents was compared to the spread of gangrene. Here in v. 2, they are depicted as having consciences that are "cauterized" — the term suggests branding with a hot iron. We are meant to think of them as being "scarred and insensitive" in their moral awareness (*syneidēsis*). In 1:19 Paul had pictured the opponents as those who had abandoned faith and a good conscience, and he accuses them of hypocrisy here (v. 2). Not surprisingly, in 1:5 Paul asked Timothy for "a good conscience and sincere [literally, 'unhypocritical'] faith." The question of whether the characterization in 4:7 of the profane myths as "old women" has a more pointed reference or is only to be read as a sexist "silly" (RSV) must remain open.

The polemic reveals once more how the author perceives the realm of demonic forces as lying just outside the community boundaries, but dangerous and capable of infiltration. False teachers "devote themselves to deceiving spirits and the teachings of demons" (4:1). The qualifications for a supervisor were hedged by the worry that he fall into the judgment reserved for the devil (3:6) or fall into the trap of the devil (3:7). Two of the opponents have been "handed over to Satan" by Paul (1:20), and some of the younger widows have already gone after Satan (5:15). Such language gives the conflict between true and false versions of the same religious movement a tensely apocalyptic tone.

Paul has once again supplied something of the content of the opponents' teaching as well as a theological rebuttal—a feature, as we have seen, distinctive to 1 Timothy among the Pastorals. In 1:19, Paul seemed to suggest that the abandonment of a healthy conscience, that is, the ability to freely decide what is good and what is not, was connected to the desire to be a "teacher of law" (1:7), namely, someone who imposes strictures on others from the outside. The same logical connection is visible here as well: those who have involved themselves with lying spirits and have damaged moral sensibilities are now proposing limits to the amount of God's creation that believers can legitimately engage (4:3). Their precepts are ascetical in character. They forbid marrying. They demand abstinence from (at least certain) foods. While the prohibition against certain foods would certainly fit within the classic observance of law in Judaism, the forbidding of marriage would not. We do know of some groups of Jews whose observance of Torah also involved certain ascetical practices (see Essenes, Therapeutae), and some Jewish mystics practiced celibacy and fasting on a temporary basis in preparation for their vision-quests (see Scholem, *Major Trends in Jewish Mysticism,* 44). The closest teaching to the present combination that we find in the NT is that of the opponents in Colossae, whose observance of Jewish worship practices (Col. 2:16) is connected to prohibitions such as "do not touch" and "to not taste" (Col. 2:21; see Francis and Meeks, *Conflict at Colossae*).

The practices here opposed by our author may have their roots in Pauline example. Thus, although the slogan "It is good not to touch a woman" in 1 Corinthians 7:1 is immediately qualified by the goodness and indissolubility of marriage (7:3–6, 10), Paul nevertheless makes it clear that celibacy is a good thing (7:7–8), though it is all a matter of the gift one has received from God (7:7). Likewise, Paul declared himself ready "never to eat meat again" if it should cause a brother to stumble in faith (1 Cor. 8:13). For Paul, however, such decisions were precisely to be from a good conscience, rather than from something uniformly imposed on all by law.

Still, in the *Acts of Paul and Thecla,* we do find a form of Christianity that takes Paul as its hero and that professes just such an ascetic lifestyle as essential to Christian identity. Paul's preaching is reduced to "continence and the resurrection," as he proclaims, "Blessed are the bodies of the virgins" (*AP* 6). Paul fasts with Onesiphorus and his family (*AP* 23), and when he does take food, it consists in bread and vegetables and water (*AP* 25). Those who argue that 1 Timothy responds to just such a movement, associated furthermore with "womanly tales," can make effective use of such evidence.

The case is not, however, completely closed. There is no link made in the *Acts of Paul and Thecla,* for example, between these practices and the teaching of the law. Neither is Thecla given a free rein to teach in the assembly by Paul, nor does she exercise authority over a man. Nor does the *Acts of Paul and Thecla* concern itself with questions of financial propriety in the way that so concerns 1 Timothy. The fact that such ascetical tendencies were present already in Judaism and are found early on in the churches of Colossae and Corinth, furthermore, makes it possible that 1 Timothy is responding to a first-generation situation.

Paul's response to the opponents is rooted entirely in the cre-

ation story: "every creature of God is good" in 1 Timothy 4:4
echoes LXX Genesis 1:31, "And God saw everything (*ta panta*)
that he had made, and behold, it was very good (*kala*)." Because
God created all things good — in this case, the human body together with all its delight and dismay — then nothing is to be
rejected as though it were evil. To reject creation is to reject God.
A more powerful statement on the goodness of the created order
would be hard to find. But notice its implication: a system of
law that proscribes some activities as evil tends to locate that
evil in the things/actions themselves; in contrast, the "good conscience" understands that it is not the thing or action but the
use of the thing or the intention of the action to which moral
value should be attached. It is not sex that is evil but the misuse of human sexuality. No food is bad, but humans can evilly
disorder their appetites.

It is because God created all things good, furthermore, that
they are to be received with thanksgiving/blessing (*eucharistia*).
The proper response to the living, creating, and beneficent God
is not a crabbed selection among his gifts (as though humans
had a superior power of discernment), but an openhearted gratitude for all of them. Only "deceiving demons" say otherwise.
Prayer and the word of God, then, do not make food and sex
"good" (which seems to be the implication of translations like
the RSV), for they are already good (*kalos*) by virtue of their creation by God. What the word of God and prayer do is "sanctify/
make them holy," that is, bring these good things explicitly
within the community that is dedicated to the "Holy God" and
that can therefore affirm a deeply ambiguous world precisely as
good, and as creation.

This is now the third example of the author's creation theology that we have seen. First, the assertion that there is "one
God" (2:5) — understood as the creator of all humans — grounds
his conviction that all humans should be prayed for (2:1-2),
since "God desires that all human beings be saved and come to
the recognition of truth" (2:4). Second, the author appeals to
the order of creation to ground his instruction that women are
to be subordinate to men (2:13). Third, in this passage, the author grounds the acceptability to Christians of all foods and of
marriage (4:3) in the goodness of all that God has created (4:4).

It seems abundantly clear that, for good or ill, our author is committed to an understanding of Christian life in which salvation and sanctification are in continuity, rather than in discontinuity, with what he sees as the order of creation — that is, with the *oikonomia theou.*

Modelling the Noble Teaching — 4:7b–16

4:7bInstead, train yourself for godliness. 8Training the body is useful in a limited way. Godliness, however, is useful in every way. It has a promise of life both now and in the future. 9The word is faithful and is worthy of complete acceptance. 10For this is why we labor and struggle, because we have come to hope in a living God who is the savior of all human beings, above all of those who are faithful. 11Command these things. Teach them. 12Don't let anyone despise your youth. Become, rather, a model to those who are faithful, in speech and in behavior, by love, by faith, by purity. 13Until I arrive, pay attention to the reading, to exhortation, and to teaching. 14Do not be careless with the special gift for service within you. It was given to you through prophecy with a laying on of hands by the board of elders. 15Pay attention to these things. Live by them so that your moral progress is manifest to all. 16Be attentive to yourself and to the teaching, and remain steady in both. For if you do this, you will both save yourself and those who are listening to you.

Notes on Translation

There are three noteworthy textual variants in 4:10. The first is the least significant, merely the addition of *kai* so that the phrase becomes "both labor and struggle." The second replaces the deponent verb "struggle" (*agōnizometha*) with the passive "we are reviled" (*oneidizometha*). Although some important witnesses contain this reading, it is surely an error, since it destroys the athletic imagery that runs through the passage (see below). The third variant replaces the perfect tense of "we have come to hope" (*ēlpikamen*) with the simple aorist (*ēlpisamen*); the reading is not well attested. In 4:12, most later MSS (but none of the best early ones) add the phrase "in the spirit" *(en pneumati)* to the list of qualities Timothy should demonstrate. A variant of potentially greater significance is found in 4:14. A few witnesses (notably the original hand of Sinaiticus) have *presbyterou* rather than *prebyteriou.* The difference is only one letter, but it marks the distinction between an "elder" *(presbyteros)* and a "board of elders" *(presbyterion).* The correction may have been made because *presbyteros* appears immediately after in 5:1, and *presbyterion* is a much less frequently used word in the NT (see Luke 22:66; Acts 22:5). Finally, in 4:15, some witnesses have *en pasin* (in everything) rather than simply *pasin* (before everyone), probably because they missed the point of Timothy's being an example in 4:12.

As in the first part of chapter 4, the diction has a rather large number of Pauline hapax legomena *(gymnazein, sōmatikē, gymnasia, eusebeia, neotēs, prosechein, amelein, epithesis, meletan, presbyterion),* but only two NT hapax *(apodochēs, agneia)* and one word found only in the Pastorals *(ōphelimos).* As in the previous section, here we find few distinctively Pauline expressions, although we can note the use of *anastrophē* (4:12) for "behavior/ way of life" in Galatians 1:13 and the same sort of hope for saving others through one's behavior (4:16) in 1 Corinthians 9:22.

Perhaps the most interesting aspect of the diction here is its employment of commonplace images for the moral life. The adjective *ōphelimos* (useful/worthwhile), for example, is found in the NT only in the Pastorals (1 Tim. 4:8; 2 Tim. 3:16; Titus 3:8), but its cognates are more widely used (see, e.g., Rom. 2:25; 1 Cor. 13:3; 14:6; Gal. 5:2) and point to the fundamental concern of the moralist, namely, the "usefulness" of profession or practice (Plato *Republic* 607D; Josephus *Antiquities* 19.2.5; see also *ti ophelos* in James 2:14, 16; 1 Cor. 15:32). Likewise, when Paul tells Timothy that his "progress" *(prokopē)* should become manifest to all (4:15), he takes a stand on a debated issue in Greco-Roman moral teaching, namely, how susceptible virtue is to progress. Paul clearly aligns himself with those who consider it possible and visibly manifested (cf. Plutarch *On Progress in Virtue* [*Mor.* 75B–86A]; Epictetus *Encheiridion* 12–13; *Discourse* III, 6).

The use of athletic imagery in hellenistic moral discourse is as well attested as medical imagery and works to capture the sense of effort required to make progress. The term *gymnasia* (training) refers first to such training for athletic contests (Plato *Laws* 648C), but can easily be applied to moral struggles (see 4 Macc. 11:20). Here Paul distinguishes between physical training and that which is applied to moral behavior: "train yourself" (*gymnaze seauton,* 4:7b) is a phrase that occurs in moral literature for just such mental and spiritual conditioning (see Pseudo-Isocrates *To Nicocles* 11; *To Demonicus* 21; see also Epictetus *Discourse* III, 12, 7). The verb *entrephesthai,* likewise, can be used for someone's "rearing," but in moral literature is applied to the process of "training" in moral behavior (4:6; cf. Plato *Laws* 798A; Epictetus *Discourse* IV, 4, 48).

For the image of the moral struggle as comparable to the Olympic Games, see Epictetus's *Discourse* (III, 22,51–52). Clearly, Paul's description of this effort as "laboring and struggling" in 4:10 fits this same context. The *agōn* is the athletic contest, classically a race or wrestling (see Herodotus *Persian War* 9.60; Epictetus *Discourse* III, 25, 3). Metaphorically, the struggle for virtue is just such a contest (see Epictetus *Discourse* III, 6, 5–7; IV, 4, 29–32). Two other terms in the passage that fit within standard moral discourse of the age are the contrasting *amelein* (to neglect/be unconcerned with; see Epictetus *Discourse* III, 24, 113) in 4:14 and *meletan* (to practice/cultivate/take pains with; see Epictetus *Discourse* I, 1, 25; II, 1, 29) in 4:15.

We now turn to some translation difficulties. The rendering of *malista* in v. 10 can easily give rise to misunderstandings. The superlative of the adverb *mala* denotes that whatever is true of something else is "particularly" true in this case (note the use in 5:17). But when the general statement concerns God's saving of all humans, the English "above all those who are faithful" might be read as indicating a special position for them, whereas the point is that God's "desire that all human beings should be saved" (2:4) is "particularly" realized among the faithful, those who have "come to the recognition of truth" (2:4; 4:3). A minor difficulty is presented by the plural *autois* in v. 16. Timothy is told to be attentive to himself and to the teaching. The Greek continues, "remain steady *in them,*" which makes grammatical but not logical sense. The RSV chooses to reduce the steadiness only to the teaching, thus, "hold to *that*" (emphasis added). But this is to miss the focus both on teaching and on character that has dominated the section. I have chosen the translation, "remain steady in both," precisely to show how this final command summarizes the point of the entire paraenesis.

Literary Observations

I have noted earlier how it is characteristic of 1 Timothy to alternate sections containing mandates for community life with sections of personal instruction to his delegate. I also suggested that such an arrangement fits within the overall purpose of the *mandata principis* letter: the commands legitimate the mission of the delegate by lending the authority of the apostle; the personal exhortation legitimates the expectation of the people that the delegate also has certain standards of behavior to meet.

In the sequence of chapters 3–4, we see that the two kinds of material are not simply juxtaposed but are more intimately connected than we might have supposed. By calling Timothy a *kalos diakonos* (good helper) of Christ Jesus in 4:6, Paul suggests that the teaching and behavior of his delegate are to serve as an example to the *episkopos* and *diakonoi* of the local community. In the present passage, we see that connection made explicit. Timothy is to make himself a *typos* whose moral progress can be manifest to all believers and whose dedication to the noble teaching and devotion to godliness can be emulated by them. It is in this sense that we are to understand 4:16: Timothy's commitment to self-improvement and to the teaching will "save himself," but it will also provide others with a living exemplar of how they also can be "saved." In the use of short exhortations, arranged antithetically, together with the themes of model and imitation, we see again the classic components of paraenesis. But now, it is not Paul who serves as the model to the delegate or to the community, but the delegate himself who is to play that role (see also Titus 2:7).

In v. 9 of this passage, we have the phrase *pistos ho logos* (the word is faithful) once again, with the added phrase (as in 1:15) *pasēs apodochēs axios* (and worthy of complete acceptance). Once more, the question arises as to the meaning and function of the phrase. In this case, as noted earlier, the reference could move backward or forward. Since the *gar* in 4:10 introduces an explanatory clause, however, the more likely referent is the statement preceding this expression. If this is so, then we find that "the word" that is faithful may well be taken in apposition to "the promise of life now and to come" (cf. "the promise of life found in Christ Jesus" in 2 Tim. 1:1).

Comment

The analysis above has shown how chapter 4 as a whole works to show Timothy as an exemplar of devotion to the noble teaching and of a life based on it. We are thereby reminded of how seriously ancient philosophy viewed the responsibility of teachers to live out their profession — it was a matter of saving the self and saving others. Since philosophy was about integrity of life and since virtue was learned by imitation, the teacher had no greater duty than to live in a fashion corresponding to the principle he enunciated. The contemporary collapse of such an understanding of moral instruction and the present-day flight from the responsibility inherent in being a teacher of others provide the grounds for reflection on the ways in which the ancient world may have been, in these respects, superior to our own.

Additional aspects of the passage deserve attention, touching on the question of the community organization in Ephesus. Paul tells Timothy in v. 14 not to neglect the special gift for service (my translation of *charisma*) that was given him. Two dimensions of the "giving" are mentioned. The first is that the gift was "through prophecy," which immediately reminds us of Paul's delivering the commandment to Timothy in 1:18 "according to the earlier prophecies made concerning you." The context for such prophecy is now located in the speech of the *presbyterion* (board of elders). The second is that this board laid hands on Timothy, which clearly suggests some sort of ritual of ordination or appointment.

Some readers can find in this reminder a logical and theological inconsistency. Their problem stems at least partially from a rigid distinction between the charismatic and the institutional, between "faith" and "order," with the assumption that in the early church one might have followed the other but that they did not exist simultaneously. In the present case, the logical inconsistency is stated thusly: if Timothy is Paul's delegate and derives his authority from Paul, then how is he also "ordained" by the local board of elders? On the basis of this objection, it can be supposed that "Timothy" is really only a cipher for the later leaders who *are* thus ordained by boards of elders. But in fact the inconsistency is more imaginary than real. There is no reason why Timothy's service in the Ephesian church could not derive both from Paul's appointment and the appointment of the board of elders — if indeed the charismatic gestures of prophecy and laying on of hands do in fact signify an appointment rather than simple gestures of empowerment by the local community's leaders. As for the imagined conflict between a process of appointment and prophetic speech, the way they could go together among a group of "prophets" is illustrated by Acts 13:2–3: "While they were worshipping the Lord and fasting, the Holy Spirit said, 'Set apart for me Barnabas and Saul for the work to which I have called them.' Then after fasting and praying they laid their hands on them and sent them off" (RSV).

The *literary* appropriateness of the mention of the *presbyterion* at this point seems clear. Paul will immediately instruct Timothy on the proper way to exhort an elder (5:1) and will tell him how to deal with problems in the presbytery (5:17–25). The need to carry out such a confrontative ministry places Timothy in an extraordinarily delicate situation. He must assert authority in the face of those who have had a role in appointing him. Paul reminds him, therefore, not to let anyone despise his youth: he is to assert his authority as real. At the same time, Timothy is reminded that the *presbyterion*'s support for his ministry is important. He is to proceed with care.

Another aspect deserving attention involves the explanatory sentence that follows "train yourself for godliness" in v. 7b. The explanation actually continues the response to ascetical teaching in 4:3–5 and forms still another theological response of 1 Timothy to false teaching. The contrast here is between a training that is useful only for the present and that which is useful forever: "It has a promise of life both now and in the future" (v. 8). That promise, furthermore, is rooted in the nature of the God in whom "we have come to hope" (v. 10). This is the living God, who can therefore give eternal life (see 1:16 and 6:12). Because God is the living one, God can be "savior of all human beings" (v. 10). There are two distinct theological points being made. First, the focus on physical asceticism in the name of religion — the forbidding of marriage and of eating certain foods — is exactly like physical training for the Olympic Games. It is an entirely this-worldly endeavor and does not pertain to the essence of faith, which is a response to the living God. Second — and more important to us in the light of our previous discussions — the *oikonomia theou en pistei* (household management of God in faith) is not *entirely* a matter of the order of creation. The "mystery of faith," after all, concerns the one who was declared righteous in the spirit and taken up in glory (3:16). The living God gives life not only now but also in the future. It is living by the measure of this reality, this life, that Timothy can save himself and save others.

Crisis in the Care of Widows — 5:1–16

⁵:¹Do not castigate an older man. Instead, exhort him as if he were your father. Act toward younger men as toward brothers, ²toward older women as toward mothers, toward younger women as toward sisters, that is, in all purity. ³Provide financial support for widows who are truly widows. ⁴But if any widow has children or grandchildren, let them learn first of all to show godliness in their own household and to give back some repayment to those who gave them birth. For this is an acceptable thing before God. ⁵Now the real widow is one who has been left alone. She has put her hope in God and continues to make petitions and prayers night and day. ⁶In contrast, the woman who lives self-indulgently has already died even though she is alive. ⁷And you should command these things so that they can stay without reproach. ⁸But if people do not provide for their own relatives, especially if they are members of their household, they have denied the faith and are worse than unbelievers. ⁹A widow should be enrolled. She should not be less than sixty years old, married only once.

¹⁰She should have a reputation for good deeds, such as rearing her children, showing hospitality to strangers, washing the feet of the saints, helping those in trouble; in short, she has been dedicated to every sort of good deed. ¹¹But avoid younger widows. For they want to marry when they have grown faithless to Christ. ¹²They earn condemnation because they have denied their first commitment. ¹³Moreover, they immediately learn to be idlers, going from house to house. They are not only idlers but also gossips and busybodies, saying things that they should not. ¹⁴I therefore want younger women to marry, to bear children, to run their households, giving no opportunity on the basis of reviling to the one who opposes us. ¹⁵For some women have already turned aside after Satan. ¹⁶If any faithful woman has widows, she should provide for them. The church should not be burdened, so that it can support those who are real widows.

Notes on Translation

The Greek text of this difficult passage is fairly stable. The singular "let her learn" (*manthanetō*) of some Western witnesses in 5:4 is surely wrong: it is the children who are to learn to practice godliness. The only other really significant variant is found in 5:16, where a number of MSS add *pistos ē* to *pistē* to form the phrase "a faithful man or faithful woman," apparently out of the assumption that a woman would not be the head of a household. In fact, however, the presence of just such a wealthy class of women in the Ephesian church seems to be part of the complex situation faced by Timothy.

The diction here is about as non-Pauline as any in the Pastorals. There are fifteen NT hapax legomena (*epiplēssein, agneia, ekgona, amoibē, monoun, anepilēmptos, katalegein, teknotrophein, xenodochein, eparchein, katastrēnian, phluaros, teknogonein, oikodespotein, pistē*). In addition, there are eighteen terms not found in the undisputed letters of Paul (*presbyteros, neōteros, presbytera, neōtera, eusebein, prosmenein, spatalan, thnēskein, arnēsasthai, hexēkonta, niptein, epakolouthein, paraitein, argos, perierchesthai, periergos, loidoria, ektrapein*), as well as two terms found only in the Pastorals (*progonos, apodektos*). Certainly, some of the unusual vocabulary is due to the subject matter: the NT is not overflowing with discussions concerning women!

There are a number of critical translation decisions that affect the interpretation of the passage as a whole. The first presents itself immediately in v. 1. Should *presbyteros* be translated as "an older man" or as "an elder"? Coming so shortly after the mention of the *presbyterion* in 4:14, the translation as "elder" would seem appropriate. Instructions on the members of that "board of elders" will also shortly be forthcoming (5:17–22). Why else would Timothy be warned against castigating an older man (the language suggests a sharp rebuke), if there were not some matter of conduct involved, such as is suggested in 5:19? On the other hand, the statement concerning the older man is followed by parallel instructions concerning various age groups of both genders, so that the instruction ends up being about the attitudes the delegate should have toward all groups in the community. The issue is made more complex because the "board of elders" was in all likelihood made up, at least in part, of such "older men." We are faced once more, in other words, with our ignorance of the ways in which the structures of the intentional community called the *ekklēsia* depended on, intersected with, or were distinguished from the relationships of the *oikos*, considered both as family and as household. That same ambiguity will be carried into the discussion of widows in 5:3–16.

The second critical decision concerns the translation of *tima* in v. 3. The RSV and other translations render the verse as "Honor widows who are real widows," and the verb *timan* definitely bears that meaning (see Xenophon *Memorabilia* 4.3.13; John 5:23; 8:49). But such honor could take on the specific form of financial support (see *timē* in Diogenes Laertius *Lives of Eminent Philosophers* 5.72; Sir. 38:1). Indeed, the commandment to "honor your father and mother" (see Exod. 20:12; Matt. 15:4; 19:19; Mark 7:10; 10:19; Luke 18:20; Eph. 6:2) bore with it the definite corollary of supporting one's parents in their old age. Indeed, an allusion to that demand perhaps appears in the passing comment of 5:4: the children who practice godliness by giving back something to their parents do something that is pleasing to God (cf. Eph. 6:2). Financial support for parents is precisely the point of Jesus' controversy with the Pharisees in Mark 7:9–

13: he accuses them of voiding the commandment to honor their parents by their avoidance of actually supporting them. Notice also that in 1 Timothy 5:17 the command that elders who govern well should receive "double honor" (*diplēs timēs*) is clearly interpreted in terms of financial support by the quotations of Scripture adduced in support of the measure (v. 18). Finally, the entire theme of this passage concerns which "widows" the *ekklēsia* should support financially (see above all v. 16). The translation "provide financial support" in v. 3 is therefore both accurate and clarifying.

In concert with the RSV, I have translated the participle *spatalōsa* in 5:6 as "lives self-indulgently." It is important to note that there is also a social-level connotation carried by the word so that it could also be rendered "luxuriously" or "ostentatiously." It is a lifestyle enabled by wealth (see Polybius *Histories* 36.17.7). Note the use of the term in LXX Ezekiel 16:49, Sirach 21:15, and especially James 5:5. The contrast with the "real widow," in other words, is not merely moral but also social and economic: the women here described are not "left alone" economically, but can afford a life of luxury and idleness.

The Greek conditional sentence in 5:8 is in the singular: "if anyone does not provide." I have translated it as plural, "if people do not provide," for two reasons. First, the plural avoids the needless repetition of the grammatically demanded "he/his" for the rest of the sentence. Second, as the reference to the "faithful woman" in 5:16 makes clear, Paul thinks in terms of both genders. The generalized "people" therefore seems appropriate. As for who might be included in v. 8 under *oikeiōn,* see the discussion by R. A. Campbell (*"kai malista oikeiōn"*).

One of the key terms in the entire passage is *katalegesthō* (let her be enrolled) in v. 9. Although it is a NT hapax legomenon, the verb is used in a variety of contexts: the enrollment of soldiers into the army, reception into the circle of the gods, acceptance into the Senate, and inclusion in a religious body. It is clear, therefore, that in the Ephesian community, Paul wants women who qualify to be registered as widows. The difficulty is exegetical: what does the enrollment signify? Is there an official order of widows, like the order of helpers? Or is this a list of those who are to receive the church's resources in exchange for their services to the church? Or is it some combination of these elements? The decision reached on this point also affects the way *paraitou* in v. 11 is translated. Does Paul mean "do not enroll" (as in the RSV), or does he mean simply "avoid," as the parallel instances in 1 Timothy 4:7, 2 Timothy 2:23, and Titus 3:10 would seem to support? See the fuller discussion below.

For the list of criteria for the "real widow" in v. 10, Paul has enclosed a series of *ei* clauses within the brackets formed by "good works." I have chosen to translate rather freely, eliminating the "if" introductions and treating the clauses as examples ("such as . . ."), with the final "every sort of good deed" serving as resumptive. The very difficult construction in v. 11 also demands an interpretive translation. I have reversed the order of the Greek clauses to put the emphasis where I think Paul wanted it: on the desire of the young widows to marry. The *hotan* clause provides the precipitant to that desire. The verb *katastrēnian* is difficult. By itself, *strēnian* means "to live luxuriously/sensually" (it is combined with *porneuein* in Rev. 18:7–9). The basic idea, then, is that they grow sensual and want to marry. But the *kata*-prefix has as its object "the Christ/Messiah" (*tou christou*). The translation must, therefore, combine the element of their sensual itch and the element of this urge turning them against — what? Paul refers in v. 12 to "their first *pistis.*" Does this mean their religious faith in Jesus as Messiah? Or does it refer to their dedication to the messianic community as "widows in service"? I have decided to translate this cluster of ideas as "when they have grown faithless to Christ" and "they have denied their first commitment."

The translation of v. 14 is complicated by the fact that the author has combined two phrases that might be taken separately or together. He says first that women should marry and bear children, "giving no opportunity (*aphormēn*) to the one who opposes us." Is this opponent human, or is it — as the next verse would seem to suggest — Satan, who lurks outside the community boundaries? But then Paul adds another phrase, *loidorias charin* (on account of reviling). We cannot be sure whether the intended meaning is that a human opponent might have an opportunity to revile the community because of the wantonness of its young women or that Satan is given an opportunity to de-

stroy or hurt the community because of the reviling that comes
upon it due to its wanton young women. It is clear, in either
case, that the author sees the result of their behavior to be both
serious and negative.

Literary Observations

The literary "feel" of this section is that of a series of *ad hoc* instructions triggered by association. I do not mean to suggest that
the commands are not purposeful, only that they appear to occur in a somewhat random sequence. Note, for example, that the
opening instruction not to castigate an elder (5:1) would seem to
connect logically to the others concerning elders in 5:17–22. But
the image of elder as "father" seems to have triggered a reflexive
"generational/gender" *topos*. What is perhaps most fascinating
about these fairly banal statements in vv. 1–2 is that they show
us once more how early Christians adopted kinship language for
the relationships in the intentional community of the *ekklēsia*.
The kinship is, of course, recognized as fictive: the elder is "as"
(*hōs*) a father, and the younger woman "as" (*hōs*) a sister. But if
these designations are taken seriously, there are implications for
the sexual activity of the community: fictive incest also becomes
a danger. Perhaps this is why, since Timothy has been identified
here as "young" (see 4:12), the command concerning "younger
women" is expanded in v. 2 to include the qualification "in all
purity."

The discussion of the widows that begins in 5:3 is by far
the most extended. Its length and complexity appear to be at
least partially attributable to the fact that "widows" in this community is a problematic category, including not only "older
women" who can be regarded as mothers but also "younger
women" who, while technically widowed because their husbands
have died, are still young and marriageable and, it is suggested,
sexually alive and interested (v. 11). The charge in v. 2 to treat
younger women as "sisters in all purity" takes on an entirely new
complexity when the sisters are not young maidens within the
shelter of the household, but perhaps young and liberated ma-
trons who are themselves householders and who are able to visit
other households at will.

Before turning to the possible historical context addressed by this discussion, we should observe that the discussion of widows is not without literary structure. The passage has four apodictic commands: (1) "provide financial support for widows who are truly widows" (v. 3); (2) "a widow should be enrolled" (v. 9); (3) "avoid younger widows" (v. 11); and (4) "I therefore want younger women to marry" (v. 14). These commands fairly well summarize Paul's position. They are interspersed with two other kinds of statements. The first type is what might be called "case law" statements in the form of conditional sentences, all of which read, "if anyone" (vv. 4, 8, 16); each of these, it should be noted, places the burden of support for those who are not "real widows" on private households. The second type of statement is descriptive of the real widow and the faux widow, respectively. They are arranged antithetically in 5:5–6, 9–13, and 14–15.

At first glance, the list of qualifications for the widows in vv. 9–10 appears to resemble that for the orders of supervisor and helper in 3:1–13, especially since the criterion of "wife of one husband" is included in v. 9. More careful analysis reveals, however, that in the case of the "real widows" the qualifications concern what they have done in the past (all the verbs are in the aorist), rather than their capacities for taking on jobs in the present. In my judgment, we find here, not an "ecclesiastical order" of women who are to perform certain tasks, but a "welfare system" that extends itself to those who are *both* genuinely needy and have proven their worthiness by service to the community.

Comment

The advent of women's history and of feminist criticism within NT scholarship has given the present passage a prominence it did not formerly enjoy. For some scholars, as I have already suggested several times, the situation addressed in 5:3–16 — or at least a certain construal of that situation — is the essential key to the sociohistorical context of the Pastorals as a whole (see pp. 20–21). In this reading, the "women's issue" is not simply one among several, but is the most important of those addressed by the author. The case is argued that 1 Timothy is

a second-century patriarchal reaction to a protofeminist movement within early Christianity (see, e.g., Schüssler Fiorenza, *In
Memory of Her,* 284–342; Bassler, "The Widow's Tale"). The "widows" are not simply impoverished women cared for by the
assembly. They are an order of women who practice an active
ministry. At least some of these women, possibly those who are
wealthier and, therefore, are on the social level of the male
"elders," are challenging male leadership by carrying out something of an itinerant mission from house to house (5:13) and
by asserting their authority to teach in the assembly, which is
tantamount to asserting their authority over men (2:12). Their
refusal to stay at home, stay silent, and stay subordinate is, in
this understanding, based on the women's claim to an authority
for leadership given by God.

The response of the author of 1 Timothy is to suppress this
movement by refusing women the right to speak in the assembly and by seeking to keep women within their domestic roles:
marrying, having children, and exercising authority within the
household (5:14). His is the classic appeal to complementary
spheres of influence for the sexes, the man's public, the woman's
private. But since the important matters take place in public,
the result is that women are trivialized along with their roles.
By reducing the order of widows to old women who are poor
and dependent, Paul helps to take the wind out of the sails of
this powerful women's movement. The older men get to rule;
the older women get to be cared for. The real issue, this argument claims, is not the sharing of possessions, but the sharing of
power. The author's resort to sexual innuendo is a disingenuous
attempt to discredit an otherwise worthy effort to serve within
the community.

Although my own reading of the situation is different, I acknowledge that the evidence is sufficiently ambiguous to give
some support to the case made by such scholars (see Thurston,
The Widows, 36–55). Certainly, something is brewing among the
affluent Ephesian women. They are wearing fancy clothing and
hairdos in the assembly (2:9–10) and are seeking to exercise a
teaching role there as well (2:11–15). In this chapter, we see
them charged with self-indulgence (5:6) and with flitting from
house to house as gossipers and busy-bodies, saying things they

should not (5:13). Neither is there any doubt that Paul proposes that younger women remain in domestic roles (5:14; see 2:15).

My disagreement with the feminist interpretation begins with its neglect of what appears to be the most obvious concern in the passage, namely, balancing the needs of the poor and the resources of the intentional community. To suggest that this passage is fundamentally about power rather than possessions is, in my view, to misread it. I also have trouble understanding the simple direction "Let a widow be enrolled" as the designation of an official ministerial order. I see it simply as a directive that those receiving community aid should be registered. Finally, I do not find the sexual innuendo to be a polemical ploy but rather a response to a very real problem.

In order to present my interpretation, two preliminary contextualizing observations are in order. The first concerns the care of widows in the ancient Jewish synagogue. From the time of the earliest legislation in Torah, through the prophets, and into the wisdom tradition, the sign of adherence to the covenant was above all the care of widows and orphans, the two groups who were chronically dispossessed and therefore impoverished in a landed, patriarchal economy (see Johnson, *Sharing Possessions,* 88–100). The tradition of "visiting orphans and widows in their distress" (James 1:27) was carried on in the diaspora synagogue through a system of community charity. For the homeless and vagrant, there was a daily plate, or distribution of food. For cases of long-term or chronic need, a community chest was used. The appointment of officials to collect for this charity as well as to distribute it was a difficult matter, for much integrity was demanded (see, e.g., *bT* ʾAbod. Zar. 17b; B. Bat. 8b). That this tradition was carried on in early Christianity is suggested by Acts 2:41–47 and 4:32–37; the conflict between the widows of the Hellenists and the widows of the Hebrews in Acts 6:1–6 also shows how difficult any such welfare system was, with an inevitable tension between the needs and desires of those cared for and the available resources of the caring community.

The second contextualizing observation concerns Paul's views concerning widows in the only other place he discusses them. In 1 Corinthians 7:8–9, Paul says to the "unmarried and widows" that it would be a good thing if they were to remain as he was (that is, celibate). But he adds as a qualifier that if they are unable to exercise self-control, they should marry, for it is better to marry than to "burn" (presumably with disordered passion). In 1 Corinthians 7:39, he declares a woman whose husband has died to be free to marry again, so long as it is in the Lord. Again, however, Paul would prefer if she remained unmarried. It is clear, therefore, that the *preference* Paul expresses in 1 Corinthians is for a life of celibacy dedicated to the Lord. On the other hand, he recognizes that this is not everyone's gift. If passion cannot be controlled, then marriage is preferable to *porneia.* In 1 Timothy 5, there is no preference for celibacy. Indeed, Paul recognizes that some younger women who had devoted themselves to celibacy after the death of their husbands grow wanton (for the problems in translating v. 11, see p. 175) and want to back out of their commitment by marrying. Paul clearly prefers that the younger women marry rather than become idlers and social gadabouts (v. 14).

Since I understand the possessions issue to be primary in this passage, I will sort through the text from that perspective and then attempt to show how the sexual dimension fits into that reading. As I suggested above, the translation of *tima* in v. 3 as "provide financial support" is critical to my case. The issue is not which women are worthy of reverence or honor, but which ones the *ekklēsia* as such is going to support with its resources. As soon as the question is posed this way, then other questions quickly follow: Who needs financial support? Who among those in need have other resources available to them? Who is worthy of the community's support? As Paul moves through these questions, we see emerging the classic problems facing all welfare systems down to the present day. First, how much help should come from the community as such, and how much from private sources? And second, what sort of behavioral norms should be invoked as a criterion for receiving community funds?

When the questions are stated so clearly, the answers come quickly. Paul wants individual households to support widows who are relatives. This is a function of godliness that is pleasing to God (5:4). Failure to do it makes one worse than an unbeliever (v. 8), and offering such support relieves the community of a financial burden (v. 16). As in the directions concerning supervisors and helpers in chapter 3, these commands show that there remains a sharp distinction between the *ekklēsia* as the *oikos theou* and the *oikos* as the basic unit of society.

One way of defining the "real widow," then, is in terms of her need and her lack of other means of support. Paul pictures her as "having been left alone" (v. 5). Having been the wife of one man, his death leaves her, if she does not have children or grandchildren with means, without resources of her own. Since Paul contrasts her state with that of a widow with children or grandchildren who can support her, we are to suppose the "real widow" to be literally alone. Her lack of resources is indicated as well by the phrase, "She has put her hope in God" (v. 5). Compare 6:17 for the contrast between hope in riches and hope in God. We presume that in her case she has no riches on which to rely.

When Paul says that to be registered on the welfare list the widow must be no less than sixty years old (5:9), we learn two things. First, we know that the list will automatically be relatively short, since life expectancy in the first-century Mediterranean was not as long as today. Second, at that age, active ministry is not ahead of her but behind her; now is the time for a life of petitions and prayer night and day (v. 5). Finally, Paul says the community should support a woman of this age and this need, who enjoys a reputation for good deeds, both domestic (raising children, providing hospitality) and communitarian (washing the feet of the saints, helping the afflicted). In effect, Paul suggests that the church should spend its resources on those who have spent their resources in the service of others (v. 10). We can note here in passing that the remarks devoted to widows in Polycarp's *Letter to the Philippians* do not tell us more about their functions. In addition to being virtuous, the widows are simply to "pray without ceasing for all people" (4.3). They are, however, portrayed as the "altar of God," a level of theological legitimation lacking entirely from Paul's practical discussion of the disposition of financial resources.

In contrast to such "real widows," Paul wants Timothy to "avoid younger widows" (5:11). He obviously means that they should not be included in the community charity roll. The reasons seem to be largely circumstantial and connected to the

behavior of some of the younger widows in Ephesus. Paul's remark about "self-indulgence" in v. 6 scarcely suggests someone
who is destitute and dependent on the community. But if such
women *are* placed on the rolls, they present two problems. The
first problem concerns the possibility they may grow restless in
their commitment to the community through a life of prayer
and may desire to marry (v. 11). Paul can hardly object to this,
since this is what he wants younger women to do in the first
place (v. 14). The difficulty seems to be the *way* in which they
place themselves in a position to marry and the fact that this
new decision represents a going back on their first commitment
to the Messiah. It is difficult to know exactly what this means,
for it is the piece of evidence that most supports seeing the widows as some sort of "order." But it may mean only that they want
to give up the life of prayer to which they committed themselves
when placed on the community dole. The second problem concerns their staying on the roll and being able to indulge a life
of idleness (note the repetition in v. 13) that finds expression
in wandering from house to house, gossiping, being busybodies, and saying things that should not be said. This mode of
behavior, indeed, may be what is leading to the desire (and the
possibility) of marrying again.

At the very least, such women strain the community's resources. But their actions also create the possibility of scandal.
Paul says that some of them have already gone astray after Satan
(5:15). He wants them to marry so that "the one who opposes
us" may not be given an opportunity (v. 14) — and that opportunity to revile would exist if the community had a board of
elderly men financially supporting a group of younger women
who lived in public idleness and self-indulgence. This is the sort
of sexually suggestive behavior that could bring a religious community into disrepute and even danger, as the devotees of Isis in
Rome discovered (see Dio Cassius *Roman History* 47.15; 53.2). I
suggest that the sexual innuendo is not part of Paul's polemic,
but touches on a real and serious possibility created by the combination of an elderly male leadership that supports sexually
interested younger women. The following warning to the rabbinic scholar in *Aboth de Rabbi Nathan* 2 captures the cultural
sensibilities involved:

Let no man be alone with any woman in an inn, even with his sister or his daughter or his mother-in-law, because of public opinion. Let no man chat with a woman in the market place, even if she is his wife, and, needless to say, with another woman, because of public opinion. Let no man walk behind a woman in the market place, even behind his wife, and needless to say, another woman, because of public opinion.

My interpretation leaves some questions unresolved. I continue to be puzzled by the meaning of "growing wanton against Christ" in v. 11 as well as by the fact that Paul never seems to consider the case of younger widows who may also be left without resources of their own — are they simply to be abandoned if they cannot find a spouse? Does he assume that, since they are younger, they would still be under the care of their parents' *oikos?* But perhaps this is to ask too much from a passage that, for all its gaps, gives us a remarkable glimpse at the problems facing the ancient church as it sought to find its place in the world, asking its members to meet their social responsibilities even as it assumed the responsibilities it inherited from the traditions of the Jewish synagogue. If Paul's discussion does not answer all our questions, it remains a careful discussion of a delicate issue in the life of an intentional community.

More Community Directives — 5:17–6:2a

5:17Elders who govern well should be considered worthy of double compensation, especially those who labor in speech and in teaching. 18For the Scripture says, "Do not muzzle an ox that is threshing," and, "The workman deserves his pay." 19Do not consider an accusation against an elder unless two or three witnesses support it. 20Those who are sinning, rebuke in the presence of all, so that the rest might be afraid. 21I am charging you before God and before Christ Jesus and before the elect angels, that you observe these matters without favoritism. Do nothing on the basis of partiality. 22Do not lay hands on anyone hastily. Do not associate yourself with

other peoples' sins. Keep yourself pure. [23]Do not keep drinking only water. Use a little wine for the sake of digestion and
for your frequent weakness. [24]The sins of some people are obvious, parading before them into judgment. The sins of some
others trail behind. [25]In the same way, good deeds are also
obvious, and deeds that are not cannot remain hidden. [6:1]Let
those who are under the yoke as slaves regard their own masters as worthy of all respect, so that the name of God and the
teaching not be blasphemed. [2a]And those who have believers
as masters should not despise them because they are brothers. Rather they should serve them better because those who
are receiving their benefaction are believers and beloved.

Notes on Translation

The citation from Deuteronomy 25:4 generated a number of textual variants in 5:18; scribes were concerned either to bring the
citation into line with the LXX (and thus changed the word
order) or into line with Paul's citation of the same passage in
1 Corinthians 9:9, which used the verb *kēmoun* rather than *phi-
moun*, the one used here. Similarly, a very few witnesses under
the influence of Matthew 10:10 replace *tou misthou* with *tēs
trophēs* for the second citation in v. 18, yielding "The workman
deserves his food" rather than "his pay." The only other significant variant occurs in 5:21, where some MSS have *prosklēsis*
rather than *prosklisis;* the difference orthographically is one letter, but the resulting text, "according to a summons/invitation,"
does not yield good sense.

The diction in this section returns to the familiar mixture
typical of 1 Timothy: there are a number of NT hapax legomena (*prokrima, prosklisis, hydropotein, stomachos, allos*) and an
even larger number of Pauline hapax legomena (*presbyteros,
diplē, katēgoria, paradechesthai, ektos, epitithēmi, pykna, prodēlos,
proagein, epakolouthein, despotēs, euergesia, antilambanein*). The
use of *prokrima* and *prosklisis* are especially striking, since the
idea of acting without partiality is Pauline, but he typically
uses the NT neologism *prosōpolēmpsia* (Rom. 2:11; Eph. 6:9; Col.
3:25). The diction, however, *is* a mixture, since many of the
phrases here are also typical of the undisputed letters of Paul:

thus, the use of *prohistēmi* in 5:17 parallels that in Romans 12:8 and 1 Thessalonians 5:12, just as the use of *kopian* for evangelism in the same verse matches Romans 16:6. The phrase *legei gar hē graphē* (for the scripture says) in v. 18 is exactly the same as Romans 10:11. For the use of *enōpion pantōn* (before all) in v. 20, compare Romans 12:17; for *enōpion tou theou* (before God) in v. 21, see Romans 14:22, 1 Corinthians 1:29, 2 Corinthians 4:2, and Galatians 1:20. The use of *phylassein* to mean "observe" in v. 21 finds parallels in Romans 2:26 and Galatians 6:13. The adjective *allotrios* (someone else's) in v. 22 is one Paul uses in Romans 14:4, 15:20, and 2 Corinthians 10:15–16. For "pure" (*hagnos*) in v. 22, see 2 Corinthians 7:11, 11:2, and Philippians 4:8; for "reckon" (*hēgeomai*) in 6:1, see 2 Corinthians 9:5, Philippians 2:3, 6, 3:7, and 1 Thessalonians 5:13; for "weakness" (*astheneia*) in v. 23, see Romans 8:26. The use of scriptural citations and allusions also found in the undisputed letters increases the Pauline "feel" of the passage, despite the large number of unfamiliar terms.

Some translation decisions: In 5:17, *timē* must be translated as "compensation/payment," since the citation of scriptural precedents to that effect leaves no alternative. On the other hand, the use of *timē* in 6:1 in combination with *kataphronein* (despise) in 6:2 points to "honor/respect" as the appropriate translation. Is it possible, in fact, that the topics have been loosely strung together by this word association?

I have somewhat reluctantly translated the phrase *on logō* in 5:17 by "in speech," since "in teaching" also obviously involves speaking. It is tempting to translate as "preaching," (cf. 4:12 and esp. 2 Tim. 4:2), but in this case, a more conservative rendering is safer since we really do not know what activities the elders engaged in. The translation of v. 20 is made complicated by the fact that we don't know how seriously to take the present tense of the participle *hamartanontes*. The RSV translation "those who persist in sin" places a heavy stress on the continuous character of the present and reads the statement against the backdrop of a charge being made against an elder. I have put the emphasis on the rebuke in the presence of all, without special attention to the persistence of the sin.

The term *prokrima* (5:21) appears as a technical legal expression on inscriptions; it means, literally, "prejudgment," whereas *prosklisis* in the same verse suggests an "inclination" (see Diogenes Laertius *Lives of Eminent Philosophers,* Proem. 20). It is used in 1 *Clement* for partisanship (see 21:7; 47:3; 50:2). The two terms together capture the sense of *prosōpolēmpsia* (favoritism/partiality) as in Romans 2:11 and James 2:1. My translation of v. 23 is fairly loose. I have Paul advising Timothy to drink some wine "for the sake of digestion [literally, "on account of the stomach"] and for your frequent weakness [*astheneias,* which could also be rendered "sicknesses"]."

The translation of *proagousai eis krisin* in 5:24 as "parading before them into judgment" tries to capture the sense in *proagein* of "going before someone" as well as the note of publicity suggested by the adjective *prodēlos.* The author almost seems to suggest that their sins (metaphorically) march before them into the courtroom! The sentence is made even trickier by a shift in syntax in the second clause. Rather than using the genitive construction "the sins of some people," the author shifts to a dative of reference in the next clause (*tisin,* "with respect to some others"). The verb *epakolouthein* means literally "to follow" (see Philo *Legation to Gaius* 185) even in someone's footsteps (Philo *On the Virtues* 64). I have tried, then, to complete the image suggested by *proagousai* by having other people's sins "trail along after": the people are visible before their sins are. Verse 25 seeks to clarify all this in terms of people's sins being obviously visible or hidden. But the adverb *allōs* makes an accurate, literal, translation almost impossible. The RSV has, "So also good deeds are conspicuous; and even when they are not, they cannot remain hidden." The phrase "and even when they are not" translates the adverb *allōs.* But the clause could be understood as meaning that *even when good deeds are not obvious, they cannot remain hidden,* which is not Paul's thought. He means that even deeds that are not good cannot remain hidden forever. My translation tries to make the point clearly.

Finally, the translation of 6:1–2a seeks to pick up the nuances of honor/shame dynamics in the Mediterranean world (see Malina, *The New Testament World,* 25–50). The following terms are all part of the same symbolic framework: *axios* (worthy; see Josephus *Life* 250; Lucian *Toxaris* 3), *timē* (honor; see Xenophon

Cyropaedia 1.6.11), *kataphronein* (despise; see Xenophon *Memorabilia* 3.4.12), *onoma* (name/reputation; see Plato *Apology* 38C; 1 Macc. 8:12), *blasphēmein* (defame/injure the reputation; see Philo *Special Laws* 4.197; Josephus *Life* 232), and *euergesia* (an act of patronage/benefaction; see Plato *Laws* 850B; *Letter of Aristeas* 205). Recognition of this is particularly important since Paul works a reversal on the conventional equations (see Comment below).

Literary Observations

In contrast to the fairly well-structured discussion of the widows in 5:3–16, this section of text really does resemble a loose collection of *mandata* without any visible organizing principle apart from the need to address certain issues in the community: in the life of the *ekklēsia*, problems connected with the pay of elders and the handling of charges against unworthy elders; in the life of the *oikos* (or at the intersection of the household and assembly), problems with slaves. As mentioned earlier, the repetition of the term *timē* in 5:3, 5:17, and 6.1 may account for the consideration of these matters in this sequence.

The most noteworthy literary aspect of the passage is the concentration of scriptural citations and allusions it contains. The Pastorals do not cite Torah often. In Titus there is no direct citation. In 2 Timothy 2:19, there is a mixed citation from Numbers 16:5, Sirach 17:26, and Isaiah 26:13, and 2 Timothy 3:8 makes an explicit allusion to the story of Moses in Exodus 7:11, 22. In the present section, we find a direct citation (as "Scripture") of LXX Deuteronomy 25:4 ("Do not muzzle an ox that is threshing"; 5:18), a clear allusion to Deuteronomy 19:15 ("unless two or three witnesses support it"; 5:19), and another allusion to Isaiah 52:5, ("so that the name of God . . . not be blasphemed"; 6:1).

There is also an allusion to a saying of Jesus in 5:18: "The workman deserves his pay." The structure of the Greek sentence could lead a reader to think that this last citation was *also* thought to be from "Scripture." So Nestle-Aland put the question *unde* (from where?) in the margin of their critical edition and suggest Numbers 18:31 and 2 Chronicles 15:7 as remote antecedents. Alternatively, since the precise wording of the statement occurs also in Luke 10:7 (and a slightly different version in Matt. 10:10), it could be argued that this "scriptural slip" points to the late dating of 1 Timothy, since the author was quoting a canonical Gospel as "Scripture." It may also be, however, that the saying from Jesus is added somewhat loosely to the scriptural citation. In either case, one of the striking things about this cluster of citations and allusions is that they are all found elsewhere in Paul. For the tradition of testimony depending on two or three witnesses from Deuteronomy 19:15, see also 2 Corinthians 13:1. For the blaspheming of the name of God from Isaiah 52:5, see also Romans 2:24. Most impressively, in his discussion of the payment of ministers in 1 Corinthians, Paul explicitly quotes Deuteronomy 25:4: *ou kēmōseis boun aloōnta* (the version in 1 Cor. 9:9 agrees with the textual variant in 1 Tim. 5:18). And Paul adds, as further support for the position that they should be supported, *houtōs kai ho kyrios dietaxen tois to euangelion katangellousin ek tou euangeliou zēn* ("Thus also the Lord commanded that those who preach the good news should live out of the good news"; 1 Cor. 9:14). This web of intertextuality suggests either that it is Paul who instinctively cites identical authorities to address identical situations or that a later writer is consciously using the Roman and Corinthian correspondence to address an analogous situation in his own day.

Comment

When discussing the community structure of chapter 3, I offered what I consider to be the most reasonable reconstruction of the *presbyterion* (4:14) as presented so fragmentarily by 1 Timothy. If indeed the main functions of the *presbyteroi* were handling the finances of the community (particularly with regard to the collection and distribution of funds for charity) and settling disputes, then these instructions take on greater vividness in light of the discussion concerning widows. For it is clear that the crisis of leadership we suspected in the case of supervisors and helpers is a serious one in the case of the elders. The most obvious way to make sense of the instructions concerning pay for the elders (5:17), the charges being made against them (v. 19), the caution against ordaining too quickly (v. 22), and the warn-

ing that some people's sins are slow to emerge (vv. 24–25) is
to conclude that some of the elders in the Ephesian community — perhaps some who had only recently been appointed —
were guilty of peculation with the community funds, perhaps
precisely those earmarked for the care of widows (5:3–16). For
a discussion of the literary structure and thematic unity of this
passage, see Fuller, "Of Elders and Triads").

Charges are definitely being made; Timothy is to consider
them only if supported by more than one witness (5:19). He is
to rebuke those who are sinning in front of everyone (v. 20).
These charges concern people whose outward appearance is perhaps good (v. 24). Timothy is warned against getting involved in
their practices (v. 22). I suspect that Paul's deep concern to make
clear who is a widow and who is not is directly connected to this
situation. We cannot go beyond the evidence, but analogous situations through the ages provide some support for thinking that
some elders may well have been supplementing their income at
the expense of the community or, perhaps worse, using the assembly's funds for the support of those women whose behavior
might bring the church into disrepute. This cluster of mandates,
even though they appear to be somewhat disjointed, provide a
sense that the crisis in leadership in Ephesus was real and was
connected not only to divergent doctrines but also to immoral
practices among community leaders.

That presbyters may have been chronically exposed to just
such temptations is suggested by Polycarp's *Letter to the Philippians.* In his listing of desirable qualities in various officials, he
singles out for mention in the case of presbyters that they "care
for all the weak, neglecting neither orphan nor widow nor poor,
but ever providing that which is good before God and man,
refraining from all wrath, respect of persons, unjust judgment,
being far from the love of money, not quickly believing evil of
anybody, not hasty in judgment, knowing that we all owe the
debt of sin" (6.1). Note that the two functions mentioned are
the care for the needy and the hearing of cases for judgment.
If, in Ephesus, elders themselves were misusing funds and were
up on charges, then the structure was indeed threatened from
within. Toward the end of his letter, Polycarp brings up the case
of Valens, an erstwhile presbyter of the Philippian community;

from the exhortations that immediately follow, it is clear that Valens's fault had to do with avarice and the misuse of funds (11.1–2).

Paul's advice to Timothy in the situation he faces shows the insight of an experienced administrator. The only piece of advice that seems a bit odd is that concerning Timothy's diet. Did Paul consider his abstinence from wine to create a lifestyle too similar to the false teachers who forbade certain foods (4:3)? Perhaps, but it is more likely that his discussion of the crisis made him mindful of the stress under which Timothy was operating, and, following the sort of commonsense medical advice of the age, recommended wine as an aid to digestion and to physical strength. The other pieces of advice can still be read with profit by anyone dealing with similar crises: the need to exercise patience, the necessity of being fair-minded and of avoiding prejudice, the insistence on fair process. But the first piece of advice is perhaps the most pertinent because it gets to the root issue of which everything else is a symptom. Paul recommends that the elders be paid sufficiently so that they have no need to practice fraud with the community funds. Simple, but effective.

In 6:1–2a, Paul addresses another sort of problem. It appears at first sight to be purely domestic, a matter of slaves not showing submission to their masters. But this is not a simple snippet from a household code, such as we find in Colossians 3:22–4:1 or Ephesians 6:5–9, which lays out the mutual responsibilities of slaves and masters. Here, the focus is entirely on the slaves. The issue, furthermore, is not one of behavior but of attitude. The slaves are despising their masters rather than considering them worthy of respect or honor. In the ancient world, with its system of patronage and honor, such attitudinal derogation was almost worse than open rebellion. And here is where we find the intersection with the life of the assembly and a hint that perhaps the ideal of "in Christ there is neither slave nor free" (Gal. 3:28) was strongly alive in the Ephesian church. The basis for the lack of respect seems to have been the fact that, in the assembly, slaves and masters were simply "brothers" and equal in their status. That this equality did not get carried over into the domestic sphere could create the same sorts of difficulties as were experienced in the case of women.

The tension between religious ideal and social reality — even in the first generation — is suggested vividly by Paul's Letter to Philemon. Philemon's slave Onesimus had run away, joined Paul, and become a Christian. Paul is returning him to his master, as the social order demands. But he wants Philemon to regard Onesimus "no longer as a slave, but more than a slave, as a beloved brother, especially to me, but how much more to you, both in the flesh and in the Lord." (Philem. 16). In this case also, both master and slave are Christians. Paul addresses himself to Philemon's attitude toward Onesimus. He wants the slave returned to him as an assistant (Philem. 12-14), but will not force the master's hand. Paul does not address the problem that will arise if Philemon chooses to keep Onesimus as his slave. He does not seem to realize that Onesimus might have attitude problems of his own! But in the Ephesian church, we see occurring just such attitudinal reactions among Christian slaves. They are "despising" their owners who are also believers, indeed precisely *because* they are believers (1 Tim. 6:2a). They think that the owners should have translated the egalitarian ideals of the assembly into the social realities of the household, but they have not.

Paul's desire that households reflect the proper subordination of ranks makes his response to this situation automatic. His criterion for supervisors or helpers is that they can manage the children of their own household (1 Tim. 3:4, 12). His expectation of women is that they raise their children in the faith (2:15), and of children that they care for their parents in godliness (5:4). The apostle's concern for the stability and order of households derives both from his clear appreciation of the hellenistic *oikos* as part of the *oikonomia theou* not in the least at odds with *pistis* (1:4) and his concern that a Christianity associated with social disorder will bring the good news into discredit (see 3:6-7; 5:14). In the present case as well, he fears that the disrespectful attitude of Christian slaves toward Christian masters will lead to the name of God being blasphemed (that is, God's own reputation being dishonored, 6:1).

What is most interesting about Paul's response is that he picks up the language of honor and shame — and reverses it. In the social system of antiquity, the masters would be the only ones to be in the position of benefactors and, therefore, also recipients of honor. When asking the slaves to serve their legal masters all the better *because* they are faithful and beloved, Paul uses a term that is startling in this context. He designates such service in 6:2a as a *euergesia,* that is, as a benefaction. By so doing, he suggests that their service is given from a position of strength and nobility and brings honor on themselves, as well as on "the name of God and the teaching" (6:1; see Danker, *Benefactor*).

Cravings for Wealth — 6:2b–10

⁶:²ᵇTeach and urge these things. ³If anyone teaches otherwise and does not attend to the healthy words of our Lord Jesus Christ and the teaching that accords with godliness, ⁴that person is deluded, understanding nothing. Instead he is sick from debates and controversies, from which come envy and strife and reviling speech, evil suspicions, ⁵the constant wranglings of people with corrupted minds. And defrauded from the truth, they think that godliness is a means of financial gain. ⁶Now godliness is a great source of gain, when it is accompanied by self-sufficiency. ⁷For we brought nothing into the world, because neither can we take anything out of it. ⁸But if we have food to eat and a covering, with these we shall be content. ⁹Now those who want to be rich are falling into a temptation and a trap, and into many senseless and harmful cravings that plunge people into ruin and destruction. ¹⁰For the love of money is a root for every kind of wickedness. By pursuing it some people have been led astray from the faith and have tortured themselves with many agonies.

Notes on Translation

Among MSS of the Western text tradition, in particular, there are a number of variants for this passage, which appear intended to improve the text by clarification, especially of obscure terms and expressions. In 6:3, for example, the original hand of Sinaiticus and some Old Latin MSS replace the difficult *proserchetai* (come to) with the much more familiar *prosechetai* (pay attention to), found also in 1 Timothy 1:4, 3:8, 4:1, 13, and Titus 1:14.

The reading *proserchetai* must be retained because it is the best attested and easily the hardest reading, but translators end up turning it in the direction of *prosechetai* simply to make sense.

The Western text makes a number of alterations also at 6:4, mainly by changing the singular *ginetai* to the plural *gennōntai* and then turning "envy" and "strife" into plural forms as well. The text adopted by this translation keeps the singular throughout. More plausible is the correction of *apesterēmenon* in v. 5 to one of several other possibilities. We can see the scribes' point: the verb *aposterein* means "to defraud" (see Josephus *Life* 128) and is used that way in 1 Corinthians 6:8 and James 5:4. But it is hard to fit into the present context. MSS, therefore, correct it in the direction of "having turned away from" (cf. 1 Tim. 1:19).

Ancient copiers also agree with present-day translators in finding the syntax of 6:7 difficult. We would expect something like, "For since we brought nothing into the world, neither will we take anything out of it." The sapiential sentiment echoes Job 1:21 and Qoheleth 5:11–15. But the presence of *hoti* at the beginning of the second clause is extremely awkward, as my translation demonstrates. Some scribes try to ease the awkwardness by supplying an additional phrase, either *alēthes hoti* (it is true that; see Titus 1:13) or *dēlon hoti* (it is obvious that; see Philo *On the Eternity of the World* 75). A fair number of witnesses also have the singular *diatrophēn* in v. 8 rather than the plural *diatrophas;* others, clearly under the influence of 3:9, add "of the devil" (*tou diabolou*) to the word "trap" (*pagida*) in v. 9; and a couple of MSS replace "many agonies" (*odynais pollais*) in v. 10 with "various agonies" (*odynais poikilois;* cf. James 1:2). As a whole, the variants show how carefully some scribes read the texts they were copying and how they were moved, when they saw what appeared to be mistakes in the copies before them, to attempt pious corrections.

The diction is once more at the far end of the continuum that can reasonably be called Pauline, with eleven NT hapax legomena (*heterodidaskalein,* nosein,* logomachia,* hyponoiai,* diaparatribai,* porismos, diatrophē, skepasma, blabera,* philargyria,* peripeirein*) and twelve Pauline hapax legomena (*proserchesthai, hygiainein,* eusebeia, epistemai, zētēsis,* eispherein, ekpherein, empiptein, bathizein, oregesthai,* apoplanan,** and *typhoun** [found only in the Pastorals]). As always, word counts alone are deceptive. I have marked with an asterisk the terms above whose use is explicable by the specific topic of polemic between rival teachers. Likewise, such terms as *porismos, diatrophē,* and *skepasma* find a home in the philosophical topos *peri autarkeias* (concerning self-sufficiency). Paul's use of *arkesthai* (to be satisfied with) in v. 8, as well as his sapiential statements in vv. 6–7, show that he is dealing with the same topic as in 2 Corinthians 9:8 and Philippians 4:11.

There are a number of translation problems that require decision. The verb *heterodidaskalein* (v. 3; see also 1:3) remains almost impossible to render idiomatically, although "teaching otherwise" works in the present context. The term recurs in Polycarp's *Letter to the Philippians* 3.1, and other *hetero-* constructions begin to emerge in second-century Christian literature (see, e.g., *heterognomēs* in *1 Clem.* 11:2). I discussed above the textual difficulty in the same verse with *proserchesthai.* A literal translation would be "does not approach the healthy words," but, half-agreeing with the MSS that replace this verb with *prosechesthai,* I have attempted a compromise, "does not attend to."

The slander in 6:4 contains a number of terms that deserve some attention. In 2 Timothy 3:4, I translated the passive of *typhoun* as "crazed." It is a word that occurs frequently in polemic between rivals, sometimes with the nuance of "puffed up" (see Diogenes Laertius *Lives of Eminent Philosophers* 6.7) and sometimes, as here, with the sense of "deluded/stupid" (see Philo *On the Confusion of Tongues* 106; Josephus *Against Apion* 1.15). The term "ailing/sick" (*nosein*) also appears in such contexts of mental unrest and instability (see Xenophon *Memorabilia* 3.5.18; Philo *Allegorical Laws* 3.211). I have translated *peri zētēseis kai logomachias* as "sick from debates and controversies," although the construction could also be taken as "having a morbid fascination for debates and controversies" (see Plutarch *On Inoffensive Self-Praise* 20 [*Mor.* 546F]). I have discussed in the commentary on 2 Timothy how medical imagery is used in such polemic. Here, we see how mental sickness is connected to "corrupted minds" (6:5; cf. 2 Tim. 3:8) and is opposed to the "healthy words" of Jesus (see 1:10; 2 Tim. 1:13; 4:3; Titus 1:9, 13; 2:1, 2). For good teaching as "healthy/sound," see Plutarch, *How to Study Poetry*

4 (*Mor.* 20F); Philo *On Abraham* 223; and Josephus *Against Apion* 1.222. Finally, I have rendered the word *diaparatribai* in v. 5 as "constant wranglings." This is the only occurrence of the term, which appears to be an intensified form of *paratribē* (irritation/ friction; see Polybius *Histories* 2.36.5).

The term *porismos* occurs in vv. 5 and 6. It is difficult to capture both the literal sense of the term and the play that Paul makes on it. For the first instance, I have given a hyperliteral rendering, "means of financial gain," since that is precisely what Paul means: some people seek to get rich through *eusebeia* (see 6:9). But in the second instance, I have generalized *porismos* to "a great source of gain," since here he definitely is not referring to financial advancement but rather to a "gain" that might be called spiritual, namely, the life of godliness itself. Here the precise sense of *meta autarkeias* is important. I have translated it as "when it is accompanied by self-sufficiency," for the point is that *autarkeia* itself cancels the materialistic sense of gain, leaving only the spiritual sense of "advancement/advantage" (cf. the remarks on physical training in 4:8).

The translation "food to eat and a covering" in 6:8 makes the plural *diatrophas kai skepasmata* into the singular, understanding the plural to correspond to the inclusive plural subject "we." The noun *diatrophē* means broadly "means of sustenance" (see Epictetus *Encheiridion* 12.1), and *skepasma* can mean either "clothing" (Aristotle *Politics* 1336A) or "shelter" (Aristotle *Metaphysics* 1043A). In the Cynic tradition, which made so much of *autarkeia*, the translation "clothing" would be more likely. Because this is the topos on self-sufficiency, I have rendered *epithymiai* as "cravings," in order to fit the overall sense of acquisitiveness in the passage.

The maxim in 6:10 finds parallels in other writings (see below) and is one of the most quoted passages in the NT. My translation is a bit more restrictive than the traditional "For the love of money is the root of all evils" (see RSV). First of all, *riza* lacks the definite article and is properly translated as "a root." Second, the phrase *pantōn tōn kakōn* should be taken as generic: "for every kind of wickedness." Certainly no ancient moralist would confine *epithymia* to the desire for money! In this case of avarice, as with other forms of vice and false teaching opposed by the letter, we find that it is found among those who were members of the community: thus, their vice has "led [them] astray from the faith" (*apo tēs pisteōs;* cf. 1:19; 4:1; 5:8; 6:21).

Finally, the translation in 6:10 of *periepeiran odynais pollais,* while not of great moment, should be mentioned. The verb *peripeirein* means literally "to impale or pierce through something" (see, e.g., Josephus *Jewish War* 3.296). Here, the wound is self-inflicted; they have pierced "themselves" (*heautous*). The phrase *odynais pollais* is in the dative case, describing either the means or the manner of being pierced: they are impaling themselves with many agonies, or they experience agonies as they pierce themselves. The RSV has "pierced their hearts with many pangs," which is literal and unhelpful: what does it mean? In this translation, I have taken some liberty and rendered it as "tortured themselves with many agonies," understanding the point to be that a life lived under such constant craving is a form of self-torture.

Literary Observations

The letter begins a turn to the end in 6:2b, but the topic that has remained just below the surface throughout the letter now becomes explicit, namely, the problems caused by wealth in the Ephesian community. In this section, Paul confronts it with respect to the attitudes of Timothy his delegate. In typical polemical fashion, he connects the mental diseases of the false teachers to a moral sickness, namely, the love of money (*philargyria,* v. 10). A sign that this is something more than conventional slander, however, is shown by the fact that the position holding godliness to be a source of financial gain (v. 5) stimulates the most elaborate theological rebuttal in the letter. After the final charge to Timothy in 6:11–16, we shall find Paul returning one last time to the issues of riches in 6:17–19.

Two aspects of the passage once again raise the issue of 1 Timothy's literary and historical placement. The first is Paul's allusion to "the healthy words of our Lord Jesus Christ" in v. 3, which he combines with "the teaching that accords with godliness." What does he mean by "the words of Jesus"? Is this, in effect, simply a generalized reference to the tradition, and virtually to be equated with "the teaching"? Or does Paul have in mind the specific words spoken by Jesus and handed down orally in the communities? Although Paul scarcely makes heavy use of such sayings traditions in the undisputed letters, he is by no means dismissive of them, quoting Jesus' words at the last supper (1 Cor. 11:23–25) and alluding to his commandment concerning divorce (1 Cor. 7:10). As we have seen, Paul seems also to be quoting a saying of Jesus in 1 Timothy 5:18 to the effect that preachers and teachers should be well paid by the community (see Luke 10:7; 1 Cor. 9:9). There are, as we know, a fairly large number of sayings of Jesus that Paul might have had in mind, if the topic is either service to others as *euergesia* (6:2a; see Luke 22:24–27; cf. Mark 10:41–45) or the fallacy of seeking life in wealth (see Luke 6:20, 24; 9:23–25; 12:22–34; 14:25–33; 16:13). We cannot be sure that Paul is thinking of any such traditions, but the use of this expression between 5:18 and 6:13, with its reference to the speech of Jesus, is at least intriguing.

The second intertextual question concerns the cluster of pronouncements in 6:6–10. The statement in v. 7 bears at least a thematic resemblance to Job 1:21 ("I came naked from my mother's womb and naked I shall return") and a stronger one to LXX Qoheleth 5:14 ("As he came from his mother's womb he shall go again, naked as he came, and shall take nothing for his toil, which he may carry away in his hand"). Such sentiments find parallels in other wisdom literature as well (see, e.g., *Anthologia Palatina* 10.58; Philo *Special Laws* 1.294–95; Seneca *Moral Epistles* 102.25). Similarly, Paul's declaration that *philargyria* is a root for every kind of wickedness in 6:10 is paralleled by even more statements from Greco-Roman moralists. Bion called "love of money the mother-city of all evils" (*philargyia metropolin pantōn tōn kakōn;* see Diogenes Laertius *Lives of Eminent Philosophers* 6.50). Other statements to the same effect — but with slightly less verbal resemblance — are found in Diodorus Siculus's *Library of History* (21.1.4), the *Sibylline Oracles* (8.17), *The Sentences of Pseudo-Phocylides* (42), and Philo's *Special Laws* (4.65).

Allusions to both 6:7 and 6:10, furthermore, are found in Polycarp's *Letter to the Philippians:* "But the beginning of all evils is the love of money. Knowing therefore that we brought nothing into the world and we can take nothing out of it, let us arm ourselves with the armour of righteousness and let us teach ourselves first of all to walk in the commandment of the Lord" (4.1). How should this occurrence be evaluated? One option is to suggest that 1 Timothy has nothing distinctive about it but is simply borrowing from broad paraenetic traditions (see Dibelius and Conzelmann, *The Pastoral Epistles,* 85–86). But in fact the specific *language* of 1 Timothy is distinctive. Of all the parallels yet adduced that share its sentiment, none puts it in exactly the same language. This observation, in turn, has consequences for the way we regard the echo in Polycarp.

If Polycarp was, as H. Von Campenhausen suggested, the possible author of 1 Timothy ("Polykarp von Smyrna und die Pastoralbriefe"), then we could imagine that the same sentiments appear in both writings because the compositions had the same author. This theory, however, ignores the fact that Polycarp introduces these lines in a way that inescapably suggests that they are found in Paul's letters:

> These things, brethren, I write to you concerning right-eousness, not at my own instance, but because you first invited me. For neither am I, nor is any other like me, able to follow the wisdom of the blessed and glorious Paul, *who when he was among you in the presence of the men of that time taught accurately and steadfastly the word of truth.* (*Letter to the Philippians* 3.1–2, emphasis added)

Polycarp here clearly distinguishes himself and his authority from that of Paul, who is portrayed as a man of a previous generation. Polycarp then adds,

> And also when he was absent *wrote letters to you, from the study of which you will be able to build yourselves up into the faith given you.* (*Letter to the Philippians* 3.2, emphasis added)

This statement makes clear that whatever Polycarp adds after it will derive from those letters. After a short transition sentence, which contains an allusion to Galatians 4:26, Polycarp cites *archē de pantōn chalepōn philargyria* (1 Tim. 6:10—not, it is true, an exact citation, but more of an echo), then he follows with a verbal

allusion to 1 Timothy 6:7 (*ouden eisēnegkamen eis ton kosmon all'*
oude exēnenkein ti echomen) before continuing with instructions
that contain further echoes of 2 Corinthians 6:7, 1 Timothy 5:5,
1 Corinthians 14:25, Galatians 6:7, 1 Timothy 3:8, 2 Timothy
2:12, Galatians 5:17, 1 Corinthians 6:9–10, and other Pauline
texts. Polycarp clearly signals that these instructions and sentiments come from Paul. As with other allusions, however, his
citation is not exact, yet it is closer to 1 Timothy 6:7 and 6:10
than any other parallel from antiquity. The evidence suggests
two things: first, Paul's language concerning possessions is sufficiently distinctive to be recognizable, and second, Polycarp is
echoing that language and not some other expression of the
same sentiment.

Comment

The recent study of Pauline Christianity shows that his urban
communities were by no means made up exclusively of the
lower orders. A not insignificant number of Paul's converts, it
seems, could be considered at least moderately, if not extrava-
gantly, wealthy (see Meeks, *The First Urban Christians,* 51–73).
In communities such as Corinth, moreover, the disparities between wealth and social standing could cause real problems in
the assembly, for example, at the Lord's Supper (see Theissen,
The Social Setting of Pauline Christianity, 145–74). A similar sort
of disruption of the egalitarian spirit by visible wealth is seen in
James's criticism of the partiality shown toward the wealthy in
the assembly (James 2:1–6). In short, the presence of wealthy
Christians within a movement that stemmed from a founder
who was intensely critical of wealth inevitably created severe
tensions (see Countryman, *The Rich Christian*).

Throughout 1 Timothy, in fact, we have sensed just such
tensions below the surface. The Ephesian community clearly
had some wealthy members, as the next passage will make explicit (6:17). Some of the members of the community were
slave-owners (6:1–3) whose servants were contemptuous of their
masters' refusal to translate equality into the household. Some
of the women in the community were able to parade in the
assembly not only in good but even in extravagant clothing,

hairdos, and jewelry (2:9). Other women used the support of the assembly to live in idleness and become social butterflies (5:13), while other real widows were not being supported by families that clearly had the means to do so (5:4, 8, 16). The presence of such wealth, I have suggested, posed a temptation to the leaders of the community. We know that charges have been made against elders (5:19–20) concerning matters that do not easily come to light (5:24–25). It is possible that the elders were envious of such pervasive wealth and were taking advantage of it. Surely the instruction that they should be well paid seems intended to forestall such temptation (5:17). And, as we have noted, Paul takes pains to note that supervisors and helpers should not be lovers of money (3:3) or eager for shameful gain (3:8). Now, all of this surfaces explicitly in Paul's charge that some are using godliness (*eusebeia*) as a means of financial gain (*porismos,* 6:5) and, lest we misunderstand him, "seek to become rich" (*boulomenoi ploutein,* 6:9) and, by having this ambition (*oregomenoi*), have been led astray from the faith (6:10).

What is Paul's understanding of the demands of "faith" in this context? His response fits within the broad lines of moral discourse in his age. On one hand, he stresses the danger and deceptiveness of the craving for wealth: people who seek it have "senseless and harmful cravings" that both torture them and lead them to ruin and destruction (6:9). On the other hand, he advises *autarkeia* (6:6). This is a central term for ancient discussions of possessions, especially in the Stoic-Cynic tradition (for selections on the topic, see Malherbe, *Moral Exhortation,* 112–14, 120, 145). As the etymology suggests, it can be translated as "self-rule" or "self-sufficiency." More positively, it can be translated as "contentment," emphasizing the willingness to be satisfied with what one has, rather than having that craving disease that always seeks more.

As a means of encouraging the Corinthians to share their material possessions in the collection for the saints in Jerusalem, Paul assures them that God "is able to make every gift abound for you, so that always, in every way, having *autarkeia,* you can yourselves abound in every good work" (2 Cor. 9:8). Paul writes to the Philippians, thanking them for a gift of money they made to him: "Not that I complain of want; for I have learned, in whatever state I am, to be content (*autarkēs*). I know how to be abased and I know how to abound; in any and all circumstances I have learned the secret of facing plenty and hunger, abundance and want" (Phil. 4:11–12). This is an almost perfect definition of *autarkeia;* ancient moralists (or at least some of them) would have demurred only when Paul added, "I can do all things in him who strengthens me" (Phil. 4:13).

It is this sort of self-sufficiency that Paul urges on his delegate. In fact, he approaches the Cynic ideal in considering food and a covering as enough to make a person satisfied (6:8). We note again that there is a certain kind of creation theology backing Paul's instruction to *autarkeia.* In this case, it is the reality that humans are born with no possessions and die with no possessions (6:7); we *cannot* take anything with us. Embedded in this simple, yet profoundly true, observation are at least three theological corollaries. The first is that true "godliness" (*eusebeia*) must begin with precisely this recognition: that human existence is itself a gift from God that cannot in any significant fashion be improved by possessions. The second is that the insensate pursuit of possessions is a flight from the truth of creation, that is, human dependence on the God who makes all things good and to be received with thanksgiving (4:3). The third is that to make godliness itself a means of gaining possessions is a peculiarly twisted perversion of the proper order of creation and of the human relationship with God.

Closing Commission — 6:11–21

6:11But you, O Man of God, flee these things! Instead, pursue righteousness, godliness, faith, love, endurance, and a gentle temper. 12Engage the noble athletic contest for the faith. Take hold of the eternal life to which you were called, and you professed the noble profession before many witnesses. 13I command you before the God who gives life to all things, and before Jesus Christ who testified to the noble profession before Pontius Pilate, 14keep the commandment spotless and blameless until the appearance of our Lord Jesus Christ, 15which God will reveal at the proper season. He is the blessed and only master, the King of kings, and the Lord of lords. [16]He alone possesses immortality. He dwells in unapproachable light. No human being has ever seen Him. No one ever can see Him. To Him be eternal honor and power. Amen. [17]Tell the rich in this world not to be arrogant and not to put their hope upon the uncertainty of wealth, but rather upon God who supplies us with all things richly for our enjoyment. [18]Tell them to do good work, to be wealthy in noble deeds, to be generous in giving, to be sharers of possessions, [19]thereby storing up for themselves a noble foundation for the future, so that they can lay hold of real life. [20]O Timothy! Protect this tradition! Avoid the profane chattering and contradictions of so-called knowledge. [21]Some have professed it; they have missed the mark concerning faith. Grace be with you.

Notes on Translation

In 6:11, a large number of MSS understandably replace the rare *praupathia* (it is found in Philo *On Abraham* 213, but not otherwise in the NT) with *prautēs* (meekness), which is common in Paul (see, e.g., 1 Cor. 4:21; 2 Cor. 10:1; Gal. 5:23). The difference in meaning is negligible. Likewise some MSS try to relieve the very difficult construction of 6:12 by adding *kai* (and) before "you were called" to create, "you were both called and professed the noble profession." See the addition of *kai* also in 6:16 ("*and* dwells in unapproachable light"). Too few witnesses support the reading to make it likely to have been original.

A desire to make the text appear more familiar may also account in 6:13 for the replacement of *zōogonountos* (life-generator; found in Luke 17:33 and Acts 7:19) with the more obviously Pauline expression *zōopoiountos* (maker of life; found in Rom. 4:17; 8:11; 1 Cor. 15:22, 36, 45; 2 Cor. 3:6; Gal. 3:21). The same motivation is clearly at work in 6:17, where some MSS replace *hypsēlophronein* (literally, "think high things," that is, "be arrogant"; found only here) with the combination *hypsēla phronein*, which is found twice in Romans (see Rom. 11:20; 12:16). Likewise, it was instinctive to add the qualifier *zōnti* to the word *theō* to create "living God" in the same verse, since that combination is found in 3:15 as well as in Romans 9:26, 1 Corinthians

9:3, 2 Corinthians 6:16, and 1 Thessalonians 1:19. The desire to conform this text to that of others may account also for the presence in some witnesses of *amēn* at the end of the letter (cf. Rom. 16:27; Gal. 6:18). The MSS that correct the final prayer to the singular you (*sou*) are probably concerned with the literary self-presentation of the letter as one written to Timothy (cf. 2 Tim. 4:22). The plural *hymōn* ("y'all") here and in Titus 3:15 may, however, fit the quasi-public character of the *mandata principis* letter.

The diction of this final passage is what we have come to expect in 1 Timothy, with a fair number of NT hapax legomena (*praupathia, anepilēmptos, aprositos, hypsēlophronein, adēlotēs, agathoergein, eumetadotos, koinōnikos, apothēsaurizesthai, antithesis, pseudōnymos*) as well as Pauline hapax legomena (*eusebeia, epilambanein, zōogonoun, Pontios Pilatos, aspilos, dynastēs, apolausis, ektrepesthai, bebēlos*), with three terms found only in the Pastorals (*parathēkē, kenophōnia, astochein*). At the same time, there are many touches that are virtually the same as in the undisputed letters: the use of *pheugein* (flee) and *diōkein* (pursue) for moral responses rather than physical ones (6:11; see 1 Cor. 6:18; 10:14; 14:1; Rom. 9:30); the use of *agōn* and *agōnizesthai* (athletic contest/struggle) for moral and spiritual effort (v. 12; see 1 Cor. 9:25; Col. 4:12; Phil. 1:30; 1 Thess. 2:2); the use of the language of "call" (*kalein*) and "profession" (*homologein, homologia*) for moral and spiritual commitments (v. 12; see 1 Cor. 1:9; 7:18; Col. 3:15; Rom. 10:9; 2 Cor. 9:13). Other turns in the passage are close to Pauline usage, but not quite the same. One can compare, for example, the inability of humans to see God in unapproachable light (v. 16) with the language of 1 Corinthians 2:9, or the ideal of being "generous in giving" (*eumetadotos*) and "sharers of possessions" (*koinōnikos*) in v. 18 with Paul's language in Romans 1:11, 12:8, 13, 15:26, 27. But as so often in the case of 1 Timothy—and in contrast to 2 Timothy in this respect—the overall "feel" of the language is inarguably one step farther from what is familiar in the undisputed letters.

The passage as a whole does not present many real difficulties to the translator. In 6:12, the double occurrence of cognate constructions (*agōnizou, agōna; hōmologēsas, homologian*) are troublesome stylistically, especially since the substantive in each case is modified by *kalos,* which, when rendered as "noble," rings falsely in present-day ears. Yet the passage is sufficiently elevated in tone — being introduced with "O Man of God" — that "Engage the noble athletic contest" and "you professed the noble profession" do not seem inappropriate. Much more difficult is how to deal with the asyndetic character of the second part of v. 12. I decided to leave the awkwardness, rather than try to smooth it out by supplying a temporal clause as in the RSV: "to which you were called when you made the good confession."

A similar problem arises in the translation of 6:13. Paul uses the verb *martyrein,* which itself means "witness/testify." Does he want "the noble profession" (*tēn kalēn homologian*) to be identified with that testimony, or is it that to which Jesus testified, as in my translation? The mention of Pontius Pilate, the Roman prefect of Palestine under whom Jesus was executed (see Tacitus *Annals* 15.44.28), is striking. The name never occurs in the undisputed letters, and although *Pilatos* is used frequently in the Gospel passion accounts, the full name *Pontios Pilatos* is found in addition to this passage only in Matthew 27:2, Luke 3:1, and Acts 4:27. The figure of the Roman prefect is developed in the *Acts of Pilate* and other apocryphal elaborations of the passion account (see Elliott, *The Apocryphal New Testament,* 164–225). As with the allusion to the saying of Jesus in 5:18 and the reference to the "healthy words of our Lord Jesus Christ" in 6:3, the present passage reveals an interest in the human Jesus that is roughly proportional to that found in the undisputed letters.

Because the second-century teacher Marcion taught a version of Christianity that was ascetical in character, indeed deeply dualistic; because his teaching had some connections to the broader movement called Gnosticism (which took its name from the Greek word for "knowledge," *gnōsis*); because Marcion authored a book entitled *Antitheses* (opposing the true teaching of Paul from that of the Old Testament); and because Polycarp of Smyrna was an avowed opponent of Marcion, it has been supposed at least since the time of F. C. Baur in 1845 (see p. 4) that the final charge in 6:20 might have particular reference to Marcion and his writing: "Avoid the profane chattering and antitheses of so-called Gnosis." Such a connection is not impossible, but it is unlikely. The fairest reading of this line is not as a specific allusion but as a continuation of the generalized polemic that characterizes the letter. The term *antithesis,* after all, has the simple meaning of "opposition" (see Plato *Sophist* 257E) and is used in logic for the opposition of propositions (Aristotle *Topics* 113B) and in rhetoric for the presentation of the thesis by opposition (Aristotle *Rhetoric* 1410A). In the present sentence, it is combined with *kenophōnia* (literally, "empty sound") that is clearly, as in 2 Timothy 2:16, being used as generalized slander. The designation "so-called" or "falsely so named" (*pseudōnymos*) has a variety of uses but no particular technical sense (see, e.g., Plutarch *On Brotherly Love* 4 [*Mor.* 479E]; Philo *Life of Moses* 2.171). As for the term *gnōsis,* there is no need to take it as a reference to a second-century movement. From the beginning of this letter, the author has scorned the pretensions of those who "want to be teachers of law, without understanding what it is they are talking about" (1:7) in contrast to those who "have come to the recognition of the truth" (2:4; 4:3). The same contrast is involved here as well.

Literary Observations

We can observe the elements of paraenesis again in this final section of the composition. First, Paul makes the familiar transition from the condemnation of false teachers to the positive instruction of his delegate, "but you" (*su de,* 6:11; cf. 2 Tim. 2:1; 3:10, 14; 4:5). Second, Timothy is portrayed as the exemplar for the attitudes Paul desires among the rich as well: his pursuit of virtue is to "take hold of the eternal life" (6:12), just as the good works of the rich will enable them to "lay hold of real life" (v. 19). Third, Timothy finds his own model in the behavior of Jesus (cf. 2 Tim. 2:8): Timothy's "professing the noble profession before many witnesses" (v. 12) is preceded by Jesus' witnessing to the noble profession before Pontius Pilate (v. 13).

The translation of 6:13–16 as a whole is a challenge because it consists of a single extended sentence. As in other places where this occurs, I have decided in favor of many short sentences in an effort to replicate in appropriate English idiom some of the rhetorical effect of the long Greek sentence. Everything from v. 15b through v. 16 is indented by the 27th edition of the

Nestle-Aland critical text, indicating its editorial judgment that this is another hymnic fragment. It is possible: the clauses are well balanced, and there are elements of rhyme, which occur frequently in hymns as well as in other forms of prayer.

We find a deliberate wordplay in 6:17–18 using variations on "rich" (*plousiois, ploutou, plousiōs, ploutein*): the rich are not to rely on riches but on God who gives richly, and they are to be rich in good works! We can note as well that there is some assonance in v. 19 in the sequence *themelion kalon eis to mellon* (a noble foundation for the future), which may help account for the choice of *themelios,* which otherwise seems a somewhat odd direct object for *apothēsaurizein* (to store up; cf. Sir. 3:4).

Finally, the closing exhortation to Timothy in 6:20–21 forms an *inclusio* with 1:3–7 and emphasizes the urgency of dealing with the threat posed by false teachers in Ephesus.

Comment

Paul concludes the letter with what at first sight appears to be an uncoordinated series of remarks (see Dibelius and Conzelmann, *The Pastoral Epistles,* 87–92). Closer examination, however, discovers it to be a well-constructed final exhortation, with the admonition concerning the rich connected to the admonition concerning the attitudes of Paul's delegate and with both rooted in the reality of God.

In my analysis of the previous section (6:2b–10), I suggested that pervasive and excessive wealth in the Ephesian church appears to underlie many of the specific problems that Timothy must address. Here at the end, Paul turns explicitly in 6:17, not to those who seek to become rich (v. 9), but who are already "rich in this world [or "age," *aiōn*]." His advice is brief, but touches on the main points of early Christian understanding concerning possessions (see Johnson, *Sharing Possessions*).

The apostle says first that the rich are not to be arrogant. He does not use the term *hyperēphania,* but *hypsēlaphronein,* "to think high things." We find the same expression used twice by Paul in Romans. In the first case, he warns the Gentiles not to "be arrogant," but to fear (Rom. 11:20); in the second, he warns the members of the Roman church not to "be arrogant" but to be lowly minded (12:16). It is, of course, the great temptation of the wealthy to assume that great possessions means personal greatness. Wealth also breeds a false sense of security. Paul warns the rich "not to put their hope upon the uncertainty of wealth, but rather upon God" (6:17). We are reminded of the poor widows who have been left alone and have put their hope in God (5:5). Paul obviously intends to make a contrast between the illusory character of human possessions and the "real life" (*ontōs zōē*) that comes from God (6:19).

Hope in God is certain because God "supplies us with all things richly for our enjoyment" (6:17). This affirmation of God's generosity and open-handed giving is strikingly similar to the characterization of God as the one who "gives to all generously and without grudging" in James 1:5. The qualification "for our enjoyment" fits within the positive view of creation elsewhere in this letter, particularly the statement that God created things "to be received with thanksgiving" and that nothing created by God as good was to be rejected but was to be received with thanksgiving (4:3–4).

The perception that God is the giver of all gifts, and generously provides all that is needed, leads to the freedom to share possessions with others. Paul's desire that the rich use their possessions this way can scarcely be stated more emphatically, since he uses four roughly equivalent terms in 6:18 to get the point across: "do good work" (*agathoergein*), "be wealthy in noble deeds" (*ploutein en ergois kalois*), "be generous in giving" (*eumetadotous*), and "be sharers of possessions" (*koinōnikous*). The motivation offered is one found frequently in Jewish and early Christian literature — that possessions shared in this life will lead to spiritual riches in the life to come (see, e.g., *m.* Pe ʾah 1:1; *bT* Shabb. 156b; Luke 6:35; 12:33–34; 16:9). In a somewhat mixed image (combining a verb for "storing a treasure" with "foundation" as an object), Paul recommends building a good foundation for the age to come and then spells out the reason why: "so that they can lay hold of real life" (6:19).

The same motivation is provided Timothy. The passage begins with the instruction for Timothy to "flee these things" (6:11), namely, the desires for wealth that lead many to destruction. Instead, he is to pursue virtue and live out the profession to which he was called and to which he has committed himself, and thereby "take hold of eternal life" (v. 12). By so doing, Timothy will follow in the path of Jesus, who before him made the "noble profession before Pontius Pilate" (v. 13). What Paul does not state is that Jesus' fidelity to death was answered by God with resurrection, so that he, too, laid hold of eternal life. That conviction, however, is certainly contained in the characterization of God as the one "who gives life to all things" (v. 13), as the one who will reveal the "appearance of our Lord Jesus Christ" at the proper season (vv. 14–15), and as the one who "alone possesses immortality" (*athanasia*, v. 16). Because this is truly "the living God" (3:15; 4:10), in other words, fidelity toward him and hope in him will find its reward in "true life." This is the "tradition/deposit" (*parathēkē*) that Paul calls on Timothy to protect and preserve (6:20; cf. 2 Tim. 1:12, 14). This is the *oikonomia theou* (God's household management) in the world that is professed by *pistis* (see 1:4). Those who seek knowledge and security on some other basis have "missed the mark concerning faith" (*pistis*, v. 21).

Works Cited in 1 Timothy

Balch, D. *Let Wives Be Submissive: The Domestic Code in 1 Peter.* SBL Monograph Series 26. Chico, Calif.: Scholars Press, 1981.

Bassler, J. "The Widow's Tale: A Fresh Look at 1 Tim 5:3–16." *JBL* 103 (1984): 23–41.

Bjerkland, C. J. *Parakalō: Form, Funktion, und Sinn der Parakalo-satze in den paulinishcen Briefen.* Biblioteca Theologica Norvegica 1. Oslo: Universitetsverlag, 1967.

Blackburn, B. C. "The Identity of 'The Women' in 1 Tim 3:11." In *Essays on Women in Early Christianity,* edited by C. D. Osburn, 1:303–19. Joplin, Mo.: College Press, 1995.

Burtchaell, J. T. *From Synagogue to Church: Public Services and Offices in the Earliest Christian Communities.* Cambridge: Cambridge University Press, 1992.

Campbell, R. A. *The Elders: Seniority within Earliest Christianity.* Edinburgh: T. & T. Clark, 1994.

———. *"kai malistia oikeiōn:* A New Look at 1 Tim 5:8." *NTS* 41 (1995): 157–60.

von Campenhausen, H. "Polykarp von Smyrna und die Pastoralbriefe." In *Aus der frühzeit des Christentums,* 197–252. Tübingen: J. C. B. Mohr (Paul Siebeck, 1963).

Chesnutt, R. D. "Jewish Women in the Greco-Roman Era." In *Essays on Women in Early Christianity,* edited by C. D. Osburn, 1:93–130. Joplin, Mo: College Press, 1995.

Colson, F. H. "Myths and Genealogies — A Note on the Polemic in the Pastoral Epistles." *JTS* 19 (1917–18): 265–71.

Conzelmann, H. *A Commentary on First Corinthians.* Translated by J. W. Leitch. Hermeneia. Philadelphia: Fortress Press, 1975.

Countryman, L. W. *The Rich Christian in the Church of the Early Empire: Contradictions and Accommodations.* Texts and Studies in Religion 7. New York: Edwin Mellen, 1980.

Danker, F. *Benefactor: Epigraphic Study of a Greco-Roman and New Testament Semantic Field.* St. Louis: Clayton, 1982.

Davies, S. L. *The Revolt of the Widows: The Social World of the Apocryphal Acts.* Carbondale, Ill.: Southern Illinois University Press, 1980.

Dibelius, M., and H. Conzelman. *The Pastoral Epistles.* Edited by H. Koester. Translated by P. Buttolph and A. Yarbro. Hermeneia. Philadelphia: Fortress Press, 1972.

Elliott, J. K. *The Apocryphal New Testament.* Oxford: Clarendon Press, 1993.

Fee, G. *The First Epistle to the Corinthians.* Grand Rapids: Eerdmans, 1987.

Fiore, B. *The Function of Personal Example in the Socratic and Pastoral Epistles.* Analecta Biblica 105. Rome: Biblical Institute Press, 1986.

Francis, F. O., and W. A. Meeks. *Conflict at Colossae.* Sources for Biblical Study 4. Missoula, Mont.: Scholars Press, 1975.

Fuller, J. W. "Of Elders and Triads in 1 Timothy 5:19–25." *NTS* 29 (1983): 258–63.

Greer, T. C. "Admonitions to Women in 1 Tim 2:8–15." In *Essays on Women in Early Christianity,* edited by C. D. Osburn, 1:281–302. Joplin, Mo.: College Press, 1995.

Johnson, L. T. *1 Timothy, 2 Timothy, Titus.* John Knox Preaching Guides. Atlanta: John Knox Press, 1987.

———. *Sharing Possessions: Mandate and Symbol of Faith.* Overtures to Biblical Theology. Philadelphia: Fortress Press, 1981.

Malherbe, A. J. *Moral Exhortation: A Greco-Roman Handbook.* Philadelphia: Westminster Press, 1986.

Malina, J. B. *The New Testament World: Insights from Cultural Anthropology.* Louisville: John Knox Press, 1981.

McEleney, N. J. "The Vice-Lists of the Pastoral Epistles." *CBQ* 36 (1974): 203–19.

Meeks, W. A. *The First Urban Christians: The Social Context of the Apostle Paul.* New Haven: Yale University Press, 1983.

Meier, J. P. "*prebyteros* in the Pastoral Epistles." *CBQ* 35 (1973): 323–45.

Mitchell, M. M. "New Testament Envoys in the Context of Greco-Roman Diplomatic and Epistolary Conventions: The Example of Timothy and Titus." *JBL* 111 (1992): 641–62.

Murphy-O'Connor, J. "The Non-Pauline Character of 1 Cor 11:2–16?" *JBL* 95 (1976): 615–21.

Osburn, C. D. "The Interpretation of 1 Cor 14:34–35." In *Essays on Women in Early Christianity*, edited by C. D. Osburn, 1:219–42. Joplin, Mo.: College Press, 1995.

Padgett, A. "Wealthy Women at Ephesus: 1 Timothy 2:8–15 in Context." *Interpretation* 41 (1987): 19–31.

Scholem, G. *Major Trends in Jewish Mysticism*. New York: Schocken Books, 1941.

Schüssler Fiorenza, E. *In Memory of Her: A Feminist Theological Reconstruction of Christian Origins*. New York: Crossroad, 1983.

Scroggs, R. "Paul and the Eschatological Woman." *JAAR* 40 (1972): 283–303.

Sterling, G. E. "Women in the Hellenistic and Roman Worlds (323 BCE–138 CE)." In *Essays on Women in Early Christianity*, edited by C. D. Osburn, 1:41–92. Joplin, Mo.: College Press, 1995.

Stiefel, J. H. "Women Deacons in 1 Timothy: A Linguistic and Literary Look at 'Women likewise...' (1 Tim 3:11)." *NTS* 41 (1995): 442–57.

Theissen, G. *The Social Setting of Pauline Christianity: Essays on Corinth*. Translated by J. Schutz. Philadelphia: Fortress Press, 1982.

Thurston, B. B. *The Widows: A Women's Ministry in the Early Church*. Minneapolis: Fortress Press, 1989.

Verner, D. C. *The Household of God: The Social World of the Pastoral Epistles*. SBL Dissertation Series 71. Chico, Calif.: Scholars Press, 1983.

Wire, A. C. *The Corinthian Women Prophets*. Minneapolis: Fortress Press, 1990.

Wolter, M. *Die Pastoralbriefe als Paulustradition*. Forschungen zur Religion und Literatur des Alten und Neuen Testaments 146. Göttingen: Vandenhoeck & Ruprecht, 1986.

Chapter Three

Titus

The pieces making up the puzzle of this correspondence called the Pastorals are here put together in still another fashion. In contrast to the bare bones of 1 Timothy, we are told more about the movements of Paul and his associates, but in contrast to 2 Timothy, there is no reason to suppose that Paul is writing from a place of captivity. The most natural way to read his remarks — if we had no other information — would be as coming from an apostle freely moving about his mission. He does not identify his present whereabouts, but says that he expects to spend the winter in Nicopolis (3:12). He expects Titus to return to him from his stint of temporary duty in Crete, when Paul sends Artemas and Tychichos to relieve him at his post (3:12). Why has Titus been left on Crete in the first place? Paul gives two reasons: Titus is (1) to amend what is defective and (2) to appoint elders in every city (1:5). Much of the letter is taken up with instructions on these matters.

As noted in the general introduction, there is nothing inherently implausible about these arrangements. We know that Paul sent delegates on just such missions. Certainly, Timothy's mission to Corinth, for example, was to "amend what was defective" (see 1 Cor. 4:16–21). Nor is there any reason to question Paul's interest in organizational matters. He would certainly have been concerned that a new part of the mission field (which is the impression we receive about Crete) have local leaders. The biggest difficulty in placing this letter in Paul's career is that his only contact with the island of Crete we know of was as a prisoner on a ship bound for Italy from Caesarea (Acts 27:1). Paul was accompanied by Aristarchus, but no mention is made of Titus

(Acts 27:2). Difficulties in sailing led to the ship putting up "at a place called Fair Havens, near which was the city of Lasea" (Acts 27:8). The impression given by Acts is that the ship put in there only for a short while. Paul wanted to stay, but because the harbor was not suitable for wintering, and because the majority wanted to move on, the ship left Fair Havens (Acts 27:11–12), never to touch land again until it met disaster. These are not the sort of circumstances under which, we would imagine, a new foundation would be made.

It is possible, of course, that Crete had communities founded at an earlier time as part of the wider Pauline circle, as the church at Colossae had been founded by Paul's associate Epaphras (see Col. 1:7; 4:12). In the same way, it is possible to take the phrase "I left you in Crete" (*apelipon se en Krētē,* Titus 1:5) not in a geographical sense but in an administrative sense, meaning "I kept you in that place." Still, the lack of positive evidence elsewhere for Paul's work in Crete makes it difficult to rely too trustingly on the evidence in this letter alone. On the other hand, it seems equally unlikely that a later pseudepigrapher, with the undisputed letters and Acts available to him, would have picked such an unlikely location for the posting of Paul's delegate.

Like 1 Timothy, Titus takes the form of a *mandata principis* letter (see the discussion on pp. 106–107). The paraenetic elements are virtually nonexistent. Instead of imitating Paul as a model, Titus is to show himself to the community as a model of good deeds (2:7–8). Stylistically, Titus is not "approximately Pauline" throughout, as in 2 Timothy, nor only "marginally Pauline," as in 1 Timothy. Instead, it alternates short sections whose Pauline diction and cadences none would deny (e.g., 1:15; 2:11–14; 3:4–7) with others whose diction and syntax are closer to those in 1 Timothy.

Another distinctive feature of this letter is the way that the instructions genuinely seem to respond to a specific social situation. As the detailed notes in the commentary proper will demonstrate, the evidence in Titus suggests that Paul's delegate was sent to a newly founded and very raw form of Christianity; note the distinctive use of the perfect tense *pepisteukotes* in 3:8b: "those who have come to believe in God." In 1 Timothy, the church at Ephesus already had supervisors, elders, and helpers in place; indeed, Paul could stipulate that the supervisor not be a "recent convert" (1 Tim. 3:6). In the present letter, Titus is to appoint elders or supervisors in every city (1:5). Not only is the native population described as mendacious and rough (1:12), but the same qualities may adhere to converts as well. The evidence in Titus suggests that in Crete the gospel is struggling to establish roots in a context of severe incivility.

The climate for evangelization is made even stormier by opponents who are competing for the religious allegiance of the populace. In 1 and 2 Timothy, it could be stated with some certainty that the opponents were members of the messianic community itself. Although that may also be the case in Titus, there is in this letter a stronger sense of competition from the outside, specifically from Jewish teachers: the opponents are "from the circumcision" (1:10), have "Jewish myths" (1:14), are teaching about laws of purity (1:15), claim to "know God" (1:16), and are concerned with the observance of the law (3:5, 9). Evidence from non-Christian sources makes the presence of a strong Jewish community on the island of Crete in the mid-first century plausible (see, e.g., 1 Macc. 15:23; Josephus *Antiquities* 17.12.1; *Jewish War* 2.103; *Life* 427; Philo *Legation to Gaius* 282). It may be that the teachers to whom Paul refers are not themselves Jewish but, like the agitators in Galatia, are Gentiles who — perhaps under the influence of Jewish teachers — want to stake a deeper claim in the heritage of Torah.

In any case, the opponents appear to be making progress. The degree of their success provides an important insight into the preoccupations reflected in this letter: they are "overturning entire households by teaching what they should not for a shameful profit" (1:11). A fragile Christian community, then, is being threatened, not only by the harsh and misanthropic character of its converts, but also by the ability of Jewish missionaries to persuade those newly converted to the messianic movement that they possess a more attractive version of God's word in the Law, a version that offers the stability of an ancient and stable civilization.

It is, of course, possible that a pseudonymous author created this situation, although the ways in which Titus agrees with, yet differs, from 1 Timothy suggests a fictional capacity of some merit. The question facing this hypothesis is what Titus really adds to 1 Timothy. The alternative position is the one advanced here. Titus is best understood when considered by itself as a genuine piece of correspondence, addressing a specific and real situation of crisis in a newly founded Pauline community.

If such is the case, then three distinctive aspects of Titus come into sharper focus. First, the characterization of the opponents and the treatment of them is sharper and more decisive, appropriate to the threat they pose. Second, the *mandata* in this letter focus, not on the institutional offices of the *ekklēsia* (there is nothing on that after 1:5–7), but on behavior within the *oikos,* for it is the basic structure of the household that is under threat both by the mores of the converts and the suasions of the rival teachers. Third, Titus advances an alternative basis for *paideia* than the law, namely, the gift of God that has been given in Christ and made available through the power of the Holy Spirit. In Titus, grace has an educative function.

As part of my attempt to break the preconceived mold of "the Pastorals," I have tried to establish connections between each of these letters and others in the Pauline corpus. Second Timothy, I suggested, looks most like Philippians, and 1 Timothy most like 1 Corinthians. Of all the letters to which Titus can be compared, the closest similarity is not to the two other Pastoral letters, but to Paul's Letter to the Galatians.

The Greeting — 1:1–4

1:1 From Paul, a slave of God and an apostle of Jesus Christ according to the faith of God's elect and the recognition of the truth in accord with a godliness **2**based in the hope of eternal life, which was promised by the truthful God before everlasting ages, **3**and which he has revealed at the appropriate time by his word in the proclamation to which I have been entrusted by the command of our savior God, **4**to Titus, a genuine child in this shared faith. Grace and peace from God Father and from Christ Jesus our savior!

Notes on Translation

The Greek text of this greeting is relatively stable. A handful of MSS reverse the order of "Jesus Christ" in 1:1 and of "Christ Jesus in 1:4 (see the discussion on 2 Tim. 1:1 on p. 42) and replace "based in hope" (*ep' ēlpidi*) with "in hope" (*en elpidi*) in v. 2. In v. 4, some MSS also add *eleos* (mercy) after the word "grace," undoubtedly under the influence of 2 Timothy 1:2. The fact that every other Pauline letter except Colossians also contains the title *kyrios* in the final phrase also influenced some scribes to add it in v. 4: "the Lord Jesus Christ our savior" (cf. Rom. 1:4; 1 Cor. 1:3; 2 Cor. 1:2; Gal. 1:3; Eph. 1:2; Phil. 1:2; 1 Thess. 1:1; 2 Thess. 1:1; 1 Tim. 1:2; 2 Tim. 1:1; Philem. 3).

In one sense, the diction of the greeting is thoroughly Pauline. Every word except the NT hapax legomenon *apseudēs* (unlying) in v. 2 occurs in the other Pauline letters, and Paul even uses cognates of that word with some frequency (see 2 Cor. 11:26; 1 Cor. 15:15; Rom. 1:25; 9:1; and esp. 3:4). Yet at the idiomatic level, some of the terms occur in phrases that are not otherwise found in Paul. *kairois idiois* (at the appropriate time; v. 3), for example, is found otherwise only in 1 Timothy 2:6, and Paul elsewhere does not use *koinos* in the sense of "shared" as it appears in v. 4, even though he uses cognates in that sense (1 Cor. 1:9; 2 Cor. 1:7; Philem. 17; Gal. 6:6). Some phrases that might intuitively seem un-Pauline, in contrast, are attested elsewhere in the apostle's undisputed letters. For the "elect of God" (*eklektōn theou*, v. 1), see Romans 8:33 and Colossians 3:12; for "on the basis of hope" (*ep' elpidi*, v. 2), see Romans 4:18 and 1 Corinthians 9:10; for "everlasting ages" (*chronōn aiōniōn*, v. 2), see Romans 16:25; for "according to the command" (*kat' epitagēn*, v. 3), see Romans 16:25 and 1 Corinthians 7:6.

The major translation difficulty presented is one frequently encountered in these letters. The entire greeting is a single, long sentence, which works both logically and rhetorically in Greek, but which makes for difficult reading in English. Contrary to my usual practice of breaking longer Greek periods down into smaller English sentences, I have decided to stay with the single complex sentence, at least in part to retain some of the solemnity of the original.

Literary Observations

Titus has the third longest greeting of any Pauline letter with sixty-five words (cf. Romans with ninety-four and Galatians with seventy-six), and is sufficiently formal to have led one commentator to regard it as the introduction to the Pastorals correspondence as a whole (see Quinn, *The Letter to Titus,* 19–20). Titus is designated in 1:4 simply as "genuine child in this shared faith," which captures nicely the kind and degree of association between Paul and this delegate suggested by the other NT evidence concerning him (see Acts 18:7; 2 Cor. 2:17; 7:6, 13–14; 8:6, 16; 12:18; Gal. 2:1, 3; 2 Tim. 4:10). We should note especially Paul's characterization of him in 2 Corinthians 8:23 as "my partner (*koinōnos*) and fellow worker with regard to you." As for the final element in the greeting, only the designation of Jesus as *sōtēr hēmōn* (our savior) is unusual.

Like the greetings in Romans and Galatians, this one expands the portion dealing with Paul's mission. In form, it resembles other passages (see esp. Rom. 6:25–27) in which the good news is couched in terms of a contrast between past and present revelation (see Dahl, "Form-Critical Observations"). Here the contrast is between the *promise* (made before everlasting ages, v. 2) and the *manifestation* (made in the appropriate season, v. 3). The element of continuity between promise and full realization is the "faith of God's elect and the recognition of the truth in accord with godliness" (v. 1) and the object of these human dispositions, "eternal life."

If indeed Titus can legitimately be read as a *mandata principis* letter, which assumes a public as well as a private readership, this formal greeting logically functions as a public legitimation of Titus in his role as Paul's delegate. If Paul has been entrusted with this preaching "by the command (*epitagē*) of our savior God" (v. 3) and if Titus is his associate or partner in the preaching, then he can indeed himself teach "with all command/authority" (*epitagē,* 2:15). In a letter that turns immediately to the problems that need attention, the greeting thus serves to establish for Titus from the start the weight of Paul's own authority and that of God's word (1:3).

Comment

Our approach to each of the Pastoral Letters has been to assume that they are real letters addressed to specific historical and social settings. Titus, therefore, is not to be reduced to a composite picture of "the Pastorals," but is to be read on its own terms. This approach becomes particularly pertinent in the case of the greeting. Are we to see it simply as a loose collection of stereotypical "Pastoral" language, or should we read it, as we do the greetings to other Pauline letters, as rhetoric crafted deliberately to address the situation at hand and to anticipate major themes in the composition? The case for reading Titus as a composition that is not only distinctive but also literarily and theologically coherent is strengthened by an analysis of the greeting based on that premise.

We see first that Paul designates himself as a "slave (*doulos*) of God" (1:1). Although Paul also uses this self-designation in Philippians 1:1 and Romans 1:1, it does not appear in the greeting of either 1 or 2 Timothy. The designation is applied, however, to the delegate Timothy in 2 Timothy 2:24. Is it entirely accidental that this image of Paul as a slave who is under the command of God (1:3) is found in a letter that addresses itself to the submission of slaves (*douloi*) to their own masters (2:9–10)? Is it only chance that makes the author focus on "faith" (*pistis*) twice in this greeting (1:1, 4) to a letter in which *pistis* figures prominently (1:13; 2:2, 10; 3:15), in which "being justified" by God's grace (3:7) is contrasted to "works" (3:5)? Is it only happenstance that "based in the hope of eternal life" occurs both in this greeting (1:2) and in that same statement concerning being justified by grace: "we might on the basis of hope become heirs of eternal life" (3:7)? Or that the recognition of truth "in accord with godliness" (*kat' eusebeian*) in 1:1 is matched once more with righteousness in 2:12: *sōphronōs kai dikaiōs kai eusebōs zēsōmen en tō nyn aiōni*?

The same sort of literary connections can be seen in the characterization of faith as belonging to "God's elect" (*eklektōn theou*, 1:1). Paul uses the term elsewhere (see Rom. 8:33; Col. 3:12), but its roots are in Torah, where such language is used for God's own people (LXX Ps. 88:3; 104:6, 43; 105:5; Hag. 2:23;

Isa. 42:1; 45:4; 65:9; Esther 8:13). By using this term, Paul links his readers to the story and traditions of Israel. He will later claim that Jesus gave himself "to purify a special people for himself that was eager to do good deeds" (2:14). But notice that the greeting also emphasizes that the promise was made by the "truthful/unlying God" (*apseudēs theos,* v. 2) and is received "according to the recognition of the truth" (*alētheian,* v. 1). The truthfulness of God stands in contrast to the lying character of the Cretan population (*krētes aei pseustai,* 1:12), but also in contrast to the pretensions of those "from the circumcision" (1:10) who are faithless and who claim to know God but deny him by their deeds (1:16), that is, are liars. The greeting thus anticipates the polemic against the Jewish teachers who claim to provide access to the tradition of God's own people through the practice of the laws of purity. Paul already makes clear that the "true" fulfillment of the promise made by God in Torah is to be found in "his word in the proclamation" (1:3).

The pertinence of these observations is sharpened when we turn to the way in which Paul uses the title *sōtēr,* first for God in 1:3 and then for Jesus in 1:4. My approach here can be contrasted to that of M. Dibelius and H. Conzelmann in *The Pastoral Epistles.* They make no comment on the use of the title in this greeting (p. 131), referring the reader instead to an earlier excursus on 2 Timothy 1:10 called "Savior in the Pastoral Epistles" (pp. 100–103). It should be noticed how this procedure collapses the witness of Titus into that of a composite impression of "the Pastorals" as a whole. The discussion of the title *sōtēr,* furthermore, proceeds mainly by trying to distinguish the use of the title both in Torah and in Paul from that in the Pastorals, which is thought to be deeply affected by "hellenistic conceptions" deriving from Greco-Roman savior cults and the cult of the ruler. The effect of the entire discussion is to collapse Titus into the other Pastorals, and the Pastorals into general hellenistic religiosity.

The special pleading embedded in such convoluted discussions should be obvious. A more straightforward approach recognizes from the start that the meaning of terms derives primarily not from their ideological background but from their specific uses. It should be clear at the outset, for example, that all of the uses of *sōtēr* in the LXX, whatever the conceptions the term might have had in the Ptolemaic empire (see Dibelius and Conzelmann, *The Pastoral Epistles,* 103), take on specific meanings from the sentences in which they are located. One would not appeal to the Isis cult in order to understand the statement in LXX Psalm 61:2, "He is my God and my savior." It is likewise bad methodology to assume that, because in some Greco-Roman texts and inscriptions the title *sōtēr* occurs in connection with *epiphaneia,* it must mean the same thing in 2 Timothy 1:10 or Titus 2:13.

Above all in Titus, the designation *sōtēr* cannot be regarded as just another honorific for the divine. Four characteristics of its use in particular should be noted. First, the title is used frequently (1:3, 4; 2:10, 13; 3:4, 6) and in combination with the verb *sōzein* (3:5) and the adjective *sōtērios* (2:11). Second, the title points to an activity that affects humans in the most fundamental way — they have been rescued from destructive attitudes and behavior (3:3-7) in order to live in a "godly" way (2:11-14). Third, the language of saving also has a polemical edge, for God's saving activity is contrasted to the effort at self-justification through works (3:5). Fourth, the attribution of the title *sōtēr* to God in 1:3 and then to Jesus in 1:4 establishes a pattern that is continued through the letter. Thus, God is called *sōtēr* in 2:10 and Jesus in 2:13; God in 3:4 and Jesus in 3:6. One could certainly argue from such usage that Titus suggests a functional equivalence between Jesus and God (see Harris, "Titus 2:13 and the Deity of Christ"). But the polemical point is even more obvious: against the claims of those from the circumcision that they offer true continuity with God's promises, Paul asserts that the promise of God had to do with eternal life. By calling Jesus *sōtēr* in such constant and close conjunction with the designation of God as *sōtēr,* Paul effectively identifies the salvation that comes through Jesus as the fulfillment of that promised by God.

In sum, the analysis of the greeting within the context of Titus as a coherent literary composition shows a complex web of intertextual signals which, taken together, create a world of meaning distinctive to this letter.

Leadership in the Assembly — 1:5 – 9

^{1:5}This is the reason I left you at Crete: that you might set right things that are deficient, and that you might, as I directed you, appoint elders in each city. ⁶Someone should be blameless, husband of one wife, having children who are believers and not liable to the charge of being profligate or disorderly, ⁷for the supervisor should, as God's household manager, be blameless: not self-willed, not irascible, not addicted to wine, not violent, not willing to do anything for money; ⁸instead, he should be hospitable, someone who loves the good, is temperate, righteous, holy, self-controlled; ⁹he should cling to the faithful word according to the teaching, so that he is able both to exhort by means of the healthy teaching and to confute those who speak in opposition to it.

Notes on Translation

In 1:5, some MSS replace the verb *apoleipein* (found also with much the same sense in 2 Tim. 4:13, 4:20) with *kataleipein* (used also in 1 Thess. 3:1), but there is not much, if any, difference in meaning. More fascinating is the addition made in 1:9 by Codex Alexandrinus. After the verb "exhort" (*parakalein*), it adds "those in every affliction" (*thlipsei*). A still fuller expansion of the same verse is offered by minuscule 460, which adds at the end of 1:9: "Do not ordain the doubly married, nor make them deacons, nor should they have wives married twice, nor should they approach the divine liturgy at the altar. Rebuke as the servant (*diakonos*) of God rulers who are unjust judges and rapacious and liars and merciless." We will see the same MS making another addition to 1:11.

After the greeting, which was so thoroughly Pauline in diction, we turn to a passage which is quintessentially Pastoral in its diction, having in these five verses three NT hapax legomena (*epidiorthoun, philagathos, enkratēs*) and fifteen Pauline hapax legomena, nine of them attested elsewhere in the Pastorals (*paroinos, plēktēs, aischrokerdēs, sōphron, presbyteros, apoleipein, philoxenos, hosios, hygianein*), and six totally absent from the Pauline corpus (*Krētē, leiponta, katēgoria, anypotaktos, authadē, orgilos).* Again, the most reasonable explanation of this shift in vocabulary is the shift in subject matter.

Even though this section of text is brief, it presents a number of translation challenges, several of them in 1:5. I have already discussed the possibilities for understanding "I left you" *(apelipon)* in the appointive rather than in the geographical sense. But the verse also has a strangely mixed construction: Titus is to "set right *(epidiorthoun)* things that are deficient *(ta leiponta)*." We would be more comfortable with either "fill up what is lacking" or "rectify what is in error." Finally, the placement of the phrase *hōs egō soi dietaxamēn* (as I directed you) leaves it unclear whether it should conclude the statement concerning the appointment of elders or introduce their qualifications.

The lack of a syntactical transition in 1:6 makes translation difficult. The construction *ei tis* (if anyone) recalls 1 Timothy 3:1, 5 and 5:4 and appears to refer to those who should be considered as elders. I have taken the liberty of translating it as "someone should be." There *is* a connective joining 1:6 and 1:7, but its presence only obscures things further. Paul begins by listing the qualities desired in elders; then v. 7 proceeds, "for the supervisor...." Does this suggest that the positions of supervisor and elder (treated separately in 1 Timothy) are here melded? The repetition of "blameless" in 1:6 and 1:7 would seem to point to a separate position now being considered. But if it is separate, why the connective *gar* (for)? It may be that the author was careless or that the positions did slide one into the other, as my reconstruction of the church structure in 1 Timothy suggested was possible.

It is also difficult to know how strongly to render some of the individual terms. Concerning the elder's children, for example, should *katēgoria* in v. 6 be taken in the stricter sense of "accused" (see Josephus *Antiquities* 2.4.3; Philo *On Flight and Finding* 36) or in the broader sense of "category" (see Aristotle *Nicomachean Ethics* 1096A)? Does the combination in the same verse of *asōtia* (see LXX Prov. 28:7; *Testament of Judah* 16:1) and *anypotakta* (see 1 Tim. 1:19) equal —in contemporary parlance— "drunk and disorderly," or does it point to a more subversive pattern of dissoluteness and rebellion? Concerning the supervisor, the combination of *authadēs* (see LXX Gen. 49:3; Josephus *Antiquities* 4.4.24), *orgilos* (see Aristotle *Nicomachean Ethics* 1108A; LXX Ps. 17:49), and *plēktēs* (see Aristotle, *Eudemian Ethics* 1221B; Diogenes Laertius *Lives of Eminent Philosophers* 6.38) suggests a person of such violent tendencies as to be scarcely in control of himself.

Literary Observations

The letter to Titus, like the one to the Galatians and like 1 Timothy, lacks a thanksgiving. The reason is the same: Paul is eager to get down to the business at hand. Indeed, the expression "for this reason" (*toutou charin*) in v. 5 that begins the body of the letter covers the reason for sending this missive as well as for Paul's leaving Titus in Crete. The twofold statement of purpose leads directly into the qualifications for the elder/supervisor. The four verses devoted to these qualifications (1:6-9) exhaust the topic of the *ekklēsia* in Titus. All other exhortations will be concerned with the behavior of the delegate or with the household (*oikos*).

We find in vv. 6-9, a list such as those in 1 Timothy 3:1-13. We have already discussed the care that must be taken in analyzing lists from the hellenistic world, since they tended to contain considerable amounts of conventional and predictable material. But a comparison of the lists in 1 Timothy and Titus is worthwhile. One lesson learned from form criticism is that, when a standard form is used and when there is deviation from that form, the variation is to be taken seriously as some sort of signal. The first thing to be stated, then, is that the lists concerning the supervisor in 1 Timothy 3:1-7 and concerning the elder/supervisor in Titus 1:6-9 contain a number of shared elements. In each, these qualities appear: without reproach, husband of one wife, hospitable, prudent, not given to wine, not violent. But there are also some significant differences that go beyond, for example, the use of synonyms for "without reproach" (Titus has *anenklētos;* 1 Tim. has *anepilēmptos*):

Titus	1 Timothy
philagathos (love of good)	*kosmios* (respectable)
enkratēs (self-controlled)	*nēphalios* (sober)
dikaios (righteous)	
hosios (holy)	
mē authadēs (not self-willed)	*epieikēs* (gentle)
mē orgilos (not wrathful)	*amachos* (peaceful)
mē aischrokerdēs (not willing to do anything for money)	*aphilargyros* (not lover of money)
	mē neophytos (not new convert)

A close comparison of these terms suggests that in Titus the qualities to be avoided are harsher and the virtues to be cultivated are more rudimentary. Finally, we see that whereas in 1 Timothy the supervisor is to run a good household and have his children in good order, in Titus the children are to be believers and not criminals. And whereas in 1 Timothy the supervisor is to be an "apt teacher" (*didaktikos*, 3:2), in Titus he is to "cling to the faithful word according to the teaching" (v. 9). Dibelius and Conzelmann comment that "the variations do not reveal a tendency in any particular direction" (*The Pastoral Epistles*, 132). Is that really the case?

Comment

The instructions concerning the leaders whom Titus is to appoint in each city give us some important clues concerning the situation to which this letter is addressed. The differences from the list of qualities in 1 Timothy cannot be dismissed. When taken together, they do reveal a tendency, which is that the foundation in Crete is new and located in a population with less-than-impressive moral character. There is no specification that the supervisor should not be a new convert for the simple reason that there are no other options; the entire community is made up of new converts. The requirement that the supervisor have children who are believers points to a situation in which Christianity has not been in existence long enough for that to be common. The necessity of noting that the supervisor's children ought not to be frequenters of night court also suggests an atmosphere of rudeness and incivility. And when we see that some of the opponents are disorderly/rebellious as well and upset entire households (1:11), the seriousness and specificity of these remarks become more apparent.

Even the personal qualities demanded of the supervisor point to a situation in Crete that is harsher and less well-developed than in Ephesus. We note that it is sufficient in Ephesus to ask that the supervisor be an "apt teacher" (1 Tim. 3:2); it is assumed apparently that he knows his catechism. Here, the supervisor is to "hold fast" to the word (Titus 1:9). This could be translated as "be concerned with preaching," but given the emphasis placed on "the word" in the greeting, it is best to take this as the supervisor's personal commitment to the right understanding of the gospel "according to the teaching." Finally, the combination of virtues to be cultivated and vices to be avoided are surprisingly rudimentary, with the strong implication that candidates *might be* people who are arrogant and violent and drunken and wrathful. This impression of a rough population will only be deepened as we progress through the letter.

Two other features of this opening set of *mandata* can be noted. The first is that the supervisor is explicitly imaged as God's household manager (*oikonomos theou*, v. 7). Paul applies the same image to himself and Apollos in 1 Corinthians 4:1–2, but it is implicit especially in the discussion of community leaders in 1 Timothy, where the *ekklēsia* is portrayed as the *oikos theou* and the mystery of faith as the *oikonomia theou* (1 Tim. 3:15; 1:5) and where good leaders are judged on the basis of how well they govern their own *oikos* (1 Tim. 3:5, 14; see Verner, *The Household of God,* 145–47). The use of the image here is particularly striking, for, as we shall see, it is the practices of believers within the social structure of the *oikos* that is the special concern of Titus. Second, the supervisor is pictured as someone who must be able to engage in controversy, capable of refuting those who speak against the teaching (1:9). Once more, this is a qualification not demanded of the supervisor in 1 Timothy and points to the critical situation in Crete, where the controversy over "healthy teaching" is upsetting entire households (1:11).

Identifying the Opposition — 1:10–16

1:10For there are many who are also unrestrained, empty talkers and deceivers. They are mainly from the circumcision. 11It is necessary to control people such as these, who are overturning entire households by teaching what they should not for a shameful profit. 12A certain one of them, one of their own prophets, said, "Cretans are forever liars, evil beasts, idle gluttons." 13This testimony is true! For this reason, refute them sharply, so that they might become healthy in the faith 14and stay away from Jewish myths and the commandments of human beings who have turned away from the truth. 15All things are pure for those who are pure. But for those who have been defiled and are unbelieving, nothing is pure. Instead, both their mind and their conscience have been defiled. 16They claim to know God. But by their deeds, they deny God. They are abominable. They are faithless and are useless for any good deed.

Notes on Translation

The textual variants in the passage are few and relatively insignificant. In 1:12 and 1:15, some scribes tried to provide smoother syntactical connections by adding the particles *de* and *men* respectively. In v. 14, the word *entolais* (commandments) is replaced in some MSS with *entalmasin*, probably due to the influence of "the commandments of men" in Colossians 2:22; other MSS replace "commandments" with *genealogiais* (genealogies; see 1 Tim. 1:4; Titus 3:9). The most fascinating variant is again offered by minuscule 460. At the end of v. 11, it adds: "Curb the children who abuse their own parents or strike them, and rebuke and admonish them as a father to children."

The vocabulary is, like the last section, a mix. There are five NT hapax legomena (*mataiologos, phrenapatos, epistomizein, Ioudaikos, bdelyktos*) and ten Pauline hapax legomena (*anypotaktos, anatrepein, Krētēs, martyria, aitia, hygiainein, prosechein, mythos, miainein, arnēsasthai*). Other expressions evoke the undisputed Pauline letters: *hoi ek tēs peritomēs* (those from the circumcision) in v. 10 occurs elsewhere only in Galatians 2:12

and in Acts 10:45 and 11:2; *panta kathara* (all is pure) in v. 15 echoes Romans 14:20; the use of *nous* (mind) and *syneidēsis* (conscience) in v. 15 is closest to Pauline passages such as 1 Corinthians 1:10 and 8:7; *pan ergon agathon* (every good deed) in v. 16 is paralleled by 2 Corinthians 9:8. We are faced with the usual choice: is the author someone who has picked up some familiar phrases from the authentic letters and woven them into his own diction, or is this the same Paul in a less familiar mode?

Some translation decisions should be noted. The translation of "unrestrained" for *anypotaktoi* in v. 10 finds a parallel in Epictetus's *Discourse* (II, 10, 1) and corresponds to the command in v. 11 to "control" (*epistomizein*, which literally means to "bridle/ curb") them. The same adjective is used for the children of the elder in 1:6. We are to understand that these people are themselves unruly and that their speech is particularly misdirected. The identification of them as being "from the circumcision" would seem to indicate that they are Jewish, although it is not clear how many of them are; the superlative adverb *malista* (most of all) is here translated simply as "they are mainly." The designation *hoi ek tēs peritomēs* is used in Acts 10:45 and 11:2, as well as in Galatians 2:12, for Jewish Christians. We cannot simply assume that the same is the case here, but it may be.

In 1:12, the phrase *gasteres argai* (literally, "idle stomachs") is translated as "idle gluttons." For the meaning of *argos* (*a-erga*, without deed), see James 2:20. For *gastēr* with reference to gluttony, see Hesiod *Theogony* 26 and Xenophon *Cyropaedia* 1.2.8. For the sake of poetic sound in the citation in 1:12, I have rendered *aei* as "forever" rather than "always," and in order to balance the sentence in 1:16, I have added the object "God" to the second clause. Finally, the translation of *bdelyktoi* in v. 16 as "abominable" is unavoidable but unfortunate, for the English term does not sufficiently capture the force of the adjective, which is cognate to *bdelygma*, used in the LXX for that which is associated with idolatry (see LXX Deut. 29:16; 1 Kings 11:6) and is therefore abhorrent to God (note its appearance with "uncleannesses" in LXX Prov. 17:15). The adjective is found in 2 Maccabees 1:27, Philo *Special Laws* 1.323, and *Testament of Gad* 3:2, but is a hapax legomenon in the NT.

Literary Observations

As in the other Pastoral letters, the opponents are described polemically. We can detect some standard features of the conventional rhetoric here — the opposition is willing to do anything for financial gain (1:11); they are foolish in speech and deceivers (v. 10), they are morally ill (v. 13), they follow myths (v. 14), their verbal profession is denied by their deeds (v. 16). The polemic here also contains a higher degree of specificity than normal, providing details to the living opposition behind the stereotype: many or most of them are of Jewish heritage or are claiming a stake in it (v. 10); they claim special knowledge of God (v. 16); they are involved with Jewish myths (v. 14); their teaching involves the keeping of commandments (v. 14); these commandments concern purity (v. 15); they are upsetting households by their teaching (v. 11).

The most striking aspect of the description is Paul's use in v. 12 of a citation from "one of their own prophets." That Paul is capable of citing a well-known tag from a poet is shown by his citation of Menander's *Thaïs* 218 in 1 Corinthians 15:33: "Bad company ruins good morals." The line quoted in v. 12 has been identified as coming from Epimenides, a Cretan poet (ca. 600–500 B.C.E.) who, according to Plato (*Laws* 642D), predicted the failure of the Persian mission ten years before it happened. He is called "friend of God and wise man" (*theophilēs kai sophos*) by Plutarch (*Solon* 12). For his reputation as a prophet, see also Aristotle *Rhetoric* 1418A and Cicero *On Divination* 1.18.34. The Greek hexameter is in Attic rather than the Cretan dialect, so it may in fact come from a later writer, although early Christian writers also associate it with Epimenides (See Jerome *Commentary on the Epistle to Titus* 1.12; Clement of Alexandria *Stromateis* 1.14).

At first, Paul's introduction is confusing, for his stating that many of them were from the circumcision could make it appear as though he were quoting a Jewish writer. But he definitely seems to have the native Cretan population in mind. Indeed, this introduction may help clarify the denotation of "from the circumcision" as referring, not to nonmessianist Jews, but to Gentiles who, under the influence of Jewish teachers, wanted to follow Jewish law. This would make the resemblance to Galatians all the more striking.

The characterization of the Cretan population — by one of its own! — is particularly harsh. That they are "idle gluttons" suggests a life devoted to pleasure; that they are "evil beasts" connotes more malicious attitudes and behavior. Such characteristics, however, are cited in 3:3 in Paul's sketch of "our" preconversion morality. The opening phrase, that "Cretans are forever liars," is picked up by the poet Callimachus (*To Jove* 8) and reflects a widespread reputation based on the claim by Cretans to have on their island the grave of Zeus (see Lucian of Samosata *Lover of Lies* 3; *Timon* 6; *Anthologia Palatina* 7.275). The Cretans' claim to possess the grave of a Greek god suggests perhaps a polemical intent of their own! And it is clear the claim was offensive to Greek ears. We shall not linger here on the logic involved in a Cretan stating that Cretans are always liars — and our author stating, "This testimony is true!"

Comment

Paul concludes his list of desiderata for a supervisor in 1:9 with "able to confute those who speak in opposition" and then turns to a description of those opponents. His reason for concern quickly becomes evident. First, the unsavory character of the local population that was already suggested by 1:6–9 here becomes explicit: even a native Cretan prophet testified truly to their coarse and evil ways. The note of violence suggested by "evil beasts" is manifested in their being without restraint and in their willingness to "overturn entire households." The characterization of Cretans as "forever liars" is here turned to polemical advantage in v. 16, as Paul declares that their claim to "know God" is contradicted by their deeds. Indeed, Paul's use of *bdelyktos* (abomination) to characterize them in v. 16 seems to be specifically directed to their claims about access to God through "purity."

The second cause of concern for Paul is precisely the appeal that a nomistic system would have for a population in societal chaos. If, in fact, these areas of Crete were given over to widespread incivility, the need for something to provide structure and stability would be obvious. And this is precisely what the Jewish law, and above all its system of purity observances, could provide, for it enables all reality to be organized into discrete realms and provides for the safe negotiation of life by regulation from without.

Paul's response to this claim, however, is that it simply does not work. Morality is not a matter of rules about things that are pure and impure by nature or decree, but a matter of the disposition of the heart. By locating the moral character of behavior in the *nous* (mind) and *syneidēsis* (conscience) in v. 15, Paul is consistent not only with 1 Timothy 1:5 and 1:19, but also with 1 Corinthians 8–10 and Romans 14. His choice of the language of "defiling" (*miainein,* v. 15) is very effective, for the verb was used for ritual defilement in the LXX (see Lev. 5:3; 11:24; 18:24; 1 Macc. 1:63). If the mind and conscience are themselves "pure," therefore, there is no part of creation that can be considered anything but "pure" (cf. 1 Tim. 4:3–4). But if the mind or conscience is "defiled," everything seen and done is likewise affected by this human disposition, becoming "defiled."

Such is the "healthy teaching" within the community to which the supervisor is to cling (1:9). And his sharp rebuke and rebuttal of the opposition is to be carried out in order that "they might become healthy in the faith" (v. 13). It will be made clearer toward the end of the letter that infinite patience is not to be expended (3:10). But if the lying character of the Cretans and the opponents of the community is made obvious in their deeds, it is incumbent on this community to reveal "the unlying God" (v. 2) who has revealed eternal life through the word of preaching (v. 3) and to demonstrate that truth through a way of life that is fitted to that promise and gift. The identification of the opponents thus serves to set up the positive instructions to which Paul next directs Titus's attention.

Household Instructions — 2:1–10

2:1But you, go on speaking about the things that are appropriate to the healthy teaching. 2Older men should be sober, dignified, temperate, healthy in faith, love, and endurance.

³Older women, likewise, should have the demeanor befitting
a priestess. They should not be gossips or enslaved to excessive drinking. They should be effective teachers ⁴so that
they might advise the younger women to be lovers of their
husbands, lovers of their children, ⁵temperate, chaste, good
housekeepers who are subject to their own husbands, in order
that the word of God might not be slandered. ⁶Exhort the
younger men, likewise, to be temperate. ⁷In every respect, offer yourself as an example of good deeds. In your teaching,
show integrity, dignity, and ⁸healthy speech that cannot be
condemned, so that the one who opposes might be shamed,
having nothing bad to say concerning us. ⁹Slaves should be
subject to their own masters, seeking to please them in every
matter. They should not talk back ¹⁰or pilfer, but should demonstrate complete good faith, in order that they might in every
respect adorn the teaching about our savior God.

Notes on Translation

In 2:5, some MSS offer *oikourous* (mistresses of household; see
Philo *Who Is the Heir* 186) in place of *oikourgous* (workers in
household). The terms can, however, be used interchangeably,
so the difference in meaning should not be over stressed. Probably under the influence of 1 Timothy 6:1, some MSS add "and
the teaching" to the phrase "word of God" in v. 5. More dramatic
variations are offered in v. 7. Scribes appear to have been puzzled
by the rare word *aphthoria* (lack of corruption; for the adjective
aphthoros, see LXX Esther 2:3) and offer several replacements:
adiaphthoria (which has much the same meaning; cf. Plato *Laws*
768B); *aphthonia* (which means "lack of envy"; cf. Plato *Protago-
ras* 327B); and, at the end of the clause, *aphtharsia* (immortality;
cf. 2 Tim. 1:10). The text as translated is the correct one. In v. 8,
we find the familiar confusion between the pronouns *hēmōn* (us)
and *hymōn* (you); contextually, both work, so the decision in this
case is made on the basis of superior attestation. Finally, in v. 10,
some MSS seek to provide a smoother transition by replacing *mē*
with *mēde,* and in place of "demonstrate complete good faith,"
one MS offers, "demonstrate complete love."

There are few distinctively Pauline turns in the language: they are the words and phrases "that are appropriate" in v. 1 (*prepei*, see 1 Cor. 11:13; Eph. 5:3), "be subject to" in v. 5 (*hypotassesthai*, 1 Cor. 14:32; Rom. 13:1), "word of God" in v. 5 (*logos tou theou*, see Rom. 9:6; 1 Thess. 2:13), "slandering" in v. 5 (*blasphēmein*, see Rom. 2:24), and "well-pleasing" in v. 9 (*euarestos*, see Rom. 12:1; 14:18). For the most part, the diction continues the pattern of the previous section, with ten NT hapax legomena (*presbytis, katastēma, hieroprepeis, kalodidaskalos, sōphronizein, philandros, philoteknos, oikourgos, aphthoria, akatagnōstos*) and eight Pauline hapax legomena, four found elsewhere in the Pastorals (*hygiainein, nēphalios, sōphrōn, semnotēs*) and four unattested in the entire corpus (*hygiēs, despotēs, nosphizesthai, kosmein*).

There are few real difficulties in translation. The adjective *philandros* (literally, "man-lover") in 2:4 can be used for a woman's having masculine habits (Plutarch *Theseus* 26) or being lewd in her behavior (Plato *Symposium* 191E), but here plainly has the sense of "loving her husband" (see Plutarch *Alcibiades* 8). In vv. 6-7, the phrase *peri panta* (in every respect) can be applied either to the young men or to Paul's delegate. It seems to work best when applied to Titus's acting as an example.

The ambiguity of the term *oikourgos* in 2:5 was discussed above: it can mean "the mistress of a house/temple" or "the keeper of the house" in the sense of "housekeeper/worker." It seems unlikely that the adjective *agathas* (good) would conclude this list, especially since it rarely, if ever, stands alone, so I have applied the adjective to *oikourgous* to make "good housekeepers." This should not, I think, be understood as a description of how well the house is managed so much as a description of their moral character as keepers/managers of the house (see Helton, "Titus 2:5 — Must Women Stay at Home?").

I have translated *en katastēmati hieroprepeis* in 2:3 as "demeanor befitting a priestess," which may be a little free, but not inappropriate. The noun *katastēma* can refer to an internal disposition (see *Letter of Aristeas* 210, 278) or external bearing (see Josephus *Jewish War* 1.40); the translation "demeanor" seeks to capture the combination. The term *hieroprepēs* basically means "worthy/fitting a sacred place/person" (see Xenophon *Symposium* 8.40; 4 Macc. 9:25). "To have the dignity of a priestess" is not an inappropriate comparison for an older woman.

The verb *nosphizesthai* applied to slaves in 2:10, which I translate as "pilfer," means "to hold back something" and is used for
the secret holding of possessions for oneself (see Xenophon *Cyropaedia* 4.2.42; LXX Josh. 7:1; Acts 5:2). Finally, it is possible
to translate the phrase *didaskalian tēn tou sōtēros hēmōn theou*
in 2:10 either subjectively as "the teaching that comes from
our savior God" or objectively as "the teaching about our savior God." Because of the *gar* clause that follows immediately in
2:11, the objective rendering given here is better.

Literary Observations

The passage is well constructed. The opening present imperative in 2:1, "go on speaking," governs the first five verses, and
the imperative "exhort" in 2:6 controls the remaining ones. The
respective commandments are couched in the form of noun
clauses following these verbs of speaking, using the accusative
plus the infinitive construction. There are purpose clauses in 2:4,
2:8, and 2:10, which demarcate the closing of sections and prepare for the major explanatory clause introduced with *gar* (for)
in 2:11. After that extended statement (2:11–14), the section is
closed by a repetition of the command to speak and instruct
in 2:15.

Titus is told to give instructions on behavior in the *oikos*. The
larger life of the assembly is not in view here. Once more, my
position is sharply different from that of Verner, who says of Titus 2, "Household relationships have been replaced by relationships in the Christian community" (*The Household of God,* 171).
Since the time of Xenophon, Plato, and Aristotle, philosophers
had written tractates "On Household Management" (*peri oikonomias*), seeking to define mutual moral responsibilities within
the social order, and particularly within the basic societal unit
of the hellenistic world, the household (see Balch, *Let Wives
Be Submissive*). The basic structure of the *oikos* was remarkably
consistent. The head of the household was the *paterfamilias,*
and under him were his wife, children, slaves, and clients. It
was an extended, rather than a nuclear, family. Authority ran
from the top down, and submission went from the bottom to
the top, with the lower orders showing respect and submis-

sion to the upper levels: wife to husband, children to parents, slaves to masters, clients to patrons (see Bradley, *Discovering the Roman Family*). The moral teaching devoted to household responsibilities *(ta kathēkonta)* also tended to be fairly standard (see Malherbe, *Moral Exhortation*, 91–93, 96–105), with particular attention given to the dynamics existing between the mutually defining pairs: husband/wife; parents/children; slaves/masters. In Colossians 3:18–4:1 and Ephesians 5:21–6:9, Paul (or a follower) addresses the dynamics for each of these pairs.

The "household code" in Titus 2:1–10 differs from those in the other Pauline letters in two obvious ways. The first is that no attention is given to reciprocal pairs. Two of the categories treated — older men and younger men — do not fit within the dyadic structure of the household's power arrangements. The only angle into "natural family" dynamics is through the instructions given to the older women, who, in addition to their own virtuous qualities, are to instruct younger women in the proper attitudes toward husbands and children, but there is no corresponding instruction to husbands and male children! Likewise, there is no instruction to masters corresponding to that given to slaves. The second distinction from the other Pauline versions of the household code is the lack of legitimating language, such as "in the Lord" or "because of the Lord" or "as pleasing the Lord," that Paul sprinkles into the directives in Colossians and Ephesians.

Comment

In this passage, we meet one of the distinguishing marks of Titus among the three Pastoral Letters. First and Second Timothy concentrated primarily on behavior in the *ekklēsia,* whereas Titus focuses on the *oikos.* Not church leaders but various age and gender groups in the extended hellenistic household are instructed. What is most startling is the banal character of the instructions. The instructions to the older and younger men could scarcely be more general. For older men, only the note that they should have "endurance" strikes a note of specificity (2:1). Younger men are told only to be "reasonable/temperate" *(sōphronein,* v. 6).

Special attention is given to those on the lower end of the

power structure in the *oikos,* women and slaves. The instructions
to older women recognize their special role in the household in
two ways. First, Paul emphasizes their responsibility to provide
a model of dignity. They are not to be gossipers and drinkers,
but are to have the bearing of priestesses! Second, Paul recognizes their authority to teach within the household (2:3). We
are reminded of the distinction drawn between the public and
private spheres in 1 Timothy 2:11–15 and the way in which Timothy's mother and grandmother were his instructors in the faith
(2 Tim. 1:5; 3:14–15). In particular, the older women have the
responsibility of being "good teachers" of the younger women.

It is through the instruction of these older women that we
catch a glimpse of the desired qualities for women in this
context. They are clearly domestic in character, and fairly rudimentary. The instruction to be good "keepers" of the house
points to their specific sphere of authority (see Xenophon *Oecumenicus*). But this authority is clearly meant to be subordinate
to that of their husbands. Perhaps we gain some sense of the specific situation in the Cretan communities from two small details
in this instruction. First, the younger women's obedience is to be
to "their own husbands." Can we detect a hint of the influence
of other male teachers making inroads into the structure of domestic authority (see 1:11)? Second, the women are to be taught
to love their husbands and children (2:4). The virtues themselves
are well attested in the literature (for *philandros,* see Plutarch *Alcibiades* 8; for *philoteknos,* see 4 Macc 14:13; 15:4; Plutarch *The
Education of Children* 20 [*Mor.* 14B]; *On Having Many Friends* 2
[*Mor.* 93F]). What is surprising is that these are qualities that
need to be taught. Is this a sign of the savageness and incivility
of the native population, that responses ordinarily thought to be
"natural" should require teaching?

The instruction to the slaves (2:9–10) likewise has the standard command to be subordinate. But does the specification of
"to their own masters" point, as in the case of young women,
to the influence or appeal of powerful allegiances outside the
sphere of the *oikos?* And while we may not find surprising the
exhortation to be pleasing in every respect, or to show complete
fidelity, the specific instructions not to "pilfer/steal" and not to
"talk back" seem, once more, so rudimentary as to suggest — if

we are to take these as real instructions for a real situation — a population that is in need of the most basic moral formation.

The overall impact of these instructions is to strengthen the conventional household structure. The emphasis is on the transmission of wisdom from the older to the younger, and on the subordination of women and slaves to those considered their social superiors. This effect is heightened by the three motivation statements (vv. 5, 8, 10). In v. 5, the behavior of the women — specifically their subordination to their own husbands — is commanded so that "the word of God might not be slandered [or blasphemed]."

In the Greco-Roman world, insubordination or instability in the *oikos* was reason enough to condemn a religious movement (see the account of the banishment of the Bacchic cult by Livy *History of Rome* 39.8–19). Thus, if the Christian household does not demonstrate the culture's sense of what is appropriate, the preaching ("word of God") can be brought into discredit. There may also be a hint of the rivalry between this Pauline mission and the law-observant mission of those "from the circumcision" which is upsetting entire households and threatening to bring the entire mission into discredit (see 1:10–11). That problem seems even more obvious in the second motivation statement. Paul has just told Titus that he must be an example of good works and virtue in every respect, and he provides this reason, "so that the one who opposes might be shamed, having nothing bad to say concerning us" (2:8). Now it is not the message but the messengers that might come under attack, though it is not certain whether "the one who opposes" is a rival teacher or some complete outsider who considers the intrasect rivalry reason enough to dismiss and seek to destroy the movement.

Finally, the behavior of slaves is given the same motivation. The Roman empire in particular was suspicious of any teaching that might cause unrest among the huge slave population (See Finley, *Ancient Slavery and Modern Ideology,* 93–122). It is fascinating, then, to see that whereas the two previous statements were couched in terms of avoiding opprobrium, this last one is cast in a positive form, "in order that they might in every respect adorn the teaching about our savior God" (2:10). The mention of "our savior God" (or "God our savior") leads in turn to the explanatory statement in 2:11-14 that makes sense of these otherwise banal instructions and provides one of the most important keys to the interpretation of Titus as a whole.

Grace That Educates — 2:11-15

2:11 For God's grace has appeared. It gives salvation to all people. **12**It educates us, so that, once having rejected ungodliness and worldly desires, we might live prudently, righteously, and in godly fashion during the present time, **13**as we await the blessed hope and the appearance of the glory of the great God and of our savior Jesus Christ. **14**He gave himself for us, so that he might ransom us from every kind of lawlessness, and might purify a special people for himself that was eager to do good deeds. **15**Speak and exhort these things, and reprove with all authority. Let no one treat you scornfully.

Notes on Translation

The text of this section is remarkably stable. In 2:11, some MSS offer variations for the adjective *sōtērios* (gives salvation), which is a NT hapax, replacing it with *sōtēr* (savior) or "our savior." The adjective is the hardest reading and is surely the correct one. In v. 13, some MSS reverse the sequence "Jesus Christ" and have "Christ Jesus." We have seen that this is a common occurrence in the Pastorals see pp. 42 and 215). In 2:15, Codex Alexandrinus has "teach" rather than "speak these things." And a few MSS replace the NT hapax *periphronein* (despise/scorn) in v. 15 with the more familiar *kataphronein* (see Rom. 2:4; 1 Cor. 11:22).

The diction is much more recognizably Pauline than in the previous section. There are four NT hapax legomena (*sōtērios, sōphronōs, periousios,* and *periphronein*) and five Pauline hapax legomena (*epiphanein, arnēsesthai, kosmikos, eusebōs, lytroun*). For many of these terms, however, Paul uses cognates: he does not use *lytroun,* for example, but *apolytrōsis* is a key term for him (see Rom. 3:24; 8:23; 1 Cor. 1:30); he does not use *periphronein* but does use *kataphronein;* he makes no use of *sōphronōs,* but does of *sōphronein* (Rom. 12:3); he does not use *epiphanein,* but does use *epiphaneia* (2 Thess. 2:8), *phainein* (Phil. 2:15), *phaneros* (1 Cor. 3:13), and *phaneroun* (Rom. 16:26). As a result, the entire passage has a "feel" that is more Pauline.

Nevertheless, the diction retains that strange mixture of elements that is characteristic of the Pastorals. The phrase *charis tou theou*, for example, is a favorite of Paul's (see Rom. 6:15; 1 Cor. 1:4; 3:10; 2 Cor. 6:1; Eph. 3:2; Col. 1:6; 2 Thess. 1:12), but Paul never speaks of its "appearing," as we find it in 2:11. Paul never uses *sōtērios* (giving salvation), but "salvation" (*sōtēria*), specifically by God's gift or favor, is central to his writings (see Rom. 1:16; 2 Cor. 1:6; 6:2; and esp. Eph. 2:5, 8). Likewise, as we have seen several times earlier, whereas Paul does not speak of life before God in terms of being "godly" (*eusebōs*), he does, as in v. 12, use *asebeia* for a life in rebellion against God (Rom. 1:18; 11:26). Paul also speaks of that life in terms of "lawlessness" (*anomia*, see Rom. 4:7; 6:19; 2 Cor. 6:14; 2 Thess. 2:7) as Titus does in v. 14. Paul frequently speaks of "desires/passions" as problematic (Rom. 1:24; Gal. 5:16), but he nowhere else refers to them as "worldly (*kosmikas*) passions" as in v. 12. The idea in v. 13 of living in expectation (*prosdechesthai*) and in hope (*elpidi*) is familiar in Paul's other letters (see Rom. 16:2 and Phil. 2:29 for "expectation"; see Rom. 4:7 and 8:20, 24 for "hope"), but not the idea of "expecting the blessed hope." The idea of being "zealous/eager" (*zēlōtēs*) in v. 14 is found in Paul (1 Cor. 14:12; Gal. 1:14), but not in combination with "good deeds" (*kalōn ergōn*). And so on. One phrase that strikes the reader as distinctively Pauline is "who gave himself for us" (*hos edōken heauton hyper hēmōn*), which so strongly echoes Galatians 1:4, 2:20, and Ephesians 5:2.

The passage demands a certain number of critical translation decisions. The first, of course, is how to render the expression *charis tou theou* in 2:11. The genitive construction is subjective, referring to an attitude or action that God has revealed, rather than one directed to God. But the precise valence of *charis* is difficult. I have chosen the English "grace," simply because it has become so neutral; unfortunately, it has also become almost devoid of significance. The term suggests two things: the *favor* shown by one party to another and the *unearned* character of that favor. The translation "gift of God" might work almost as well. In the same clause, the decision must be made between "the saving grace of God has appeared to all" and (as here) "the grace of God has appeared, giving salvation to all." They are equally inclusive, but the second translation plainly emphasizes that the *salvific* character of God's gift extends to all humans.

Another decision involves the appearance of *tou megalou theou kai sōtēros hēmōn Iēsou Christou* in v. 13. I have separated "great God" and "our savior Jesus Christ," since it seems more natural for the Greek construction to be read that way. But it is possible to read them as equivalent: "our great God and savior, Jesus Christ." Although the NT generally is chary about the application of the title *theos* to Jesus, it is equally true that Paul understood Christ in terms that were more than human and attributed divine qualities and attributes to him. In Romans 9:5, in fact, Paul may also have applied the title of *theos* to Christ. It is not the impossibility of Paul's theological thinking that directs my translation, only my sense of how the Greek might more naturally be read (see Wainwright, "The Confession 'Jesus Is God' "; Harris, "Titus 2:13 and the Deity of Christ").

Literary Observations

In form, this passage most resembles those other kerygmatic statements in the NT that appear as highly compressed summaries of God's work as experienced in the world (see, e.g., Rom. 3:21–26; 2 Cor. 5:16–21; Gal. 4:1–7; Eph. 2:1–10; Col. 1:15–20; 1 Tim. 2:4–6; 2 Tim. 1:9–10) and is correctly recognized as a particularly rich and powerful expression of Christian soteriology. The statement is structured by diverse agents and different temporal moments. The primary agent is God, whose "favor" toward humans works to save them; in remarkable unity (and perhaps identity) with *ho theos* is Jesus Christ, certainly savior and, as we have seen, perhaps also "God our savior." The third agent is humanity itself, which has been shaped to be a specific people and is now capable of living in a certain fashion. Temporally, we see that God/Christ have worked in the past: God's favor "appeared" and Christ "gave himself." But they continue to work in the present, for the grace "educates Christians" so that they can "live in the now age" in a new manner. Christians have already received the gift, live now in a new fashion, and await the future "blessed hope" that will come from the "glorious appearance" of God and Christ.

Two kinds of intertextual echoes can be detected in the statement as well. The first, as I noted above, is the distinctively Pauline expression, "He gave himself for us" (see Gal. 1:4; 2:20; Eph. 5:2). It is remarkable that the critical text of Nestle-Aland (27th ed.), which sedulously notes all cross-references in the margins, should so completely miss this one. The reason must surely be that the authentic Pauline letters are not regarded as the appropriate point of reference for the Pastorals, and, perhaps even unconsciously, the editors do not even "hear" the echoes that are there.

The second echo is scriptural. The last part of the statement, found in the purpose clause of 2:14, is filled with the language of Torah: "ransoming" (*lytrōsētai*), "cleansing" (*katharisē*), "chosen people" (*laon periousion*), "zealous" (*zēlōtēs*). There are, in fact, several specific passages from the LXX that this statement particularly recalls. In LXX Psalm 130:8, we read, "and he himself will ransom Israel from all its lawless deeds" (*kai autos lytrōsetai ton Israēl ek pasōn tōn anomiōn autou*). In LXX Deuteronomy 14:2, we find, "because you are a holy people to the Lord your God, and the Lord your God has chosen you so that you become for him a chosen people out of all the nations on the face of the earth" (*hoti laos hagios ei tō kyriō tō theō sou, kai se exelexato kyrios ho theos sou genesthai se autō laon periousion apo pantōn tōn ethnōn tōn epi prosopou tēs gēs*). Likewise in LXX Exodus 19:5, "You will be to me a chosen people from all the nations" (*esesthe moi laos periousios apo pantōn tōn ethnōn*). Finally, in LXX Ezekiel 37:23, "I will rescue them from all their lawlessnesses in which they have sinned, and I will cleanse them, and they will be for me a people" (*rhysomai autous apo pasōn tōn anomiōn autōn hōn hēmartēsan en autais kai kathariō autous kai esontai moi eis laon*).

What is most intriguing about this kerygmatic statement in vv. 11–14, however, is that it takes the form of an explanatory clause: "for (*gar*) the grace of God has appeared." Determining the precise significance of that construction leads us to the interpretation of the passage in its present context.

Comment

The placement of this magnificent kerygmatic statement is not accidental. The author did not suddenly feel the need, after so many practical instructions, to insert some theology. The position and the wording of the statement are alike carefully constructed. In order to grasp this, we can begin with the position. Verse 11 begins with the particle *gar* (for), which signals that the statement to follow should be understood as foundation or explanation for what preceded. What went before in this case, we recall, was a set of instructions notable mainly for its banality, causing us to wonder what sort of population required instructions at such a rudimentary level. That passage ended with the third of the motivational clauses. If slaves behaved properly (not being refractory and not pilfering), then they would adorn the teaching "about our savior God" (2:10). This kerygmatic statement, in turn, provides the *didaskalia* concerning the saving gift of God.

The connection to the instructions is direct. Everything in the letter to this point has suggested that before their conversion, these Christians had been dominated by "every sort of lawlessness," were driven by "godlessness" and "worldly desires," and had not, in fact, been capable of living lives of prudence, justice, and godliness. Their good behavior in the household "adorns" that teaching because it shows the gift to have been real. It is by the appearance of the grace of God that they are able to live during "the now age" in an entirely different manner. When looking at the instructions, we wondered what sort of world required young women to be taught to love their husbands and children. It appears that civilization, and culture, are not necessarily "natural" and that the habits of the heart that build communities of meaning and of meaningful relationships can be forgotten and lost or abused and destroyed. Sometimes civilization needs to be taught for the first time to the savage heart or relearned by the heart grown savage.

This brings us to the most important word in the statement, the participle *paideuousa* in v. 12. It is in the present tense, meaning that the action is contemporary and continuous. It is active, and its subject is "the grace of God." Most significantly, the verb *paideuein* in this context must mean precisely "educating in human culture." The cognate noun *paideia* can be taken as symbolizing the entire complex world of meaning that we call Greek culture — the world based on cities and the rational exchange of discourse and the replacement of violence with legal process (Plato *Republic* 376E; Aristotle *Politics* 1338A; see Jaeger, *Paideia: The Ideals of Greek Culture*). In the hellenistic-Jewish writing the *Letter of Aristeas,* we find this sense of the verb: "lovers of learning... are beloved by God, for they have educated (*pepaideukotes*) their minds toward what is excellent" (287; see also Plato *Laws* 741A; Xenophon *Memorabilia* 1.2.1; Josephus *Jewish War* 7.343; Acts 7:22). Paul's point, then, is that in this instance grace itself educates in humanity. How it does this will be spelled out more fully in 3:4–7.

The statement here also has a polemical application. I noted above the intensely scriptural tone of the purpose clause in v. 14: "so that he might ransom us from every kind of lawlessness, and might purify a special people for himself that was eager to do good deeds." Remember the challenge from the side of those "from the circumcision," who are advancing a solution to the incivility of Crete based on the observance of law, in particular on the laws of purity (1:10–15). The language of 2:14 appears to be deliberately shaped as a rebuttal to their position. Through the death of Jesus, God has "ransomed/redeemed" them from all their "lawlessness." The term *anomia* is particularly apt, for the sociological term *anomie* (lack of norms) seems to describe perfectly the situation Titus faces. But instead of providing them with a code of pure and impure, God has directly "purified them." We remember the statement in 1:15 that to the pure all things are pure; Paul here claims that God has purified for himself a special people, distinguished not by its external code but by its internal capacity to live "in the now age" with prudence, righteousness, and godliness. They are a people, in short, "eager to do good deeds." And because of this, they are able to live within the structures of society in a positive rather than in a destructive way. Those who think that this is a meager accomplishment may not have checked the headlines from any major city newspaper lately.

Newness of Life in the Holy Spirit — 3:1–8a

3:1 Remind them to be submissive to rulers and authorities, to be obedient, to be ready for every good deed, **2**to slander no one, to be peaceful, reasonable, showing complete meekness toward all people. **3**For we also were once thoughtless, faithless, deceived, enslaved to a variety of passions and pleasures, living a life of wickedness and envy. We were hateful and we hated each other. **4**But when our savior God's kindness and love for humanity appeared, **5**he saved us — not on the basis of the deeds which we in righteousness had accomplished, but according to his own mercy — by means of a washing that led to rebirth and new life from the Holy Spirit, **6**which he poured out on us abundantly through Jesus Christ our savior, **7**so that, having been made righteous by his grace, we might on the basis of hope become heirs of eternal life. **8a**This saying is reliable.

Notes on Translation

In 3:1, the lack of copulatives bothered some ancient scribes as much as it does the present-day translator, with the result that many MSS supply *kai* (and) between *archais* (rulers) and *exousiais* (authorities). The only other recourse is to turn one of the two substantives into an adjective: "ruling authorities" or "rulers in authority." The combination *archai kai exousiai* in Paul is predominantly used of superhuman spiritual powers (see 1 Cor. 15:24; Eph. 1:21; 3:10; Col. 1:16; 2:10), but is found elsewhere with reference to human rulers (see, e.g., Luke 20:20); compare Paul's reference to the imperial power as "those holding authority (*exousia*)" in Romans 13:1 and the command in 1 Timothy 2:2 to pray for "kings and all those in high places."

The only other significant textual variants are found in 3:5, where some MSS understandably felt the urge to supply the preposition *dia* (through) before the phrase "Holy Spirit," and in 3:7, where some MSS offer the aorist active *genōmetha* rather than the aorist passive *genēthōmen* for the verb "to become"; in both cases, the difference in meaning is negligible.

The diction of the passage is, once more, closer to Paul's other letters than we find in some other parts of the Pastorals. There is only one NT hapax legomenon (*stygētos*), but there are nine Pauline hapax legomena (*hypomimnēskein, peitharchein, hēdonē, poikilos, philanthrōpia, epiphanein, palingenesia, amachos, diagein*); of these, *amachos* and *diagein* are found only in the Pastorals. It is not simply that the other words are attested in the undisputed letters, but that they are used frequently and in the manner they are deployed here. No argument need be made about such signature Pauline terms as *charis, ergon, dikaiosynē, dikaioun,* and *klēronomos.* But there are also many small touches that resonate with Paul's usage elsewhere. The use of *hypotassesthai* for subordination in 3:1 (and in 2:5, 9) is precisely the same as in Romans 13:1, 1 Corinthians 16:16, and Colossians 3:18. The expression "to be ready" (*hetoimos einai*) in v. 1 is found in 2 Corinthians 9:5 and 10:6, and "for every good deed" (*eis pan ergon agathon*) in 2 Corinthians 9:8. Paul uses the verb "to slander" (*blasphēmein*) as it is used in v. 2 in Romans 14:16 and 1 Corinthians 10:30. For *epieikēs* (reasonable/gentle) in v. 2, see Philippians 4:5, "Let your reasonableness become known to all people."

Paul also uses *praytēs* (meekness) consistently as a virtue (v. 2; see 1 Cor. 4:21; Gal. 5:23; 6:1; Eph. 4:2; Col. 3:12. The most striking use is in 2 Corinthians 10:1, where he speaks of the *praytēs* and *epieikeia* of Christ (see Leivestad, "The Meekness and Gentleness of Christ"). And so on, for other terms in the passage: *anoētai* in v. 3 (see Gal. 3:1, 3; Rom. 1:14); *apeitheis* in v. 3 (Rom. 1:30); *planōmenoi* in v. 3 (1 Cor. 6:9; Gal. 6:7); *douleuein* in v. 3 (Rom. 6:6; 7:6; Gal. 4:8-9); *epithymia* in v. 3 (Rom. 1:24; 6:12); *kakia* in v. 3 (Rom. 1:29); *phthonos* in v. 3 (Rom. 1:29; Gal. 5:21); *sōzein* in v. 5 (1 Cor. 15:2; Rom. 5:9-10). Paul speaks easily of God's "kindness/sweetness" (*chrēstotēs,* v. 4) toward humans, as in Romans 2:4, 11:22, and Ephesians 2:7, as well as of God's *eleos* (mercy) toward them, as in Romans 9:23, 11:31, 15:9, and Ephesians 2:8.

Even some of the terms that may not be quite as familiar find a place elsewhere in Paul. The term *loutron,* which I have translated in v. 5 as "a washing" — and which seems without question to be a reference to baptism — is found in Ephesians 5:26 in the same connection, but in 1 Corinthians 6:11, we also find "you were washed (*apelousasthe*), you were sanctified (*hēgiasthēte*)," again with probable reference to baptism (cf. Boismard, *Quartre Hymnes*). Similarly, the noun *anakainōsis,* which means literally "renewal/new-again" and which I have translated in v. 5 as "new life," is found in Romans 12:2. Finally, the verb *ekchein* (to pour out) in v. 6 is found (in the form *ekchynnomai*) in a remarkably similar construction in Romans 5:5: "the love of God has been poured into our hearts through the Holy Spirit."

Two key nouns in this section are not attested elsewhere in Paul but are widely used in hellenistic literature. The first is *philanthrōpia* (literally, "love for humanity"), which is found only in v. 4 and in Acts 28:2, with reference to the hospitality of the Maltans. It is a quality that is sometimes ascribed to God (or the gods), as in Lucian of Samosata *(Twice Accused* 1), Philo *(On the Cherubim* 99), and Josephus (*Antiquities* 1.1.4), and it is attributed to the Spirit of Wisdom in Wisdom of Solomon 1:6. When used of human rulers, it is sometimes combined, as here, with *chrēstotēs* (kindness; see LXX Esther 8:12k–l; Philo *Special Laws* 2.141; Josephus *Antiquities* 10.9.3). The quality of *chrēstotēs* is frequently attributed to the Lord by the Psalms (see LXX Ps. 24:17; 30:19; 67:10; 103:28).

The second noun is *palingenesis* (literally, "rebirth"), found in the NT only in v. 5 and in Matthew 19:28. Matthew uses it to refer to the "new age" of the Son of man; a similar "public/ cosmic" sense of *palingenesis* is found in Josephus (*Antiquities* 11.3.9) and Philo (*Life of Moses* 2.65). The term is also used of personal "rebirth," whether by reincarnation (see Plutarch *Isis and Osiris* 72 [*Mor.* 379F]), the future life of the soul (Philo *On the Cherubim* 114; *Hermetic Tractate* 13.3), or a new way of life in the present through divine intervention (see Apuleius *Metamorphoses* 11.21). It is clear that in this passage the sense is closer to this last meaning, as found also in John 3:3, 5, Romans 6:4, and 1 Peter 1:3, 23: baptism initiates a person into a new way of life that is touched by the power of God, and is, therefore, of fundamental "newness."

Literary Observations

The structure of this passage is similar to that of 2:1–15, in that it begins with a fragment of the household code (3:1–2) and grounds the attitudes it advocates in the long sentence that begins with *gar* (for) in 3:3–7.

Titus's reminder to "them" (presumably all the believers, not simply the slaves of 2:9–10) that they should be submissive to rulers and authorities is for two reasons only superficially similar to the instruction in 1 Timothy 2:2 to pray for kings and those in high places. First, that instruction concerned the practice of prayer; second, it did not deal with living under state authority as much as with referring that authority to the care of God. Titus 3:1–2 is much closer to Romans 13:1–7. There also, Paul advocates "submission" to every ruling authority, with no hint that any other attitude was appropriate to Christian life.

Both passages are part of the larger household code, *peri oikonomias*. The empire, after all, was envisaged in terms much like the individual household, as the Greek term for empire, *he oikoumenē*, suggests. Just as in the individual *oikos*, the paterfamilias was the head, with all authority moving downward from him and all submission moving upward, so it was in the larger world of the *polis* and the all-encompassing *oikoumenē*. By the time of Paul, the empire had been in existence for over three hundred years. It was as much a fact of nature and a subject of divine providence, as the cycle of the seasons. Philosophers no longer debated alternatives or utopias, but rather worked at what the social order required by way of obligation from the individual: what were *ta kathēkonta*, or social duties, of the good citizen?

Just as Titus 1:2–3 is an example of a revelation formula, with its contrast between the past and the present, so does 3:3–7 find its formal parallel in other "conversion formulas" in Paul's letters. In such statements, there is a sharp contrast drawn between a former way of life and the present. In personal terms, we can count Paul's autobiographical statements in Philippians 3:2–11 and 1 Timothy 1:12–17 as examples. Even closer are those statements sketching the common experience of Christians before and after their conversion (see Rom. 6:17–19; Col. 3:5–11; Eph. 2:2–10). The most striking parallel is 1 Corinthians 6:9–11 (RSV): "Do not be deceived; neither the immoral, nor idolators, nor adulterers, nor sexual perverts, nor thieves, nor the greedy, nor drunkards, nor revilers, nor robbers will inherit the kingdom of God. And such were some of you. But you were washed, you were sanctified, you were justified in the name of the Lord Jesus Christ and in the Spirit of our God." As in our passage, we find the vice-filled lives before conversion, the turning point marked by baptism, justification, and the Holy Spirit.

The passage closes with the expression *pistos ho logos*, which we have found to be characteristic of the Pastoral Letters (see 1 Tim. 1:15; 3:1; 4:9; 2 Tim. 2:11). In this case, the formula clearly refers to the statement preceding, rather than that following. I have translated it as "This saying is reliable."

Comment

Even for readers who otherwise do not find much to value in Titus, the two kerygmatic passages in 2:11-14 and 3:3-7 are treasured as particularly rich — because remarkably compressed — soteriological statements. And they *are* soteriological: cognates of "savior" occur five times within them. Small wonder that they have figured prominently in the great "appearance" feasts of the Nativity and Epiphany, for each contains the verb *epephanē:* in 2:11, it is the saving grace that teaches how to live; in 3:4, it is the very attributes of God that grace communicates.

The soteriological passages are similar also in the rhetorical role they play within the letter. We saw that 2:11-14 connected the capacity for civilized behavior to the educative power of grace, thus providing the religious underpinning to the household directions in 2:1-10: the good behavior of people in the *oikos* adorned the teaching about God the Savior because it demonstrated how God's gift could empower and direct a new way of acting in the "now time."

In 3:1-2, Paul completes the household code he began in 2:1-10 by offering advice concerning behavior in the wider world, specifically regarding rulers and those in authority. We expect the exhortation to "be submissive," for that is standard in an imperial civilization constructed on the cultural premises of Hellenism (see also Rom. 13:1). But Paul goes on to elaborate the internal dispositions that should motivate such submission, and it is at this point that the instruction takes on complexity and depth.

First, we observe that these attitudes are remarkable for their irenic quality. The willingness to obey (*peitharchein*) means that submission is not forced but willing. Likewise with "ready for every good deed": the Christian's participation in the social order is not reluctant or passive, but one that is eager and active. Most striking, however, are the other four qualities advocated. They are not to engage in that brutal form of verbal murder called slander (*mēdena blasphēmein*), but are to be *amachos* (peaceful, literally, "not battling"), *epieikēs* (reasonable/gentle), and their *praytēs* (meekness/gentleness) should be demonstrated to all.

Second, these peaceful attributes stand in contrast with what we have learned about the native population from which this nascent Christian movement drew its followers. We saw earlier that the Cretans were called liars, savage beasts, idle gluttons (1:12), that care needed to be taken lest the supervisor/elder had children who were rebellious or dissolute (1:6) or lest he himself was addicted to drink, wrathful, violent, or greedy for gain at any cost (1:7), that slaves had to be warned not to pilfer from their masters (2.10) and that young women had to be taught to love their husbands and children (2:4). Now, Paul makes explicit what these hints have already suggested: that his readers were once (*pote*) a people of the most inhumane and harsh character (3:3). In a move that might be a rhetorical identification with his audience, or may indeed reflect his own view of his past (cf. 1 Tim. 1:13), Paul includes himself in this description of a populace sunk in the most misanthropic kinds of vice. We see, furthermore, that the specific vices named represent the opposite of the positive qualities he has sketched in 3:1–2: rather than *peitharchein* (faithful in obedience), we find *apeitheis* (faithless); instead of *epieikēs* (reasonable), we have *anoētoi* and *planōmenoi* (senseless and deceived); instead of readiness for every good work, we see enslavement to various passions and pleasures; rather than *amachos* and *praytēs* (peaceful and meek), we have "hateful and hating each other." The point can hardly be made more clearly that the *internal capacity* to live "prudently, righteously, and in godly fashion" (2:12) was not theirs without the *charis* (gift) from God the savior, who *saves* them precisely by giving them these capacities.

Third, the kerygmatic statement of 3:3–7 shows that humans have been gifted with the power to live gentle and peaceful lives because they have been gifted with a new life and rebirth that comes from a God who is defined by these same qualities. Paul emphasizes in this statement once more that they were not justified out of deeds that they themselves had accomplished (3:5); instead, their righteousness came about by God's saving act and was by gift (*charis*, "grace," 3:7). There may be embedded here some slight element of polemic against the opponents who are advocating a righteousness based on the observance of law. Paul emphasizes as well the reality of this gift. It is a rebirth and a newness of life that comes from the Holy Spirit, that is, God's own spirit. As elsewhere in Paul, the gift of the Holy Spirit is closely connected to the conviction of being "heirs" not simply of a promised land, but of "eternal life" (see 1:2; Rom. 8:12–17; Gal. 3:1–19; 4:1–7; Eph. 1:11–14).

But most of all, Paul's language makes clear that this Spirit bears within it those capacities that are God's own. Thus, it is God's "kindness (*chrēstotēs*, v. 4) and love for humanity (*philanthrōpia*, v. 4)" that were revealed "through Jesus Christ our savior" (v. 6), and it was by "mercy" (*eleos*, v. 5) that God saved them. These terms were not chosen at random. Paul wants to make clear that the ability to live with gentleness and kindness within the structures of society is derived from the way God has shown Godself to be towards humans and that those who have been baptised into this community of the Messiah and have had this Holy Spirit poured richly over them can learn a new way of being human from this gift (2:11–14). Because of the hope of eternal life, which transcends the structures of this world, Christians are able to engage their social obligations, not with the savagery of misanthropy learned from their environment, but with the sweetness and kindness they have learned directly from God.

Final Exhortation and Directions — 3:8b–15

3:8b And I want you to insist on these things, so that those who have come to believe in God might set their minds on engaging in good deeds. These things are honorable and are useful to people. ⁹But avoid inquiries and genealogies and conflicts and battles over laws. For these are not useful and they are foolish. ¹⁰After one or two admonitions, avoid a factious person. ¹¹You know that a person such as this is twisted and, self-condemned, goes on sinning. ¹²Whenever I send Artemas or Tychichos to you, make haste to come to me in Nicopolis, for I have decided to spend the winter there. ¹³Diligently prepare Zeno and Apollos for their journey so that they lack nothing. ¹⁴And even our own people should learn to apply themselves to good deeds for cases of urgent need, so that they not remain unfruitful. ¹⁵All of those here with me send you greetings. Greet those who love us in faith. Grace be with all of you!

Notes on Translation

Textual variants are of a minor character. Some MSS supply the definite article *ta* before *kala* in 3:8b, to yield "these are the noble things", the difference in meaning is minimal. In 3:9, two MSS replace "genealogies" with "fights over words" (*logomachias*), probably under the influence of 1 Timothy 6:4. A number of scribes were confused by the odd wording of 3:10, which literally runs, "The factious man after one and a second admonition avoid," and tried to "correct" it by changing the word order to one that seemed more suitable to them. Finally, the very short farewell is expanded in a variety of ways by some MSS; the Nestle-Aland text (27th ed.) properly takes the shorter reading as the correct one.

The diction presents the usual Pastorals pattern. In 3:8b–10, where the topic is the opposition and the style is polemical, there are a large number of New Testament hapax legomena (*phrontizein, hairetikos, ekstrephein, autokatakritos*) and Pauline hapax legomena (*zētēsis, nomikos, periistesthai, anōphelēs, paraitesthai*), including two terms found only in the Pastorals (*diabebaiousthai, genealogia*). In 3:12–15, in contrast, where the subject is Paul's plans and the movements of his delegates, the only NT hapax legomena are proper names (*Artēmas, Nicopolis, Zēnas*), and the only Pauline hapax legomena are *nomikos* and *leipein,* with the rest of the vocabulary found elsewhere in Paul's letters.

The translation of *kala erga proistasthai* is uncertain. It is strange, first, that the same phrase appears in both 3:8 and 3:14. In the first instance, it is preceded by the verb *phrontizein,* which makes for an awkward sentence if *proistasthai* is to be translated as "be concerned for," but that rendering is preferable to the options of "give aid" or "be at the head of," so I have translated, "set their minds on engaging in good deeds." But in the second case, the context is clearly that of giving assistance to others, yet the translation "give aid" is still difficult because *kala erga* is the direct object. In this case, therefore, I have translated, "apply themselves to good deeds," hoping that the context will make clear that the "good deeds" in this case clearly means providing financial assistance, whereas in 3:8, the meaning can be construed more broadly (see Van Unnik, "The Teaching of Good Works").

Another term that contains within itself a financial implication is *propempein* in v. 13. It can mean, simply, "to see someone off on a journey" (see Acts 15:3; 20:38; 21:5). But in other contexts, it clearly means "to outfit for an expedition," that is, provide people with the resources required to make a journey (see Rom. 15:24; 1 Cor. 16:6; 2 Cor. 1:16; 3 John 6). That this is the meaning in 3:13 is clear from the added phrase, "so that they lack nothing." I have, therefore, translated somewhat freely, "Prepare Zeno and Apollos for their journey."

Literary Observations

The division of the passage at 3:8a is artificial, and was done here simply for the sake of a more even distribution of text. In fact, 3:8a comments on the kerygmatic statement of 3:3–7, "This is a reliable saying," and 3:8b continues without pause, "and I want you to insist on these things" (that is, the instructions just given in 2:1–3:7 together with their theological backing). The body of the letter actually ends at 3:11; Paul then begins to give practical directions concerning his movements and those of his delegates.

The final charge to Titus, then, should be read against the backdrop of the soteriological statement that precedes it. The charge itself is, typically, arranged antithetically: the positive focus is characterized as "honorable and useful to people" (3:8); the negative concentration on debates is called "not useful and foolish" (v. 9).

The final flurry of business reminds us much more of the conclusion to 2 Timothy than that to 1 Timothy. The detailing of names and destinations is also a feature of Romans 16:1–23, 1 Corinthians 16:1–24, Colossians 4:7–18, 2 Timothy 4:9–22, and Philemon 23–24.

Comment

Paul's final charge in 3:8b–10 reminds us again of the situation his delegate faces. Paul speaks of those "who have come to believe in God" (*hoi pepisteukotes,* v. 8b). The perfect tense suggests a stance only recently taken. This is a young community created out of materials that are raw and unpromising. Its members need to be strengthened in their fundamental identity and to learn how to translate the gift they have received from God into a new way of living in the world — that is, righteously, temperately, and in godly fashion (2:12). This means that they must set their minds on "engaging in noble deeds" (*kala erga,* literally, "good deeds"; v. 8b).

The new converts do not need to be distracted by intellectual debates and religious controversies. Nor does the delegate, who is warned away from them (3:9)! We note that as Titus is to provide a good example in every respect (2:7), so is he in this one: *his* insistence on the basics and *his* avoidance of controversy provide a model of how the community itself should focus on the translation of gracious gift into grace-filled living within the structures of society. Paul's way of using his final polemical slur against the opposition is entirely in accord with protreptic discourse, which seeks to provide a negative foil for the positive ideal. Here, the contrast is between the doing of good works, which is noble and "useful for people," and intellectual debates, which are foolish (or empty, *mataioi*) and "not useful." I have noted earlier in this commentary that the criterion of "usefulness" is fundamental in ancient discussions of morality. In 2 Timothy 3:8, the Scripture is said to be *ōphelimos* for teaching; in 1 Timothy 4:8 godliness (*eusebeia*) is said to be *ōphelimos* for everything; now good deeds are declared *ōphelimos* for other people (3:8b).

The "inquiries" (*zētēseis*) and "conflicts" (*ereis*) and "legal battles" (*machas nomikas*) and "genealogies" (*genealogias*) further support the identity of the opposition as "from the circumcision" (1:10) or at least preoccupied with the sort of debates that characterize talmudic discussions. The "battles over law" fits within the framework of talmudic debate. The reference to "genealogies" is sometimes connected to Gnostic speculations about the *pleroma,* but could as easily be found within pharisaic circles, either with reference to biblical genealogies, the chain of rabbinic tradition, or speculations about the origins of the world (see Johnson, "Gnosticism in the Rabbinic Tradition").

More significant than the origin of these agitators is their effect. By enticing members of the community into such harsh debates, they are, in effect, eliciting precisely those antagonistic and aggressive qualities that were so destructive of themselves and their society before they received the gift of "our savior God's kindness and love for humanity" (3:4). This result is plain. Rather than living lives positively engaged in the *oikos* and the *oikoumenē,* these debates are "upsetting entire households" (1:11). The "factious person" (*hairetikos anthropos*) is the one who insists on such divisive debates even when their consequences becomes obvious. Such a person would rather be right than be righteous, would rather maintain theoretical integrity than the health of the community.

Paul tells Titus to admonish such a person once or twice, but then simply avoid him (3:10). His final commentary is a sad one: such a person simply is twisted inside and can't stop doing what is foolish and useless (3:11). As in other cases where the integrity — or even simple survival — of a community is at stake, Paul is not loath to employ the techniques of shunning and excommunication (cf. 1 Cor. 5:1–8; Gal. 4:30; 2 Thess. 3:14–15; 1 Tim. 1:20).

Paul returns to the doing of "good/noble deeds" once more in 3:14. As I mentioned above, the clear implication in this passage is that such deeds include the sharing of material possessions. Paul specifies in particular "cases of urgent need" (*anankaias chreias*). His expressed desire that they "not be fruitless" also echoes language elsewhere that has a financial connotation (see Rom. 1:13; 15:28). The most immediate application would seem to be providing the resources for the journey soon to be undertaken by Zeno and Apollos, for Paul desires that "they lack nothing" (3:13). But Paul's desire that they share their material possessions extends beyond this situation to "urgent needs" in the plural. Grace, said Paul in 2:12, "teaches" how to live. That grace, said Paul in 3:4, was about "kindness and love for humanity." Now, Paul says, "let our people learn" (v. 14). The final line in this letter, then, may have more point than at first appears: "Grace be with all of you!"

In this reading of the Pastoral Letters, I have placed the correspondence within the context of Paul's ministry and tried to make sense of them as authentic letters. At the same time I have tried to give readers a sense of what reading them from another context might mean and have attempted to provide them with the data that must be considered. Ultimately, each reader must decide which hypothesis makes most sense of the correspondence. What is most important is that the literary independence and integrity of each of these letters be respected, for only if they are read separately do we adequately apprehend their literary fashioning, and therefore also their religious perceptions.

Works Cited in Titus

Balch, D. L. *Let Wives Be Submissive: The Domestic Code in 1 Peter.* SBL Monographs Series 26. Chico, Calif.: Scholars Press, 1981.

Boismard, M. *Quartre Hymnes Baptismales dans le première epître de Pierre.* Lectio Divina 30. Paris: Editions du Cerf, 1961.

Bradley, K. R. *Discovering the Roman Family.* New York: Oxford University Press, 1991.

Dahl, N. A. "Form Critical Observations on Early Christian Preaching." In *Jesus in the Memory of the Early Church,* 30–36. Minneapolis: Augsburg, 1976.

Dibelius, M., and H. Conzelman. *The Pastoral Epistles.* Edited by H. Koester. Translated by P. Buttolph and A. Yarbro. Hermeneia. Philadelphia: Fortress Press, 1972.

Finley, M. I. *Ancient Slavery and Modern Ideology.* New York: Viking Press, 1980.

Harris, M. J. "Titus 2:13 and the Deity of Christ." In *Pauline Studies,* edited by D. Hagner and M. Harris, 262–77. Exeter: Paternoster Press, 1980.

Helton, S. N. "Titus 2:5 — Must Women Stay at Home?" In *Essays on Women in Early Christianity,* edited by C. D. Osburn, 1:367–76. Joplin, Mo.: College Press, 1995.

Jaeger, J. *Paideia: The Ideals of Greek Culture.* 3 vols. Translated by G. Highet. New York: Oxford University Press, 1939.

Johnson, L. T. "Gnosticism in the Rabbinic Tradition." *Resonance* 4 (1969): 5–17.

Lievestad, R. "The Meekness and Gentleness of Christ: II Cor x.1." *NTS* 12 (1966): 156–64.

Malherbe, A. J. *Moral Exhortation: A Greco-Roman Handbook.* Philadelphia: Westminster Press, 1986.

Quinn, J. D. *The Letter to Titus.* Anchor Bible 36. New York: Doubleday, 1990.

Van Unnik, W. C. "The Teaching of Good Works in 1 Peter." *NTS* 1 (1954): 92–110.

Verner, D. C. *The Household of God: The Social World of the Pastoral Epistles.* SBL Dissertation Series 71. Chico, Calif.: Scholars Press, 1983.

Wainwright, A. N. "The Confession 'Jesus Is God' in the New Testament." *Scottish Journal of Theology* 10 (1957): 274ff.

Index of Ancient Writings

Index of Modern Writers